THIS IMPORTANT BOOK CAN CHANGE YOUR LIFE!

THE MAGIC POWER OF YOUR MIND

Do you want to feel better, live longer, enjoy greater health, wealth and happiness? This book can help you achieve these goals.

THE MAGIC POWER OF YOUR MIND reveals the astonishingly simple methods of unlocking the forces within you—ESP, hypnotism, telepathy, clairvoyance and autosuggestion. It shows you how to put your inner mind to work to help you overcome any obstacle and enable you to succeed in anything you do.

"The most valuable book written in many a day for those desiring to use the untapped resources of their minds . . ."

—Louis M. Grafe
author of "Get Rich In Spite Of Yourself"

THE
MAGIC POWER
OF
YOUR MIND

Walter M. Germain

PAPERBACK LIBRARY, Inc.

New York

PAPERBACK LIBRARY EDITION

First Printing: *October, 1967*
Second Printing: *July, 1968*

To my sons:

Preston
Robert
Albert

This Paperback Library Edition is published by arrangement with Hawthorn Books, Inc.

Paperback Library books are published by Paperback Library, Inc. Its trademark, consisting of the words "Paperback Library" accompanied by an open book, is registered in the United States Patent Office. Paperback Library, Inc., 315 Park Avenue South, New York, N.Y. 10010.

The author wishes to express his gratitude for permission to reprint selections from the works of the authors and publishers listed here:

Rebecca Beard, EVERYMAN'S SEARCH, published by Harper & Brothers.

Alexis Carrel, MAN THE UNKNOWN, published by Harper & Brothers.

Robert Collier, RICHES WITHIN YOUR REACH, published by Robert Collier Publications, Inc.

Walter Coutu, THE CRIMINAL PERSONALITY, published in Vol. VI, No. 4 of Federal Probation.

Theron Q. Dumont, THE MASTER MIND, copyright by Annie Rix Militz, published by Crusader Publications.

Eileen J. Garrett, TELEPATHY, copyright 1941, Farrar, Straus and Cudahy, Inc.

Napoleon Hill, THINK AND GROW RICH, published by Combined Registry, Chicago.

Thomson J. Hudson, A SCIENTIFIC DEMONSTRATION OF THE FUTURE LIFE, published by A. C. McClurg & Co.

Leonid Kotkin, M.D., EAT, THINK AND BE SLENDER, copyright 1954 by Dr. Leonid Kotkin, published by Hawthorn Books.

Donald A. Laird, INCREASING PERSONAL EFFICIENCY, published by Harper & Brothers.

Pierre du Noüy, HUMAN DESTINY, published by Longmans, Green & Co., Inc.

Norman Vincent Peale, THE POWER OF POSITIVE THINKING, copyright 1952 by Prentice-Hall, Inc.

Grantly Dick Read, CHILDBIRTH WITHOUT FEAR, published by Harper & Brothers.

J. B. Saul, EMOTIONAL MATURITY, published by J. B. Lippincott Company.

John A. Schindler, M.D., HOW TO LIVE 365 DAYS A YEAR, copyright 1954 by Prentice-Hall, Inc.

Thomas Sugrue, THERE IS A RIVER, published by Henry Holt and Company, Inc.

Elmer Wheeler, THE WEALTH WITHIN YOU, copyright 1955 by Elmer Wheeler, published by Prentice-Hall, Inc.

ACKNOWLEDGMENTS

This book is the outgrowth of extensive research study made during my association with the Saginaw (Mich.) Police Department as Inspector in charge of juvenile crime prevention. I wish to express my thanks to Jacques Romano of New York City for his special counsel on various phases of psychic phenomena. To Joseph Sadony, Valley of the Pines, Montague, Mich., I offer my gratitude for his encouragement. Above all, I want to thank Fred Kerner of New York City for his invaluable editorial assistance.

CONTENTS

How This Book Can
Work Magic In
Your Life

The moment you picked up this book, you held the key to rebuilding your life.

In the pages that follow, there is set forth in plain terms knowledge that is scientifically sound, easy to understand and easy to apply to your own affairs.

As you read these pages—and as you fill in the very important sections that deal with you alone—you find out:

1. How to make of your life anything you want it to be.

2. How to free your days of the deadly monster, monotony, and fill your days with interest and pleasure and health and love.

3. How to make happiness a habit with you.

4. How to use every hour of the day—even your sleeping hours—to add years to your life and life to your years.

In the sixteen carefully arranged chapters that make up this book, you will read exactly how these things are possible. You will see they are possible for you.

Hardly a person has not said to himself: "If only I could change myself and do better!" And it is not only older people who look back and sigh over wasted decades. Young people, too, look back and realize they are not using their full powers, and think: "If only I could change myself!"

This book shows you how to change yourself from within.

You have the power now. This books shows you how to find it.

THE ONE GREAT KEY: YOUR SUPRACONSCIOUS MIND

There has been a great deal of recent interest in the subject of reincarnation. The Bridey Murphy experiment—which stirred the current curiosity—does little, however, to prove reincarnation and much to prove the existence of the Supraconscious.

The Supraconscious is able to tap what is known as the "collective unconscious," and in this way any person can relate incidents out of the past with a facility that is awe-inspiring.

The "collective unconscious" and its great motivating power, the Supraconscious, are part of God's Golden Gift to man—the brain.

This marvelous organ is divided into two parts—the Conscious and the Supraconscious.

The Conscious is that part of your brain used every day during all your waking hours. It operates through the five senses of sight, smell, taste, touch and hearing. It thinks—on a conscious level—and controls much of your planning and living.

When you go to sleep, or when you are hypnotized, or when you find the secret of reaching beyond your limited, Conscious mind . . . then your marvelous Supraconscious takes over.

There is absolute proof that the Supraconscious gives the power of hypnotism, clairvoyance, autosuggestion, telepathy and teleaudience. For your Supraconscious, unlike the limited Conscious part of the mind, works through a sixth sense and keeps in touch with the Supraconscious minds of all other people.

HISTORY PROVES THE EXISTENCE OF THE SUPRACONSCIOUS

The accumulated knowledge of mankind was transmitted from generation to generation long before there were means of writing down this information.

History proves that civilizations separated by vast seas and continents and unable to communicate with one another in any way, apparently did develop the same discoveries. Why? How?

Because in the mind of every living man the Supraconscious is constantly at work—at once receiving and transmitting all knowledge to all other Supraconscious minds, and thus to all other men.

Your Supraconscious is a storehouse of knowledge so vast we hardly can look back to the beginning of it. Here lies the memory of the whole human race—the accumulated wisdom of the ages! This vast accumulation never ends, never pauses.

The Supraconscious is the secret of the child prodigy, the adult genius, the wise man of history and of today. It is the secret of those people who seem to be guided by an inner voice that never fails them . . . the happy people, the successful people, the people who attract love, the people who find their way out of difficulties, the people who seem always to live in the sun.

The Supraconscious, unlike your limited Conscious mind, always knows how to put together facts so that they lead to correct conclusions.

The Supraconscious remembers everything. Your Conscious minds feeds information to the Supraconscious and then may forget it. But the Supraconscious never forgets.

The Supraconscious is the secret of the "hunch" that sometimes guides us—and can be developed into a constant, dependable guide.

The Supraconscious can by-pass the limited Conscious mind and take absolute control of the functions and conditions of the body. The story of Alois Swaboda is an excellent example of how this occurs.

A FAMOUS STORY OF MIND OVER MATTER

The late Dr. Daniel Boone Herring, "Sage of the Desert," told me the story of Swaboda, whom he first met in 1899 in Omaha. Herring was at that time an inspector for the Pinkerton Detective Agency and first noticed Swaboda, then fifteen years old, taking his fill at a free-lunch counter in a saloon.

After seeing him eat the same way a second day, Herring arranged to get the youngster—whom he discovered was dying of consumption—a menial job at the saloon. The boy explained that he had hopped trains from New York, his birthplace, after his parents died of tuberculosis, determined to see the cow country. Three months later, his strength improved through regular eating, young Swaboda hopped another freight and continued on his way.

It was five years later that Herring next saw Swaboda, this time in New York City. He was robust and well dressed and looked little like the person who five years earlier was dying of tuberculosis. Herring said the boy was as robust as a timber wolf and his muscle control was fantastic. He was able to control every muscle in his body, down to the smallest.

Swaboda explained that a bum who came into the Omaha saloon one day to "mooch" a lemon started him on the trail to physical perfection. The bum sucked the juice from the lemon, and as he did Swaboda realized that the sight of a man

11

doing this made him drool at the mouth. He reasoned—correctly—that thinking can make all the organs of the body function perfectly. Swaboda thus discovered the magic power of the Supraconscious.

The boy went to Wyoming, got a ranch job there, and within the next few years built himself up to physical perfection. He had made the great discovery that cell structure can be renewed through the power of suggestion by the Supraconscious.

THE SUPRACONSCIOUS IS THE KEY TO ACHIEVEMENT AND SELF-BETTERMENT

In this book, you can read the almost incredible story of Edgar Cayce of Virginia Beach, Virginia. Here was a man who, although he hardly knew what he was doing, was able to tap the powers of the collective unconscious—the wisdom of many gifted healers—through his own Supraconscious mind.

Edgar Cayce, often working at a distance from the people he treated, was responsible for curing thousands of persons, in some cases those who had been given up as incurable by the most learned men in the medical profession.

Read the story of Mrs. John H. Curran of St. Louis. Mrs. Curran, a woman who had little education, tapped the knowledge of another woman, Patience Worth, who lived three centuries earlier in England. Actually, she found all the knowledge of this other woman in her own Supraconscious. She wrote volumes of poetry and many best-selling novels—which she could not possibly have done through her own Conscious mind.

Read how Anne Wiltha of Windermere, England, has through the powers of her Supraconscious found the ability to become a competent artist in oils and water-colors. Yet Mrs. Wiltha never before had touched paints in her life. In fact, she had never even shown an aptitude for drawing!

There is the story of an English girl who spoke ancient Egyptian and helped linguists decipher the writings of that lost civilization. She did not learn ancient Egyptian in school; she found it stored in her Supraconscious.

There is the story of Theresa Neumann who, after much suffering, was miraculously cured. In her waking moments she could speak nothing but the dialect of her own German village. But going into a trance she carried on whole conversations in ancient Hebrew, ancient Greek and Aramaic, the languages spoken in the Middle East at the time of Christ.

THE FAMOUS ATTEST TO THE POWER

Over and over, the world's famous and capable people have credited their ability to a power beyond their Conscious minds—the power we know as the Supraconsicous.

Thomas Alva Edison tells how "messages" came to him, directing his work to success. This was his Supraconscious.

Robert Louis Stevenson spoke humorously of the "brownies" that guided him as he wrote his masterpieces. This was his Supraconscious.

Today, G. C. Suite, director of research at the General Electric Company, tells how he and his staff get their best creative ideas from the limitless Supraconscious.

Railroad pioneer Arthur Edward Stilwell's story of how he learned of the necessity of building a railroad in the West and how he avoided disaster by listening to the warnings of his Supraconscious is startling reading.

These stories, and countless others, show how you have within you the power to do with your life what you will.

The gift of the Supraconscious is effective in healing, in learning, in getting other people to do what you want, in making yourself a better person.

THE NEW PSYCHOLOGY LEADS TO UNLIMITED ACCOMPLISHMENT

In the pages that follow, a new world is opened to you.

In them is described the new psychology that will help you to understand yourself better. And having thus achieved understanding, you stand on the threshold of unlimited accomplishment.

This book shows you how to make what you want out of your life.

The true stories you read about other people are only the first step you take in understanding yourself.

As you go deeper into this book you will find you can form more and more definite ideas about what you want in life and how to attain it—whether your wants are simple or complex, whether they depend upon other people or upon you alone.

Remember, your Supraconscious can be controlled. The way to control it is to use suggestion.

By the time you reach Chapter III you will be ready to learn the power of suggestion. You will see how to put it to work. You will see why it has been called the hidden, Golden Gift of mankind!

You will read of the control the Supraconscious has over your Conscious mind and your body. You will see how to benefit others as well as yourself.

In Chapter IV you will begin to learn about the Supersense —or the "sixth sense" as many people call it—which explains the marvelous power of the Supraconscious to gather the knowledge you need.

THE MARVELOUS POWER OF YOUR MEMORY

Chapter V gives you a startling new concept of something very familiar to you—your memory.

It will stagger you to realize how much you remember from your own experiences, let alone other persons'. How can you learn by experience if you don't instantly remember your experience? You can. You'll see how. You have knowledge enough to change the world—lying in the unexplored recesses of your mind, half forgotten!

When you reach Chapter VI, you really will cross the threshold to mind power. Mind power, while it always has been the possession of mankind, only recently has become the basis of medicine's latest treatment. Medical science is finding out how great a power for health lies in the right kind of thinking.

Do you find it difficult to control your thinking? Mind power —your mind power—is waiting for you to use it. Down through the ages, mind power has turned the ill into the well, the infirm into the active, the miserable into the happy.

THE GIFT OF GIFTS—A LONGER LIFE

Chapter VII adds the final gift to health and happiness— the gift of longevity.

And not only that, but the gift of active, rewarding years not clouded with senility. Your increasing years can be your golden harvest years.

In Chapter VIII you'll read how to use the power of prayer to keep body and mind functioning in health. See how the right kind of prayer becomes an education in self-understanding and in making the greatest use of yourself. You are given five simple rules that help you generate this ability.

HOW ABOUT HAPPINESS?

Is happiness a matter of happenstance? Or is it a controllable matter, a state over which you have the power of creation or destruction?

The pages from Chapter X onward outline how you can develop the Happiness Habit. Happiness is a habit, and like all habits it remains for you to develop it. It is just as simple, too, to develop as any other habit.

Chapter XI lists for you the rules of understanding disease —and conquering it. There is no medical jargon or psychological terminology to bog you down. In this chapter, in the plainest English, you will be shown how emotions can be destroyers equally as well as builders of health.

You will be shown the difference between the "knowing" of your emotions and the "understanding" of them. You will be given five easy rules to follow in your battle of health against disease and of ease against "dis-ease."

The new psychology discussed from Chapter XII onward, the psychology of "positive-negative" thinking, is the means to a new and better life for you. It is the key to the question of whether or not you can live your life over again.

THE CLUE TO THE SOLUTION

There are hidden powers, magic powers, within you. This much has been shown thus far.

But how are you to use them? How are you to dig down into the complexities of the Supraconscious and find these powers and utilize them?

In Chapter XIII you will find the clue to the solution of this problem. The section that starts here shows where these powers lie within you and how you can reach into yourself to tap them and, when you have found them, how to make them work for you and your betterment.

The use of these powers is based on a seven-point hypothesis. This is:

1. The Supraconscious is constantly amenable to control by the power of suggestion.

2. The Supraconscious is incapable of independent reasoning by the processes of induction.

3. The power of the Supraconscious to reason deductively from given premises to correct conclusions is practically perfect.

4. The Supraconscious is endowed with perfect memory.

5. The Supraconscious has absolute control of the functions and conditions of the body.

6. The Supraconscious has the power to communicate by means other than the recognized channels of the five senses.

7. The Supraconscious is capable of intuition and perception of the laws of nature.

MAKING YOUR LIFE THIRTY-THREE PER CENT LONGER

All these propositions are scientifically proven. They are the basis by which you are going to discover the magic power of your mind. They are the basis by which you are going to use the magic power of your mind. They are the basis by which you are going to make an entirely new life for yourself with this magic power.

Once you have acquired this knowledge, the problem then is to make the greatest use of it. That can only be done by increasing your life to a full twenty-four-hour day every day. Only by using every single minute of the entire day can you make the greatest use of these magic powers. Chapter XIV outlines for you the method of making your life-function thirty-three per cent greater than it now is.

Your life can be vital and you alone can make it vital. There are twelve simple rules of living, a dozen easy ways of making yourself life limitless, happiness habitual, and giving yourself the wealth that is health.

A WORD TO THE UNUSUALLY WISE

Many people who read this Introduction will say it is an old story, told since the dawn of history, proved over and over again. Otherwise, how can we have human progress? Otherwise, how can even a fortunate few know happiness, serenity and success in whatever form they interpret success?

That is true. The secret is old. That is why we can depend on it.

But the approach is new. Never before has the Supraconscious been explained this way. Never before has it been tied so closely to the problems of modern life. Now, at last, you

16

need not be a saint or a genius, nor need you take years of your life to understand what is going on.

Never before have the ancient truths been clearly revealed in the new concept of positive-negative thinking (Chapter XII). Nor has the wonderful habit of happiness ever been shown in the easy-to-use form that is explained in the pages beginning with Chapter X.

Yes, a secret known to the Sphinx may be repeated in these pages—but never before has it been made so clear-cut, so easy to use—for anybody, anywhere, right now.

Nevertheless, if you already have the understanding—if you already know the magic power of your mind—start making this book work for you immediately.

Skip the first two chapters. Start reading with Chapter III.

Of course, when you buy this book as a gift for the many persons you want to help, or when you tell them about the book, instruct them—the neophytes in the mysteries of the mind—to read the book from the beginning.

So . . . for the unusually wise, this book begins with Chapter III.

For those who wish to be wise, and are wise enough to know it, it begins with Chapter I.

For anyone who reads it, this book leads to the same conclusion:

You can find and use and improve the limitless power of your Supraconscious.

And when you have done this, you'll know you never before were really alive.

How To Remake Your Life:
An Introduction

"If only I had my life to live over again!"

Have you ever thought that? Have you ever found yourself dissatisfied with what you have made of your life? Have you ever wondered if anything could be done about it?

You are certainly not alone in your wondering. The desire to try to make a life over again is universal. Most people, however, think that the question "Can a life be made over?" is purely a rhetorical one.

Actually it is not.

You can remake your life. The secret is the magic power of your mind.

Within the pages that follow you will find just what that magic is. You will discover your brain and learn how to use it. You will discover the power of suggestion.

You will have your eyes opened at the wonders of your Supraconscious and your Supersense.

There is a great storehouse of memory in your brain. You have to draw upon it in remaking your life. You will be shown how to do this. And you will learn the truth of the theory of "mind over matter."

Your mind controls all the matter of your body. And you, with complete control over your mind, have within your very grasp complete control over your body. The ramifications of this are obvious.

An entirely new life is open to you. And, best of all, you will learn the secret of living longer so that you can attain the fullest enjoyment out of your new life.

You will learn of the great powers that prayer and faith hold for you. You will acquire the ability to be happy, to make happiness and to use happiness for your own advantage.

All these "hidden powers" of the brain are a magic key to helping you live your life over again. This magic is the source of health, of happiness, of longevity, of success, of anything you want out of life.

19

This magic power of your brain is within the grasp of your understanding and the reach of your powers. It is no abracadabra; it is no mumbo jumbo. It is pure, solid, scientific fact. It is proven knowledge which man has had available for generations but, more often than not, has failed to use.

The magic power of your mind lies within that portion called the Supraconscious. The Supraconscious level of the mind is the greatest wonder of nature. It is a vast memory machine; it is a powerful controlling unit; it is the segment of man's brain that automatically "runs" the human engine.

In comparison with the conscious level of the mind—that portion of your brain with which you think and consciously control your actions—it is massive, for it embodies the thinking processes of all time and of all men.

It is a powerful, superior, "upper level" thinking machine. It is "above" and "beyond" anything that man has realized heretofore. It is truly the Supraconscious.

The Supraconscious, the communicator with the "collective unconscious," as psychologist Carl Jung termed it, is the possessor of man's "hidden power." It is the means by which you can become consciously creative through employing the heretofore unused faculties of your mind. It is the means through which you can reach the solution to individual problems ordinarily unattainable by conventional mental processes.

The wise Greek philosopher Socrates admonished: "Know thyself!"

When you know as much about your own human organism as you do about the car you drive, you will discover the truth of what people have termed "miracles." These "miracles" are nothing more than a natural product of natural law.

Natural law is yours to use, and its natural products are yours to create. The power of miracles is within YOU.

Your emotions, not your intelligence, rule your behavior. This is the magic of using your Supraconscious.

"Habit, not reason, governs the lives of most people," wrote Dr. Walter Coutu in *The Criminal Personality*. Knowing this, you will understand better how the human organism works. You will understand why human conduct is the response to varied stimuli.

"If you would care to understand human behavior," Dr. Coutu said, "investigate the stimuli which produce it."

You would not have an idea, a hope, a fear or a desire without the stimulus to bring such a reaction. You would not get hungry or thirsty or angry; you would not want to go fishing; you would not get an impulse to steal; nothing is possible unless there is the "push"—the stimulus.

And emotions play the leading role in offering you these stimuli. Writing in *How to Live 365 Days a Year*, Dr. John A. Schindler says that "your emotions affect a group of organs in your body called the endocrine glands even more than they affect your nervous system. These glands govern and regulate body functions.

"When the glands are activated by such depressing emotions as defeat, futility and discouragement, their production of hormones is changed and this can cause a great many ailments."

These depressing emotions which you experience are negativisms. Their natural enemies are your positive thoughts.

The positive thinking done by one eighty-year-old man shows distinctly that you do have your life to live over again —if you truly desire it.

This man died under the wheels of a truck which struck him down as he was crossing a street. When an autopsy was performed, pathologists found that the man's lungs were scarred with healed tuberculosis lesions. His stomach showed signs of long-forgotten ulcers. His arteries were hardened. His kidneys were damaged.

Yet his widow said he'd always believed he would feel better the next day.

This man had not fretted about aches and pains that would have made invalids out of others.

"Unpleasant emotions get you down," Dr. Schindler writes. "They often can make you sick.

"Pleasant emotions often can make you well—and keep you well."

You must fight fire with fire. You must fight "bad" emotion with "good" emotion.

Learn the emotion of love.

Learn to love God and your fellow man.

And above all, know thyself!

The means to this knowledge is yours to discover, yours to use, yours to benefit by. It is all in the following pages.

Go, then, and learn!

Learn of happiness, learn of health, learn of wisdom, learn of power.

A POSITIVE PROGRAM TO REMAKE YOUR LIFE

Your life is governed by habit. Your habits are governed by you.

Read every page of this book with the greatest care. Don't skip a word. Don't fail to absorb an idea.

Make your first habit that of reading some portion of this volume every day until you form positive habits that will work for you.

I

The Magic In Your Mind

Man is the most miraculous of all the living things on this earth!

Yet despite this undeniable fact, you have powers within you that you have not utilized.

You have within you the power to do anything you desire. You have the power to change your life so that you can accomplish all the things you want of it.

You are the owner of a power that, when you begin to use it, will open up the road to happiness and health, to wealth and long life.

Yes, you as a member of the human race are a part of that God-given miracle: man.

While all other living creatures have risen to heights of "adaptation to environment" in order to survive, your ancestors outstripped this mode of living.

Man has conquered his environment. More than that—man has continued to seek conquests as he discovers and utilizes the mysteries of life.

You can make these discoveries and utilize these powers. These are powers which are vast—far vaster than you realize at this moment. And before you are through reading these pages you will see how great they are and how easily they are to be tapped for your advantage.

So miraculous is this thing called man that—despite his great development as we have been able to trace it in history—he has hardly scratched the surface of his own abilities.

Were we to draw a picture of comparison, it might be fair to say that man has penetrated no deeper into himself than the depth of his own skin. Beneath, and yet to come, lie many things: the "flesh," the "bones" and finally the "heart" of the matter.

The miracle that is man is no less a miracle than that of the mysterious setting in which he is found—the universe. The resources that man possesses are as untapped as the unknown resources of the universe.

Don't let the picture get out of hand. When you think of

the resources of the universe, you conjure up a picture of things far beyond the ability of man's powers so far.

But the resources of man are near at hand. They are within himself.

That self is YOU.

Your resources are yours alone to utilize. Yet you probably have done nothing even to investigate what potential you possess. And this potential is so great that once you start to use it, there are no limits to what you can do.

You have a Golden Gift.

You use it every day—but you do nothing with it. Does that sound impossible? Well, take, for example, a child with a pencil. Each day the child takes up his pencil and scribbles. He cannot write, he cannot compute, he cannot draw. So, while he uses the pencil every day, he actually does nothing with it.

What, then, is your Golden Gift whose powers you use so casually?

Your Golden Gift is your brain.

In your brain lies the power to make use of all your untapped resources.

And your Golden Gift is more "Golden" and more of a "Gift" than that. Your brain not only supplies the power to use your potentialities—it also holds all the resources you possess.

Your Golden Gift, your brain, your mind, is the most vital of all your possessions. It is your greatest asset.

What the chapters that follow will show you is how to use this Golden Gift. You can use your mind and you can bring forth great powers from it.

Your Golden Gift can bring you longer life, better health, greater wealth, increased happiness, more vitality. In short, your brain gives you the power to control all the essential aspects of a full life and full living.

Before you jump into learning the secrets of using the Golden Gift, let us look back a great many centuries in a few short moments. You have to understand the meaning of this power. You have to study just what man is and what his mind is. You have to discover where man comes from, and why he has a mind.

There are many theories regarding man's beginning. But to realize that man, of all the living things on earth, has the Power of Mind makes it plain that man is the work of some great creative force.

His beginnings were purposive. And the greatest challenge that faces man—the challenge you will take up as you progress from chapter to chapter in this book—is to discover what that purpose is and utilize the power of that discovery.

The theory of man's beginnings varies according to who tells it.

Scientists trace this planet to its earliest days, each arriving at his own theory of how the universe we know came about. When it comes to the beginnings of life on our planet, however, most are agreed that the first faint stirring of life was a somewhat jellylike organic mass which floated on the waters of the sea.

Those who take the Bible literally are faced with less of an enigma than the scientists. For them the issue is final: the opening words of the Old Testament relieve them of any uncertainty. "In the beginning God created the heaven and the earth." Thereby was God's thought transmuted into fact.

The fundamentalist belief may not help us to understand ourselves as well as the scientific theory of the evolvement of man. But, in any case, man's evolution is part of an Infinite Plan in which man either progresses or regresses by his own efforts, both individually and collectively.

What matter if we believe that man's start was millions of years ago in the development of a single organic cell in the ocean or that he sprang full-grown from the mind of the Creator in some Garden of Eden? Each theory recognizes the prime cause—a Creator. Each theory hinges on the fact that some power brought to this earth the first germ of life. The creation of this miracle is no less wonderful regardless of the belief: whether it started in some lowly form of plant life and developed through countless ages to the highest product of today's civilization, or if the whole were created within six days.

To understand better why we behave as we do, let us look at earliest man as we have been able to trace him.

Our ancestors showed intellectual superiority over other animals that roamed the earth. The early man's ability to stand upright made him better able to do many things. Primarily he was able to put his forelimbs to uses no other animal could. Too, the height he thus achieved made it possible for him to see farther and over a wider area. He therefore was able to protect himself far more easily.

Using his eyes rather than his more limited sense of smell to see dangers far away, he also was able to use his arms and hands to ward off and fight these dangers when they were close at hand. Best of all, however, was the fact that his intelligence permitted him to make even greater use of his arms and hands. They became creative weapons and aided man in his fight for survival.

Kill or be killed was the law of the primeval world. Man's brain was in those early days necessarily motivated by greed, fear and anger. It was these things that made the instinct of self-preservation the first law of nature. Survival of the fittest became the primary driving force of human life.

Why have I started out to show you the beginnings of mankind? Simply because by looking at these beginnings you can see how primitive greed, fear and anger have left their mark on man. It is quite obvious that most of the mental and physical afflictions of modern man stem from these earliest conflicts.

It is important to understand that these primary urges of survival are buried deep in our biological background. Note that I use the word "understand." "Knowing" these things and "understanding" them are entirely different. We must understand and recognize certain basic facts if we are to utilize the power we possess.

Learned men in the past, discovering that the human mind is capable of amazing potentialities, did not recognize them as coming from the brain. These powers were attributed to the soul. Man's soul, according to the ancients, was in his solar plexus. We still have in our everyday language the reminder of this belief. The Greek word for diaphragm, the muscular section of the body that separates the abdomen from the chest cavity (in front of which is the nerve center we call the solar plexus), is "phren." Its current usage as part of such words as frenzy, frantic, the no-longer-credited "science" of phrenology, and even schizophrenia, is evidence of this original meaning.

We know today that the inner power of man—his wisdom —emanates from the mind.

Biologist Michael F. Guyer has stated that "man is an animal; but an animal with an analytical directing consciousness." Man, however, also possesses a deeper consciousness. This deeper consciousness—the Supraconscious—has resources so astounding that they have often in the past—and even in this very age—been attributed to soul power or to so-called supernatural sources.

Herein you will have shown to you, backed up with concrete evidence, that the power and wisdom that are man's stem from his Supraconscious. The Supraconscious, the root of your mind's power, is a vast storehouse of memory from which you can tap uncalculated amounts of wisdom. It is the storehouse of what psychiatrist Carl Jung calls the "collective unconscious"—the sum total of all man's knowledge, wisdom and power since his creation. It is a storehouse you can easily enter; it is a storehouse of treasures you have the ability to use; it is a storehouse whose contents will give you the power to Do.

Psychology, the science of mind, deals chiefly with the conscious mind, the so-called objective or analytical mind. But psychology sheds little light on the complexity of human impulses. It tells little about the perplexities that are the impulses, the emotions and the feelings of the human.

Psychology—or, as it should be called now, the old psychology—is an abstract consideration of human thoughts and behavior. For your purposes, it is entirely too academic to be of real help. It cannot help you solve the practical problems you are called on to face every day in the complex situations of modern society.

Man has a multiple nature. Most of his mental processes do not take place in the realm of the mind known as the conscious. Therefore any interpretation of human thoughts and conduct that deals only with the conscious perception and the reasoning processes of mind is entirely too limited in scope of understanding to be of use to you in comprehending yourself.

As the majority of your mental processes take place in the Supraconscious, the process of conscious reasoning alone will not enable you to understand fully the true motives of what you think and do. Much less will the processes of conscious reasoning help you to understand the effects that the "emotional" thinking of the Supraconscious has on your very health and well-being.

Consciousness is only the end result of the hidden processes of the human oganism. The true nature of these hidden processes usually remains unknown to you, or at least obscure in the mental realm of the Supraconscious.

The idea that man is endowed with a brain that functions as if he were fashioned with a dual mentality is not new. This dualism of the mind has been a matter for speculation by philosophers through many ages.

The ancient Greek philosophers believed that the dual character of man's mental apparatus represented a division of body and soul. Thus all mental phenomena were interpreted in terms of the so-called supernatural, the powers of gods or devils.

27

Victor Hugo seemed to grasp the real truth when he wrote: "I sense two natures within me." Certainly Robert Louis Stevenson, the great literary genius, had a clear understanding of human nature when he conceived his famous novel *The Strange Case of Dr. Jekyll and Mr. Hyde*.

In the seventh chapter of his Epistle to the Romans, Saint Paul confessed that he seemed to possess a double nature. He wrote:

"For the good that I would I do not: but the evil which I would not, that I do.

"Now if I do that I would not, it is no more I that do it, but sin that dwelleth in me.

"I find then a law, that, when I would do good, evil is present with me.

"For I delight in the law of God after the inward man:

"But I see another law in my members, warring against the law of my mind, and bringing me into captivity to the law of sin which is in my members.

". . . So then with the mind I myself serve the law of God; but with the flesh the law of sin."

Several centuries before Saint Paul recorded his illuminating introspections, Plato likened man to a charioteer driving a white horse and a black horse, one noble and the other ignoble.

Man, then, does have a double nature. One part of it is emotional, or animalistic. The other part is spiritual, or intellectual. But while this has been accepted fact for centuries, it has only been recently that scientists have started to discover the psychological and neurological significance of this multiple nature.

As wonderful as has been man's physical evolution, it has been surpassed by the growth of his mental faculties.

Most people are inclined to believe that man's conscious mind represents his greatest mental advancement. There is no doubt as to the greatness of this. But in comparison to the vast development of man's Supraconscious, the growth of the conscious is infinitesimal.

For in man's Supraconscious lie outstanding powers. Therein lies vast wisdom. And all these powers and this wisdom are there to be used. They need only to be tapped. You need only to realize that they are there and that they can be used. You will then find that these powers and this wisdom are yours to do greater things with, yours to achieve things you have dreamed of but you never believed possible.

In your Supraconscious lies the key to success, the clue to happiness, the formula to health.

Your Supraconscious mind contains a vast storehouse of "how to do it"—how to do anything you want to do.

Your Supraconscious mind is even more than a storehouse of knowledge, of wisdom and of power. It also is a transmitter and receiver of ideas from the Supraconscious minds of others.

By opening the channels of your Supraconscious, you stand on the threshold of life as it should be lived.

Living will take on new meaning, new wonder, new power, new belief, new health.

Your Supraconscious holds the secret of your new life.

A DAILY EXERCISE TO GET TO KNOW THE MAGIC IN YOUR MIND

Every night before you fall asleep there are simple exercises which you can perform to help you open the channels to your own Supraconscious:

1. Lie flat on your back and relax every muscle in your body. Start with the ends of your toes and little by little work your way upward until you are completely untensed.

2. Concentrate mentally on having a full night's relaxed and peaceful sleep.

3. When you have reached the depth of conscious relaxation and well implanted the idea of fear-free sleep, gently move into the position in which you normally sleep.

If you have performed these exercises perfectly, you will find yourself falling into a restful, calm sleep almost immediately and discover that the next morning will present itself to you in a brightness you have never before known.

II

How To Generate Brain Power

The power to create a new life for yourself lies within your own brain.

Your brain has capacities that have been proven and used—but used by few persons so far.

Now the time has come for these capacities, these powers, these abilities, to be shown to you—for the simple purpose of illustrating to you how they may be used and how you may benefit by them.

All these great and wondrous gifts of God are contained in the organ that is absorbing these words right at this moment —your brain.

Your brain is the one thing that has made man different from other of God's creatures. Yet so new is the conception of man's thinking organ that the Greeks didn't even have a word for it.

Man had progressed through countless centuries and numberless generations to that first great golden age of Greek civilization. Yet these people, who are credited with having had a word for everything, called the brain merely "the thing in the head."

To the Greeks, the brain was completely negligible. In seeking the whereabouts of the mind, the learned men of ancient Greece chose the solar plexus. It seemed to them that the rhythmic movements of the midriff were closely linked with what went on in what was their concept of the mind.

It took two thousand years for the brain to emerge from the darkness of man's ignorance of himself. By the time the anatomists discovered the brain, it was already believed to be the possible secret storehouse of man's intelligence. By then thinkers had moved the habitation of the mind from the diaphragm to the head. Shakespeare, writing of the brain, called it that "which some suppose the soul's frail dwelling-house."

But the anatomist could do little more than weigh the brain. He discovered that the "gray matter" in man weighed about fifty ounces, in woman about forty-five ounces. He made sketches of the complicated series of nerves and cells that his knife revealed.

It was not until the latter part of the nineteenth century that the dawn started to break over the knowledge of the brain. Two medical officers of the Prussian army, wandering among the stricken men on the Sedan battlefield in 1870, had the brilliant—if somewhat ghoulish—notion of testing the effect of electrical current on the exposed brains of some of the casualties.

There began the first medical experiments that led to discovery of what the brain truly is.

It seems strange that in the entire history of man and his miraculous development it has been only within the last eighty-odd years that there has been serious realization of the intricacies of that wonderful Golden Gift, the brain.

In reality man has two brains. But these are not like the two brains of one species of dinosaur of millions of years ago. That enormous animal had one small brain in the head and a second at the base of the spine so that it could control its huge body without taxing its "higher" brain.

Man's two brains are together. The second is but a development of the first. As man has grown emotionally, as he has learned to reason and to think, so he has developed a newer section of the brain.

It is man's brain, the wonderful "enchanted loom," that has made him rise above the other species. This "enchanted loom" which helps him spin his imagination has given man the ability to reason. Without it, he would be no better off than the lion, the elephant or the monkey. Without it he could have progressed no farther than his simian "relative" the ape.

Man's imagination, the product of his newer brain, has enabled him to think out things before he does them. Therefore, if he is in error, he need not actually commit the error. He can discard that process before making the error and utilize his brain, his imagination, to try another means of solving the problem.

While the animal's power of thinking is limited to "I sense, therefore I am," man can deduce. His reasoning makes him the master of his surroundings. He can expand thinking to "I know, therefore I am." Man "knows" because he has a brain to utilize. He is not dependent on his senses purely. He takes what his senses convey to him and weighs them with reason. The result is knowledge and, eventually, understanding.

Like the animals around him, man has his original brain—

the racially older instinctive and emotional brain. Man's difference, his Golden Gift, is his newer thinking and reasoning brain.

The basal ganglia make up the older forebrain. The cerebral cortex and the middle portion make up the newer forebrain.

In the middle section of the basal ganglia is found the thalamus. This controls the involuntary functions of the body through the medium of the autonomic or sympathetic nervous system.

The cerebral cortex controls the voluntary actions of the body by means of the frontal lobes and the motor, or cerebrospinal, nervous system.

The process called thinking is one which involves both sections of the brain and both sets of nervous systems. But your thinking is divided into two sections.

You are most familiar with "conscious" thought. This is the thinking you do in everyday life. This is the thinking you are utilizing now as you read this. It is purely surface thought. It is basic thought.

You have, however, a power that is easily utilized in your thinking. Yet it is one which few people know about and fewer bother to develop. This is thinking on the "Supraconscious" level.

Supraconscious thinking is the key to the development of the Golden Gift of the brain. In the Supraconscious mind lie powers that will be unfolded for you as you read further in this book. They are powers which require no special learning to develop. They require no special key to use. They require no special payment for the profits you will reap.

The Supraconscious mind is your silent partner in achieving the greatest, and up-to-now only dreamed-of, successes in life. The average man has little concept of the tremendous power that lies beyond the level of the brain's consciousness.

By learning to use this potential correctly you can place at your disposal an abundance of energy you little realized existed in yourself. You can give yourself great new mental powers— the real purpose of the Golden Gift. And you can bring about for yourself a completely new concept of living: a way of happier and longer life.

To say that you do not use the Supraconscious now is not a fair statement. You do, but so lightly as to leave it lying much as a rich field that is not seeded for crops. All your conscious thoughts and actions are produced by the combined reactions of the dual mental apparatus and the double nervous system to those things that affect your senses. That is to say, you react to what you see, hear, smell, taste and touch.

But, as was pointed out before, this is just the same as what happens to an animal. It senses, and bases its "thinking" on the sensations. You have the power of discrimination and judgment. This constitutes your thinking to the point of knowing, and your knowing to the point of understanding.

In man the responses to sensory perception are channeled to the thalamus. It is the thalamus that is the principal source of human feelings and emotions. The patterns and the habits of so-called "emotional thinking" are channeled in this area of the brain by both the Supraconscious and the "collective unconscious."

In his recent book, *Release From Nervous Tension,* Dr. Harold Fink makes it clear that the thalamus—which he terms the "interbrain"—is the seat of man's deeper intellect, the Supraconscious.

The function of the thalamus is to act as a sort of bridge between what takes place inside of you and outside of you. Thus you are able to register "like" or "dislike" upon having one of your five senses react to a stimulus. At this instinctive "wish level" of the consciousness, the natural response of your "emotional thinking" is to seek pleasure (that is, security) and avoid pain (or insecurity).

In people who think sanely and live wisely, the reactions of sensory perception of outside stimuli first pass through the thalamus. Then they are "telegraphed" through the cortex, where feeling impulses are analyzed and modified in the light of reason. The conscious thoughts are then sent once again to the thalamus, where they are transmitted into physical action.

Sometimes one's "emotional thinking" is dominated by negative attitudes of feeling. These are offshoots of man's primitive impulses of greed, fear and anger. If these negative feelings dominate the thinking it is difficult, sometimes impossible, for the powerful emotional impulses to be adequately controlled by one's ability to reason. Thus one is deprived of one of the great powers of the Golden Gift.

How this negative thinking causes a malfunctioning of the autonomic nervous system and produces psychosomatic illness is discussed in a later chapter. You will also be shown how positive attitudes of feeling are responsible for producing good health and peace of mind. This is accomplished by the harmonious functioning of the human organism. Along these same lines it will be shown how meditation, and prayer, can produce what are commonly called "miracles of faith healing" through the simple means of extreme acceleration of the processes of organic repair.

One of the greatest examples of the everyday use of the Supraconscious is in your judgment of people and things. You may be inclined to make snap judgments. More often than not, these judgments are correct. What is the basis of this perception within you? Are you consciously so perceptive? Obviously not, for if asked, or if you seek to determine for yourself what you based your opinion on, you seldom can say.

"I just felt it, that's all," is a common answer to such a question.

What does play a part in this system of judgment, however, is the Supraconscious level of the mind. You react consciously to a person upon meeting him. Similarly you react to a situation. These reactions are filed in the brain and from its deepest depths the pattern of opinion is formed, based on these conscious reactions. This pattern is flashed to the conscious mind and you have formed an opinion.

Few people suspect that the Supraconscious is the storehouse from which they draw these judgments. It has been the development of our "cultural reasoning," as Frederick Pierce points out, that has hidden from us the fact we do use the Supraconscious in our thinking.

The quicker you are to realize that you can probe beyond the boundaries of the conscious, and allow yourself to do so, the sooner will you be starting to use fully the power that you have hidden within you.

Biologists have pointed out that while reason—the power to think consciously—has been responsible for man's attainment of mastery over his destiny, man is primarily not a rational being.

Man "relies on reason only where its usefulness is forcibly and immediately brought home to him." The rest of the time man relies on what is termed "instinct." That is, he depends for his reactions upon what his innate self knows. What the Supraconscious has learned over the countless years of man's development determines the driving power that enables him to do what he does do, whether it is good or bad.

Man's innate nature is the end product of numberless years of collective environmental experience. This experience is as much a part of man's heredity as his biological constitution.

As far as can be determined, in using the processes of the Supraconscious, man is using the oldest part of his brain from the point of view of usage. The thalamus was the dominant part of the brain in the species for unknown generations before humans were obliged to reason in order to exist and progress.

During the many centuries of uncivilized existence in which man's principal business was to keep alive amid the dangers lurking all around him, the thalamus acquired all the "feeling" guidance of wild animals. In other words, the thalamus acquired the traits of animal instincts, or just "plain instinct."

The daily association and competition with other humans and animals in a continual struggle for existence was responsible for the development of the instinct of survival in humans: self-preservation and sex.

The things that early man needed, or desired, he took. This frequently involved mortal combat. Primitive life made man an instinctively predatory creature with strong human impulses to satisfy the inherent desires and appetites of his primitive nature by fair means or foul.

When primitive instincts of self and sex cause negative emotions, such as anger, fear, lust and the like, to dominate the "reasoning" mind, these Supraconscious attitudes of "feeling" motivate the human conduct called misbehavior.

This is what C. Judson Herrick, the famed neurologist, called "thalamic dominance." It is a state of mental disorder in which one's "feelings" usurp one's sense of reason.

Human aberrations and psychosomatic ills—which, it will be shown to you later, frequently culminate in some form of degenerative disease—usually are the end products of "thalamic dominance," the cause of negative "emotional thinking."

But that is only one side of the story of human nature. Biologists see the picture in the perspective of man's baser nature. They overlook the primary reason why man's early ancestors gradually learned to walk on two feet when they descended from the trees, while the species known as monkey continued to use all four limbs.

In this you see the guiding hand of a Great Creative Force —the evolution of spirituality. The potential good in man's nature is vastly greater than most people suspect.

There has been plenty of evidence of unsuspected power and wisdom. The life of Jesus Christ is the best example. But, because of man's basic incredulity, unusual manifestations such as intuition and the extraordinary ability to be able to effect cures in oneself or others have generally been attributed to "power of soul" or "supernatural" sources.

Yet the answer is an obvious one: man's evolution is a threefold one. As well as a physical and intellectual growth, there is also a spiritual growth. The spirit manifests itself through man's deeper consciousness—his Supraconscious, the power of the Golden Gift.

There are countless cases that bear out the powers of the Supraconscious. Within the covers of this book will be submitted as many cases as space permits to convince, with actual evidence, the unbiased reader that the Supraconscious mind does possess ample powers to bring renewed health, longer life, greater happiness and new successes.

You have already been shown that the interaction of thalamic "feeling" attitudes and "reasoning" conclusions of the cortex produces finished thoughts, words and actions. The interaction of the dual mentality can produce three conditions: normal, abnormal and extranormal.

In the normal state, the human organism functions harmoniously and the individual enjoys peace of mind and a state of good health. In this state of well-being the mastery of one's own destiny is achieved by the uses of reason only.

The abnormal state disrupts harmonious functioning of the human organism and causes imbalance of the body's mechanism. This state usually robs one of peace of mind and causes ill health, as I shall prove in later chapters.

The extranormal state is produced by synchronous interaction of positive "feeling" attitudes and "reasoning" reactions of the cortex.

This is a state of mental perfection. In it the individual has the benefit of all the reasoning powers of his conscious mind. This is combined with the emotional force and the perfect memory of the Supraconscious mind added to the marvelously logical arrangement of its psychic resources.

In short, all the elements of intellectual power are in a state of intense and harmonious activity during the extranormal state of the mind.

It is this state of mind which produces real genius. It is this state of mind in which the inventiveness of Thomas Edison, Henry Ford, Guglielmo Marconi, George Westinghouse, Albert Einstein and Charles Kettering blossomed. It is this state of mind which has delivered the insight and know-how for almost every great achievement in science, industry and the arts.

It is into this area of thinking that you are going to delve. For by correctly using this potential, you can gain the benefits of health, wealth and happiness without striving. These benefits are reachable without your having to travel laborious routes.

They are yours by simply recognizing the Supraconscious level of the mind and permitting it to function under the proper conditions.

When, through the practice of self-discipline and self-control, you have attained the state of self-mastery, you will then enjoy the benefits of your intellectual and spiritual heritage.

Once the biological effects of your physical evolution—that is, your animal nature—have been uprooted by sane thinking and wise living, you will reflect in your thoughts and actions the true way of life—that exemplified by the Infinite Mind. Keeping "in tune with the Infinite" will lead you to living a life that is useful, purposeful and rewarding.

The Supraconscious is a veritable "genie" of the brain that can either be a good servant or a bad one.

The Supraconscious is wise and powerful beyond all the comprehension of the human. It is for this reason that people often refer to this hidden power of the Golden Gift as soul power.

Call it what you will. It is, regardless of what you call it, WISDOM and POWER far beyond the reason of man to comprehend fully except in the light of Divine heritage and as an instrument through which the intelligence of the Infinite operates.

The purpose of the writer is to provide you with sufficient knowledge of the basic mechanism of the great power of the Golden Gift so that you can use your Supraconscious as a good servant instead of a bad one.

To this end it is essential to establish a working hypothesis. Without such a hypothesis you cannot begin an exact study of the Supraconscious. In the field of psychological investigation, and more especially in the field of parapsychology, a satisfactory scientific working hypothesis has not yet been formulated that embraces all the psychological phenomena known to mankind these many centuries.

It was for this reason that the late Dr. Alexis Carrel, famed for his thirty-three years of brilliant biological research at the Rockefeller Institute for Medical Research, commented:

"The importance of intuition in mental life requires an investigation of metaphysic phenomena, and the application of scientific method to the study of telepathy and clairvoyance."

For our working hypothesis, then, I will use the findings of the late scientist Dr. Thomson Jay Hudson as he outlined it in his book *A Scientific Demonstration of the Future Life*. Dr.

Hudson compiled a great deal of data concerning the mind and its Supraconscious aspects.

In Dr. Hudson's time, however, it was believed that man's apparent dual nature was that of body and soul. And he, naturally, attributed the powers of the Supraconscious to the soul.

It is only the advances of psychiatry in the field of medicine which has shown us the truth that the "hidden power" of man emanates from his mind, not his soul.

While psychiatry has, however, drawn its conclusions from the studies of abnormal psychology, thus presenting the negative side of human nature, my theory is built on human nature's positive side.

The positive, or constructive, side is based on the contention that man is essentially good, due to the Godliness of his spiritual evolution as manifested in positive "emotional thinking."

The conclusions of our working hypothesis concerning the extraordinary powers of the Supraconscious are based on three things.

First I have utilized the information pertaining to mental phenomena as disclosed by the science of hypnosis. Secondly, I have used the results of Dr. Carrel's study of the so-called "miracles" of faith-healing. Finally, the conclusions are based on my own analysis of personal experiences in telepathy, clairvoyance and clairaudience.

These various experiences can be definitely classified in the category of the parapsychological science of Extrasensory Perception, so designated by Professor J. B. Rhine of Duke University.

The seven propositions of the working hypothesis upon which this study of the Supraconscious is to be based are:

1. The Supraconscious is constantly amenable to control by the power of suggestion.

2. The Supraconscious is incapable of independent reasoning by the processes of induction.

3. The power of the Supraconscious to reason deductively from given premises to correct conclusions is practically perfect.

4. The Supraconscious is endowed with a perfect memory.

5. The Supraconscious has absolute control of the functions and conditions of the body.

6. The Supraconscious has the power to communicate by means other than the recognized channels of the five senses.

7. The Supraconscious is capable of intuition and perception of the laws of nature.

These seven propositions will be embellished upon and discussed fully in the chapters to come. How you can recognize these powers of the mind and how they can be put to use for your advantage will be discussed and studied.

By understanding and appreciating the seven points of this working hypothesis, you can set about creating a new life for yourself.

These are the seven major facts that science has discovered and that you will learn in the following chapters.

These are the seven planks of the platform that forms the basis of the teachings you are to absorb in the ensuing pages.

These are the powers of the mind that have been recognized. They are powers that you can and will recognize. They are powers that you will quickly put to use for your own advantage.

These are the propositions that you will learn to understand.

These are the means by which you are going to set about NOW to create a new life for yourself.

A PLAN TO GENERATE THE POWER
IN YOUR BRAIN

Now that you have learned the secret of relaxation and calm sleep and have opened the channels to your Supraconscious, the seven-point hypothesis of this study must be implanted into your mind so that you can begin to use the powers of your Golden Gift immediately and with success.

Clip from the last section of this book the page on which the seven propositions of the working hypothesis are printed. Each night after you have achieved muscular relaxation and freed your conscious mind of the day's petty cares, read the seven-point lesson.

At first it will be best to read it aloud. Later you will find that silent reading will accomplish just as much, for by that time you will have acquired the gift of concentration and absorption.

III

How To Use Your Power
of Suggestion

What does suggestion mean to you?

Does it mean something you would like? Or does it mean something you would want?

To achieve what you want, you must want enough to achieve!

This is the truth you will learn. This is the secret of achieving all the things you have up to now only dreamed about.

You will learn to change your conception of suggestion. Suggestion is no longer that passive thing that only touches lightly on those things you would like for yourself. Suggestion now will become the means of getting for yourself all the things you rightly should have.

The most important of the seven propositions of the working hypothesis outlined in the last chapter is the first: the Supraconscious is constantly amenable to control by the power of suggestion.

This is a statement of far-reaching effect. The power of suggestion, the power you will have over your own self, is the greatest of all the powers of the brain.

You will learn to realize its full effects and the meaning of the Great Answer.

What is this Great Answer?

It is the faculty of understanding and utilizing for your welfare and for the good of mankind the powers of the Golden Gift.

With the Great Answer you will understand the causes of most of your mental, physical and behavior difficulties. But more wonderful still, with the Great Answer you hold the clue to cure.

Before you turn skeptically away and say, "Bosh!" think for a moment on the Supraconscious powers that your mind now has over your body in its everyday workings.

Deny, if you can, that, through the control of your Supraconscious, your body is constantly replenishing for itself those cells that are used up most quickly—the corpuscles of the blood stream. Thousands of red corpuscles are manufactured constantly to carry the life-giving oxygen through the arterial and veinal stream of the body. And countless white corpuscles, with disease-fighting and infection-curing properties, are produced and sent to those areas of the body with amazing rapidity where needed—and when needed.

These powers of the body, or rather of the mind over the body, you readily admit—though you rarely, if ever, think of them. Why, then, be skeptical when it is suggested that the Golden Gift holds greater powers of self-help that you have not yet tapped?

These powers need only be touched off by suggestion from within the self—that is, suggestion by the conscious level of the mind to the Supraconscious level.

The power of suggestion—or, as it should be called, the Law of Suggestion—goes back far in our history of medicine. Just how it was discovered is not only interesting, it is also helpful in our search for the knowledge of the self.

Just as the magic of ancient times was the primitive origin of religion, it was also the forerunner of scientific investigation. Among the wonderful tales of the earliest of investigations into things scientific are those concerning magnetism.

The discovery of the magnetic attractions of metals became the embodiment and the symbol of the invisible forces of nature. The Swiss savant, Theophrastus Bombastus von Hohenheim, who called himself Paracelsus (1493-1541), was the pioneer experimenter in the powers of the magnetic attractions. Paracelsus believed that he had truly uncovered the hidden power of nature.

As were so many scholars of that day, Paracelsus was both physician and physicist. He sought to employ the magnet in efforts to cure diseases in his patients. Because of its drawing powers, he believed that this force could be used to draw disease from within the human system.

The magnetism theories of Paracelsus found many devotees, among them a Jesuit priest, Father Kircher. This priest ground up magnetic lodestone and had his patients swallow the powdered stone. He then applied a poultice of iron filings over the diseased part. His assumption was that when he then held a magnet to the poultice, he attracted the iron filings and the lodestone fragments within the patient's stomach, thus drawing out of the body the affliction.

With superstition a common form of belief in those days,

the theory of magnetism gave rise to a widespread belief in marvels, miracles and magical cures. Such cures, attributed to magic, were of numerous forms. Belief in them was virtually universal.

The cult of the magnet reached its height in the eighteenth century when Friedrich Anton Mesmer sought his medical degree. In 1773, he presented to the Faculty of Medicine at the University of Vienna a thesis on *The Influence of the Stars and Planets as Curative Powers*.

It was Mesmer's theory that the moon, sun and stars all affected the human organism through an invisible fluid which he termed "animal magnetism." He said that this valuable substance could be derived from a magnet or lodestone. Further, he stated, all cellular structures had an affinity to the magnet.

Whatever cures Mesmer effected—with the help of another Jesuit priest, Father Hell—were due obviously to the power of suggestion on his patients. By telling them of the cures he was going to work, he was able to convince them these treatments would work and thus was able to achieve results.

Mesmer eventually discovered that the use of the magnet itself was no longer necessary to curative powers. His theory of animal magnetism was embellished. By transferring the power of this animal magnetism of his own body, he claimed he was able to affect the vital forces that flowed through other persons' bodies and could cure them of disease.

Mesmer's fame spread. But while he was forced to leave Vienna, for reasons never suitably explained, he continued with his experimentation in Paris for a long time. His success was boundless. The fame of his cures spread rapidly. Thousands of invalids sought him out.

He soon claimed the ability to magnetize anything he touched. His technique for transferring the animal magnetism of his body to affect the vital powers of a patient became known as mesmerism. That was the direct forerunner of what we today call hypnotism.

Medical opinion in Mesmer's time was that every disease had its natural cause rising to a crisis. Mesmer's belief was that by reducing the crisis, the period of the disease could be shortened. Thus the illness could be "drawn away" from the body.

As Mesmer's popularity grew, he was forced to seek some form of mass production in order to treat the hordes who sought him out for help. It is related that he would have a number of patients in the same room. They would wait for him for at least a half-hour. All the while soft music was heard from an anteroom.

Then Mesmer would enter. He was clad in a long robe and carried a wand. He would touch and address his patients one at a time. Thus he spread excitement and expectation. He made passes, strokings and other gestures with his hands and with his wand. These means of conveying his influence were supposed to be the media of the curative effect.

The act of mesmerism eventually came to mean pointing of the extended fingers of the mesmerist's hands. From the fingers the magnetic force was suppose to flow into the patient. The mesmerist controlled his patient by staring into his eyes with a compelling gaze.

For a long time it was actually believed that the mesmerized persons were in actual communication with the spirit world.

An ardent admirer of Mesmer was the Marquis de Puysegur. After Mesmer's treatments fell into disrepute for some time, this former student of the Viennese doctor in some experiments discovered that one of his subjects went into a state of mental trance.

De Puysegur called this "artificial somnambulism." The effect was in complete contrast to Mesmer's results. The Viennese doctor caused hysterical outbursts. His French pupil's results were calm, peaceful sleep. Whether Mesmer knew of this induction of light sleep is not known. But if he was aware of it, he made no use of it.

De Puysegur's discovery demonstrated a basic contention of hypnotism: that a state not unlike sleep can be produced artificially in an entirely awake person. Further, it proved that during this state the thoughts and the actions of the subject are to a great degree subservient to the direction of the practitioner. Thus he showed that suggestion was indeed a power—a power that can be made to do great things for man.

At the same time that de Puysegur was conducting his experiments, yet another Jesuit priest, Father Gassner, was conducting work in southern Germany. This work was spectacular from the point of view of scientific experimentation and cure.

A prominent Manchester surgeon, Dr. James Baird, fathered the scientific evaluation of hypnotism. Skeptical at first, he learned that hynotism was not trickery nor charlatanism. He dismissed the "magic fluid" theories and went about to discover the actual physical cause of the state of hypnotism. He, in fact, coined the word hynotism, coming from the Greek word "hypnos," meaning sleep.

There were other experimenters in hypnotism. But bringing the history of this phenomenon up to the time of Dr. Baird is sufficient to prove that experiment in this field has shown incontrovertibly that man possesses a dualism of mind—the conscious and the Supraconscious.

When a person is hypnotized, his power to reason objectively with the conscious mind is literally put to sleep. He can neither hear, see, smell, taste nor feel, in the accepted meaning of the senses. He is completely dominated by the will of the practitioner who induced the hypnotic state.

With the conscious level of the mind of the hypnotized person in abeyance, the Supraconscious level is then free to be aroused. It can be brought to a state of intense activity and extranormal powers.

This is done solely by suggestion.

The power of suggestion, as induced by the hypnotist, affects the Supraconscious of the patient. As this is the functioning brain of the moment, it is the power that affects the entire thinking of the patient.

That the Supraconscious can do this is proof that it is indeed the hidden key of the Golden Gift.

Were the Supraconscious not to possess extraordinary powers and vast wisdom, it would not be able to function as it does in these circumstances.

This hidden key becomes apparent to onlookers during an experiment in hypnotic functioning. The onlooker is given the opportunity at that time of seeing how great the Golden Gift is. The onlooker is shown how suggestion can stimulate the Supraconscious and control the functions of the body in ways that seem to be completely unbelievable and virtually incredible.

The onlooker is given insight into what his own Supraconscious can do, what powers it possesses, and how he himself can control those powers by utilizing suggestion on them.

To the casual observer, the mind of the hypnotized person appears to be completely transformed. It appears to possess powers and attributes not normally enjoyed by the individual during his conscious awareness.

The hypnotized person's memory becomes extremely keen. In fact, hypnotic experiment has shown that the memory of the Supraconscious is virtually perfect. Remember the fourth proposition of the working hypothesis: the Supraconscious is endowed with a perfect memory.

It would be well for you to recollect at this point the Divine

Plan of man's evolution. Recalling this fact should make you aware of that man's physical development in the world has virtually ceased. All further development now is in the world of the powers of the brain.

The first step in evolution of man was the process of organic evolution. Then came the process of development from the protoplasm through countless stages to the culmination in the wondrous animal that is man.

For at least a million years or more the dominant aspect of evolution has been in the direction of intellectual and spiritual progress and development. The process of physical development has virtually ceased. Life has progressed in eons past from the lowest form of animal life to that high level that you now know.

Now your progress must be almost solely in improvement. It is reasonable to assume, from what you already know, that the attributes of Infinite Intelligence, the intelligence of the Divine Plan, are embodied in each one of us.

But it is up to you to make proper use of this great power, this Golden Gift of God. You can take this Golden Gift and use it in a constructive way. Or you can utilize this power in a destructive way. That decision is one that lies with the conscious mind. But the question of using the power of the Golden Gift is answerable only by the Great Answer: the ability to understand and utilize for your welfare and for the good of mankind the powers of the Golden Gift.

You must utilize the powers of the Supraconscious for the welfare of mankind, for it is human nature's inexorable law that failure to progress means retrogression.

The experiments of hypnotism show simply that the Supraconscious is a part of the make-up of every person. The experiments prove that the Supraconscious need only be awakened to be used. Hypnotists have no great power over their subjects or patients. They have only the realization and recognition of the Supraconscious. They have insight into the powers of the Golden Gift.

Hypnotism shows completely how scientifically correct is the first proposition of the hypothesis: the Supraconscious is constantly amenable to control by the power of suggestion. This power of suggestion is not necessarily one that requires outside influence. It is a power that you can use to influence yourself.

Suggestion, or rather self-suggestion (often called auto-suggestion), is the key to the lock on the Golden Gift. What you can have done by your Supraconscious is limited only by what you want to have done.

Through the powers of the Supraconscious you hold the gift of health, you possess the power of happiness, you own the secret of vitality. Full life and complete living are the priceless possessions you have been endowed with. They are yours to use—if, and when, you want to use them.

See how strong suggestion is. When you read a novel, note how the Supraconscious mind can transport you into a land of imagination and make your conscious self a part of that land of fantasy. "Daydreaming" is a similar process. But hypnosis is the most dramatic demonstration.

In hypnosis, a person accepts as absolute truth every statement made to him by the hypnotist, other than requests to do anything against which the subject has a moral barrier. Thus, if the hypnotized person is told that he is the King of England, he will accept the statement as fact and immediately start behaving with the air of importance and dignity befitting to that station of life.

Similarly, a person hypnotized and told that he is someone of lowly station will assume an attitude of such a person.

The power of suggestion in respect to the hypnotized subject is so great that a person can be made to believe that he is almost anything animate or inanimate. The subject will act the part suggested with remarkable fidelity to nature—to the extent of his knowledge of the person or thing suggested.

Experiment has shown that even a person who has little or no ability to mimic and imitate naturally will, if told he is a person whom he knows intimately, proceed to give an almost-perfect imitation of that person. The subject will imitate his friend in gesture, mannerism and even in voice and intonation.

Experiments that prove the Supraconscious is aware of the moral barriers have had interesting results.

In a private exhibition for psychiatrists a hypnotist recently used an age-old trick which has, presumably, always worked successfuly. A person was placed in a deep hypnotic state and then offered a knife and told to stab the hypnotist. The patient accepted the knife without comment but when preparing to drive the knife into the hypnotist's body, suddenly hesitated, looked confused, laughed nervously and dropped the weapon.

Another experiment inadvertently showed this response. A woman was told to turn on the radio after coming out of the hypnotic state. Upon return to the waking state, the woman became quite nervous. She arose from her chair a number of times and walked toward the radio and then back.

Asked what made her so jittery, she said she had an almost irresistible compulsion to get some music on the radio. But, she said, she realized that it was quite late and the music might awaken the baby next door.

In hypnotism a person's conscious faculties are placed temporarily in abeyance. What happens is that the person hypnotized goes into a state resembling sleep. In this state only his body remains awake and this remains under the control of the Supraconscious level of the mind—for the Supraconscious never sleeps.

Experimental hypnosis provides conclusive proof of the fifth proposition of our working hypothesis: the Supraconscious has absolute control of the functions and conditions of the body.

The experiments of hypnosis also show that all humans, through the veritable storehouse of memory that the Supraconscious is, have a perfect memory. The fourth proposition of the working hypothesis—the Supraconscious is endowed with a perfect memory—is thus proved.

It has been shown by hypnotic experiment that the Supraconscious makes and keeps an accurate record of even the smallest detail of everything you see, hear, smell, taste and touch. This record disregards not a single detail—details of which your conscious mind is unaware.

The Supraconscious has powers of observation that astound the average person. While the conscious, even at its best, can only record a limited number of details of anything, or any scene, at any given time, the Supraconscious records so quickly and thoroughly that it could be likened to motion-picture film with sound track.

Many of you, I am sure, have played a child's game in which a number of objects—perhaps twenty or twenty-five—are placed on a table and after one minute's observation you have to remember as many as possible. Do you recall how few you could recollect?

Have you ever been called upon to testify in court as to what occurred in an accident or tried to reconstruct a scene? It is almost embarrassing to many people when they discover their conscious memories are so faulty.

Journalism professors at universities often use a trick to show students how faulty so-called "eyewitnesses" can be. Suddenly, without warning, during a lecture, a strange person will force his way into the classroom, fire a gun perhaps, or do some other overt and obvious act, and leave quickly.

When asked to describe accurately what happened and to give a clear picture of the perpetrator, most of the students find themselves at variance with their classmates on the details. Sometimes even major details blur in the conscious memory.

But the Supraconscious records with instant action and minute detail.

The late Dr. Morton E. Prince of Boston carried on numerous experiments that proved conclusively the magnificent powers of the Golden Gift's Supraconscious level.

For example, Dr. Prince once gave a young man a newspaper and told him to read a short item near the center of one page. After reading the item several times, the young man was asked to repeat as closely as he could the wording of the item he read. He was able to recall the item with a fair amount of accuracy.

Then, under hypnosis, he was asked the same question. Not only was he able to repeat the item word for word, he was able to repeat—word for word—the contents of the entire page. Every single item on that page had impressed itself on the memory of the Supraconscious. Yet the young man had only read the one item and concentrated on it expecting to have to recall its wording.

In another experiment with a young woman, Dr. Prince introduced the woman to a man with whom she conversed for some time. He left the room, and Dr. Prince asked the woman to describe the clothes the man wore.

She was able to come up with a detailed description of his wearing apparel. Then under hypnotic spell the same question was asked. Her answer astounded even Dr. Prince, though he was expecting greater detail in her description. This time she went into minute details of his clothing, even describing carefully the stripe in the cloth of the suit he wore. She also apparently noticed the man with whom she spoke had false teeth, something her conscious did not notice, it was later determined.

In a third unusual experiment Dr. Prince had a young woman walk past one display window of a large department store. Some time later she was asked what articles had been shown in the window. This she was unable to do. She explained that she had been looking straight ahead when she passed the window and had only caught a slight glimpse of it out of the corner of her eye.

How could she be expected to have seen or remembered anything on display in that window, she protested. But placed under hypnosis she proved to be quite mistaken. She had seen quite clearly what was in the window and had seen it with the Supraconscious, not the conscious level of her mind. Questioned again in hypnosis, she described the entire window display in minute detail.

I have witnessed a number of experimental hypnotic demonstrations. Each, though I knew full well what to expect, astonished me more, for it offered more and more conclusive proof of the powers of the Supraconscious.

One of the most interesting demonstrations I ever witnessed was conducted by Dr. Gerald M. P. Fitzgibbon of Trenton, New Jersey. Dr. Fitzgibbon was demonstrating before a large audience. He called for volunteers from the audience and selected ten, after rejecting a number of persons who in preliminary testing showed marked resistance to being hypnotized.

In rejecting the persons he did, Dr. Fitzgibbon stressed strongly that no person can be hypnotized against his will. Co-operation is the essence of hypnosis. Complete willingness is necessary with the understanding by the subject that there are no harmful aftereffects of the hypnosis, either mental or physical.

Dr. Fitzgibbon went so far as to point out that each person hypnotized would benefit physically, mentally and morally from the experience through posthypnotic suggestion in which the Supraconscious would direct the body to some beneficial doing.

The ten subjects were asked to seat themselves on the stage and fix their attention to the bright lights overhead. Dr. Fitzgibbon then walked back and forth behind the row of chairs in which the subjects were seated and said in a monotone:

"You are going to sleep . . . Relax and sleep."

As he continued to intone these remarks in a level, unchanging voice it was apparent within a very few minutes that the nine men and the one woman on the platform had gone into a hypnotic sleep.

Dr. Fitzgibbon then demonstrated by hypnotic control how remarkable the Supraconscious is. His experiments showed the power of the universal Law of Suggestion and proved to an amazed audience how perfect is the memory of the Supraconscious level of the mind.

In the state of hypnotic "sleep," Dr. Fitzgibbon was able to communicate with his subjects through their Supraconscious. He controlled this communication consciously. Any or all of the ten persons on the platform would respond to his bidding and comply implicitly with his every command.

He told them that each had a violent toothache. Instantly every subject grimaced in real anguish. Several held their hands to their faces as if to ease the agonizing pain.

This painful session was ended, and the audience was amused at the group's changing responses to the suggestion given their Supraconscious that they were uncomfortable first from excessive heat and then from extreme cold.

A moment later they were told that a talent scout from a Hollywood motion picture studio was in the audience and was offering a contract to the person making the funniest face. The facial contortions they dreamed up had the spectators convulsed with laughter.

The most startling experiment, proving the great control of the Supraconscious over the functions and conditions of the body (reread the fifth proposition of the working hypothesis), involved a young man in the group of ten hypnotized subjects.

This man was told by Dr. Fitzgibbon that at the count of two he (the subject) was going to make his body completely rigid. Dr. Fitzgibbon directed the man to stand and then counted, "One . . . two."

In seconds the young man's body visibly became stiff. His rigidity resembled a state of rigor mortis. Four volunteers from the audience carefully lifed the young man off his feet and placed him, stiff as a board, between two chairs. His head and shoulders rested on one chair and his feet on the other. His body resembled a bridge between the two chairs.

Dr. Fitzgibbon then kneeled on the man's midsection. The body remained rigidly firm. Dr. Fitzgibbon then jumped up and down on the subject. The young man's muscles, responding to the hypnotic suggestion and the power of his Supraconscious, held tightly.

This experiment, as I pointed out before, was probably the most important as far as it proved the powers of the Supraconscious over the functions and conditions of the body. Certainly—and you can attempt this yourself, at home—you could not will your muscles to this control consciously. It is obvious that the muscular segments of the body in the conscious state of mind are controlled by what scientists call "conditioned reflexes."

In a conscious state of control the muscles of the body, no matter how rigidly they may be held, would "give" to the weight placed upon them. The muscles could not even hold up the body that encompasses them, let alone remain rigid while another person jumped on the midsection.

The demonstration of muscular rigidity showed how through outside suggestion a condition of catalepsy was produced. Catalepsy is muscular rigidity growing out of hysteria and dementia praecox, conditions in which the Supraconscious takes hold after the conscious level of the mind loses control in a mentally ill person.

By artificially producing a cataleptic state, Dr. Fitzgibbon proved the power of the Supraconscious and the truth of the working hypothesis' fifth proposition: the Supraconscious has absolute control of the functions and conditions of the body. This proposition will be further expounded in Chapter VI, "Your Mind Can Control Matter." There I shall tell you how the Supraconscious powers can be either constructive or destructive and how to overcome fear.

Dr. Fitzgibbon's next experiment on that stage disclosed the truth of the fourth proposition of the working hypothesis: the Supraconscious is endowed with a perfect memory.

The hypnotist selected a man of about forty from among the subjects on the stage. The man's head was nodding in his state of hypnotic "sleep."

Dr. Fitzgibbon directed him:

"Tell me the name of the city and the street address where you lived when you were ten years old."

The man promptly gave a street and house number in Buffalo, New York.

"Where were you on the Fourth of July when you were ten?" Dr. Fitzgibbon then asked the man.

"In Niagara Falls," came the reply.

"Where did you eat your noonday meal in Niagara Falls on the Fourth of July when you were ten?"

"In the picnic grounds."

"At what time did you eat your lunch in the picnic grounds at Niagara Falls when you were ten?"

"At eleven o'clock."

Dr. Fitzgibbon then tested the true powers of the memory and observation of the Supraconscious.

"If there was a bookcase in the house in which you lived in Buffalo when you were ten years old, tell me the name of the fourth book from the right on the third shelf," he requested.

There was no reply from the man. Dr. Fitzgibbon repeated the question in a more commanding tone. The man then mentioned the name of a book pertaining to motorcycles.

The memory powers of the Supraconscious have been demonstrated in other experiments. I recall seeing one hypnotist place a middle-aged man into hypnotic sleep. Then he brought him back quickly through his younger years.

"You are now twenty years old. You are now fifteen years old. You are now ten years old. You are six years old. What is your name?"

The man gave his full name—John Bruck.

"Write it for me," the hypnotist asked, handing the man a piece of chalk and leading him to a blackboard.

The man wrote the name in a rather round first-grade-style script.

"You are five years old," the practitioner said. "What is your name?"

The man again gave the same name.

"Write it for me," he again requested.

This time the man struggled over printing his first name only.

"Write your other name!" the hypnotist commanded.

After a long wait, during which the man fondled the chalk uneasily, the subject said: "I can't."

"You are now three years old," the hypnotist then said. "What is your name?"

The subject replied only: "Johnny."

"Write it for me," the man was told once again.

Again a long pause and then the man said in a small voice: "I can't write!"

Substantiating the perfection of the Supraconscious memory in this man was the discovery a few days later of a trunk containing some of the man's schoolbooks as a child. Several showed distinctly the manner in which the subject wrote as a child at several of the ages through which he "lived" in the hypnotic state. These conformed exactly with the results of the experiment.

A wonderful demonstration of posthypnotic suggestion ended the experiment I described earlier given by Dr. Fitzgibbon. This experiment showed further just how great the power of suggestion is and how the Supraconscious can maintain control over us despite the actions of the conscious level of our mind.

The ten subjects on stage were told individually to do and say certain things after they "awakened" from their hypnotic "sleep." Upon being brought back to the conscious level, each of the subjects was obviously unaware that any posthypnotic suggestion had been implanted in their Supraconscious.

Each, to the complete delight of the watching audience, did exactly as he or she had been told to do—the very word, the very act.

The one woman among the subjects was told to leave the platform and then approach the hypnotist and ask him:

"Will you dance with me?"

Dr. Fitzgibbon then brought her out of the hypnotic "sleep." She immediately left the platform. Then she walked over to Dr. Fitzgibbon and asked:

"Will you dance with me?"

One of the younger men in the group was told to go to a piano off stage and strike the E key nine successive times. He was brought back to the conscious level and immediately did as he had been told to do while his Supraconscious was under the direction of Dr. Fitzgibbon.

A more astounding exhibition of the posthypnotic suggestion on the Supraconscious mind's ability to remember quickly and perfectly was tried with another man. Dr. Fitzgibbon told him that upon "awakening" he would walk to the front of the platform, pick up a certain commercial product and repeat a fairly long and highly technical sales talk.

Dr. Fitzgibbon read the sales talk to the hypnotized man—once—and then brought him back to the conscious level. The subject did precisely as he had been instructed and repeated word for word the technical terminology in the prepared talk used for sales promotion.

The scientific knowledge that we have garnered from hypnosis proves without any question of doubt or argument three of the propositions of the working hypothesis:

The Supraconscious is constantly amenable to control by the power of suggestion.

The Supraconscious is endowed with a perfect memory.

And the Supraconscious has absolute control of the functions and conditions of the body.

Paracelsus believed that the discovery of magnetism had led him to the discovery of nature's "hidden power." Little did he know it, but despite the fact he did not discover the "hidden power" of nature, he had discovered the "hidden power" of human nature.

The most astonishing thing about the "hidden power" of human nature is that it can be controlled through the use of the Supraconscious. And the veritable miracles that the Law of

Suggestion can influence on the Supraconscious of a human are not limited to the will of others.

That power of suggestion, the utilization of nature's Law of Suggestion, is one that you yourself can use to work "miracles" for yourself.

The things that can be wrought by the powers of the Golden Gift can be done by self-suggestion. The first proposition of the working hypothesis—the Supraconscious is constantly amenable to control by the power of suggestion—applies not only to the directions it receives from an outside source. That proposition applies just as strongly to the will of your own conscious mind in directing the Supraconscious.

The power of self-suggestion, or autosuggestion, is most effective just before you go to sleep. It is then that the many inhibitions of your conscious awareness are least active. It is then that you are most receptive to the push you need to "contact" your Supraconscious and bring it into full play.

Thousands of cases can be cited to illustrate the obvious fact that while a person is asleep the mind beyond the conscious level—that is, the Supraconscious—is more vigilant than it appears to be during waking hours.

A case in point was first published more than seventy-five years ago. Since that time countless similar instances have been noted and the results of these published irrefutably.

The only conclusion you can draw from these cases is the proof of the third proposition of the working hypothesis: the power of the Supraconscious to reason deductively from given premises to correct conclusions is practically perfect.

The case I wish to tell you was published in 1881 in *New World*. Here is an exact transcript of that account:

Jennie Lawson is a member of the second class in the Eighteenth Street Grammar School.

Friday last a number of arithmetical examples were given out for solution, but three of them (in percentages), requiring long processes of division, resisted all Jennie's efforts to secure the correct answers.

This circumstance seemed to distress the child, and after working through them again and again without success, she went home determined by persistent effort to find out where her error was, and she continued to strive until long after the rest of the family had retired.

Towards midnight her mother, who slept in an adjoining room, called to her daughter that she had better go to bed, lest she should be late in rising the next day. The girl at once retired and in a few moments was fast asleep.

About an hour afterwards, Mrs. Lawson was again awakened by a sudden noise in her daughter's bedchamber, which was then in entire darkness. She called, but receiving no answer, arose to see what was the matter.

Jennie was sitting at her desk, and had apparently just completed some work on her slate, the noise having been made by the falling of a ruler from the table to the floor. The girl was fast asleep. Mrs. Lawson did not wake her up at that time, and on the following day it was afternoon before the girl could be aroused from the deep sleep in which she seemed to be.

Upon awakening, Jennie spoke of the problems, and expressed her intention of making a further trial of their solution. Upon getting the slate, she found them completely solved in her own hand, each line neatly ruled, and the figuring without the slightest error. At this she was greatly surprised. Her last knowledge of the puzzling examples was of leaving them unsolved on the night before.

Of her performance in her sleep, she knew when she awoke absolutely nothing, and her mother, not having mentioned the incident, left her the more bewildered.

Yesterday the girl brought her work to school, and related the incident attending it to her teacher. The room was entirely dark, the girl soundly asleep, during the working out of the test examples, She had never before shown any symptoms of sleep-working, nor have any of her relatives been so affected.

Were this the only piece of evidence available, it should be sufficient to convince you that your mind actually thinks beyond the conscious level while you yourself are asleep. The working of the Supraconscious in the case of Jennie, who solved difficult arithmetic problems while asleep, is but one of so many that it is impossible to count them, let alone recount them.

In my experience with such cases of "sleep thinking" as that of Jennie's I have found that the Supraconscious level of the mind always reasons deductively from established or given premises.

In a published newspaper account of an interview with Dr. Herman Baruch, famous psychologist, the scientist stated quite flatly that his more famous brother, Bernard Baruch, the millionaire advisor to presidents, has the ability to go to sleep thinking about some knotty problem and awaken with the correct answer to the question that perplexed him.

Just how long it took for this great philanthropist to develop the faculty of self-suggestion and how much arduous effort and diligent practice it required to make full use of the power are unanswered questions.

Baruch may have been led to the idea from the work done at the Coué's Children's Clinic in Nancy, France. There mothers are instructed to whisper constructive suggestions into the ears of their sleeping children.

This "whisper method" was used successfully by a friend of mine who assisted his son in mastering a certain academic subject that the youth had previously failed. The night before the semester's final examination, the father sat beside the sleeping boy's bed and read aloud, over and over, that section of the studies that the boy had found too difficult to learn.

The boy's father reported to me later that his son wrote a perfect paper the next day.

Some day in the not too distant future there seems no doubt that school children will learn all their lessons in this manner. Homework will be cut to a minimum with all memorizing being eliminated by having the lessons played on phonograph records while they sleep. One manufacturer of school equipment has perfected a recording machine for this very purpose.

It has been shown how a "hypnotized state of mental susceptibility" can be produced by lulling the conscious level of the mind into a drowsy reverie. In this state the Supraconsicous level of the mind is highly amenable to suggestion.

Upon getting into bed at night, you should assume a comfortable position, relax completely and thoroughly and close your eyes. In this way you can induce in yourself this state of receptivity on the Supraconscious level.

Relaxation, while often thought to be a difficult thing to accomplish with thoroughness, is actually a simple process. It requires conscious effort. But without conscious effort, you cannot reach to the Supraconscious level of the mind.

In a supine position, you must concentrate on each muscle one at a time in every part of the body. Starting at the feet, concentrate on easing the tenseness of the toes. When they are relaxed, ease the semirigidity of the muscles in the feet.

Slowly move your thoughts upward in your body, relaxing each muscle as you pass it consciously. Your legs, your diaphragm, your arms, your chest, your neck—all loose and relaxed and ready for a state of self-induced hypnotic sleep.

Now you are ready to introduce to yourself a state of Supraconscious receptivity.

In this state you can deliberately introduce into your Supraconscious any desired idea. The powerhouse of the dynamic machinery that is the Supraconscious will transform this idea into a reality providing there is adequate emotional fusion.

To assure contact between your conscious and your Supraconscious in the beginning of your experiments with this great power of the Golden Gift, repeat the suggestion night after night until you feel certain that the emotional fusion has been forceful enough and that the Supraconscious level has been reached and has accepted the idea.

I have found that emotional fusion is the key to penetration of the Supraconscious from the conscious level. That is, the greater the degree of emotion attending the induced self-suggestion, the more certain will be the acceptance of the idea being introduced to the Supraconscious.

There seems no doubt from experiences I have had and from experiences other people have reported that the intensity of emotion is the key to the catalytic action of the Supraconscious.

Emotion? you ask. Yes, I reply; emotion in the sense of "transference" and of "agitation of the feelings." That is to say that a deep emotional force is built up to reach the Supraconscious level—whether consciously or not—through an intense feeling of desire.

Wanting to achieve is necessary for achieving. Remember the words of Matthew VII:7—"Ask, and it shall be given you; seek, and ye shall find; knock, and it shall be opened unto you."

A desire to accomplish must be deep within you before you can begin to scratch the surface of success.

The desire to utilize the great benefits of the Golden Gift must be effectively transferred to the Supraconscious level of your mind.

I stated a few paragraphs ago that the desire can either be conscious or unconscious. What we are trying to achieve, however, is conscious transference of ideas to the Supraconscious level. A classic example of how great this power of transference of desire can be is one in which the subject willed the desire to the Supraconscious level completely unconsciously.

The example concerns the case of the "Miracle Girl of Konnerseuth," Theresa Neumann, who meditated on the

Crucifixion of Christ with a burning desire to share His sufferings on the cross.

Theresa was born in 1898, the eldest of ten children of a villager who was both tailor and farmer. She was a perfectly normal healthy child. As a child and young woman, she was quite indistinguishable from her companions in a strongly Roman Catholic village.

"She was industrious and obedient," it was said of her, "chaste and possessed of good moral qualities, pious and adamant in her principles."

In the spring of 1918, her spine was injured in a fire. Complete paralysis of her limbs and blindness eventually resulted. But suddenly, on May 17, 1923, the day of the beatification of St. Theresa of the Child Jesus (to whom Theresa prayed much) she regained her eyesight.

On September 30, 1925, the anniversary of the saint's death, she regained the use of her limbs. She was cured without outside aid of appendicitis in November, 1925, and of pneumonia in February, 1926.

In 1926, on Thursday, March 5, to be specific, a wound opened under her heart and began to bleed profusely. The stigmata appeared for the first time while the young woman was in ecstasy.

From that time on she suffered, on different occasions, every agony that it is recounted befell Christ from the time He started His passion until He died on the cross.

The marks of nails appeared on her hands and feet. The imprint of a crown of thorns showed on her forehead. Her eyes bled.

The following Sunday the stigmata started to shrink. But on the next Wednesday they became gradually more and more pronounced. On Friday they bled again while Theresa went through the agonies of the Crucifixion.

One of the features of the ecstasies which Theresa went through that puzzles most investigators is the language she used. Throughout most of her vision, she spoke in her village dialect. But when she seemed to be quoting directly the figures surrounding Christ, she lapsed into a language of which she had absolutely no knowledge.

Language experts identified the tongue she spoke in quoting these persons in her vision as ancient Aramaic, the language spoken at the time of Christ. And, they pointed out, she clearly made use of small variations in the language as it was spoken at that very time.

In the vision of the angels, she claimed to hear them cry out: "Kadosh, Kadosh, Kadosh." This is Hebrew—not Aramaic—for "Holy, Holy, Holy."

She claimed to hear the apostles shout when Judas betrayed Christ: "A sword; down devil of a fellow; thief! Thief! A sword; down devil of a fellow!" This she kept on repeating in a combination of the Aramaic and ancient Greek languages.

When Jesus was being flogged in her vision, she wept and was shaken by such convulsions that it seemed her frail body would collapse under the blows of the whip.

When not in ecstasy, Theresa appeared to be perfectly normal mentally. She was not in the least a psychotic personality, as all who met her testify. Her health was of the best.

It appears that there is no great difference between natural sleep and that state of "sleep" produced by suggestion—which is most often called a trance. In the trance state, the conscious level of the mind becomes as fully inactive as it does in natural sleep.

When the conscious level is inactivated, the Supraconscious level can hold full sway over the processes of the body and mind.

This scientific explanation of the miracle of the stigmata is in no way intended to detract from the power of God and the sanctity of Theresa Neumann. Both, on the contrary, are clearly manifested to the unbiased observer in the phenomenon of her stigmata.

Nor do I intend to cast any reflection on the cloistered groups of devout women called Stigmatists. These religious women, who for years have concentrated their thoughts on the life of Christ, have so completely focused their mental energies on His sufferings on the cross, and so vividly pictured His wounds in their "mind's eyes," that their "emotional thinking" actually changed the chemical and physical cellular structure of the tissues. This made nail marks appear in their hands and feet as well as the spear wound of the crucified Christ.

These Stigmatists devote their lives to emulating the life of Christ. They fix their conscious thoughts during long periods of meditation on the wounds of the hands, feet and side of Christ. They concentrate on these wounds so vividly on the conscious level of the mind that the mental picture of these very wounds is transmitted to the Supraconscious level of the mind.

By the emotional fusion of these thoughts with the Supraconscious, these devout women are sometimes able to suggest to their Supraconscious the very wounds of Christ in their own bodies. The emotional fusion sometimes provides the catalytic action that has been known to manifest itself in reproducing these very markings on their own flesh.

The action of the Supraconscious in these Stigmatists is again convincing evidence of the fifth proposition of the working hypothesis: the Supraconscious has absolute control of the functions and conditions of the body.

This is no different from that biological process of the sympathetic nervous system that is known as metabolism. What medicine has discovered about the human metabolic processes is ample proof of the powers that the Supraconscious of the Golden Gift can use for you.

Let us suffice to say at this point that it is the metabolic processes of the body that replenish the blood cells when they are needed. This process of organic growth and repair is explained more fully later. You have just been given a peek at the wonders of the human body that are controlled by the Supraconscious.

Having this knowledge should lead you naturally to the understanding of the powers that are about to be explained to you. Once you can use your own conscious powers to reach the Supraconscious level of your Golden Gift, you hold within your own hands virtual control of the power of longer, healthier life and greater, fuller happiness.

In the chapters that follow, you will learn how your own metabolic processes can be speeded up by positive "emotional thinking."

This is a form of concentration, exactly like prayer and meditation, which will lead you to the limits of producing phenomena you probably never believed possible of yourself.

You now understand that you have within you the power to use the Law of Suggestion.

You now know that you possess the Great Answer: the power to understand and utilize for your own welfare and for the great good of all mankind the powers that have been Divinely granted to you as the Golden Gift.

With the Great Answer you have open to you the road that leads from your conscious to the Supraconscious.

You have discovered the road that leads to using the Supraconscious—your own as well as that of others—for the greatest good.

The Infinite Plan was not conceived for ill and evil. It was created for good.

Thus with constructive thinking, with positive planning, with purposive creating, you can utilize the Golden Gift's treasure house of the Supersense.

HELPING YOURSELF WITH SUGGESTION

Autosuggestion is the secret to autoconditioning.

You have now learned—and used—the ability to reach your Supraconscious. The next step in helping yourself do whatever you desire is to "plant" the suggestion of this desire in your Supraconscious.

1. Before falling asleep, relax completely and open the passageway to your Supraconscious.

2. Now repeat to yourself a positive thought expressing a positive desire.

3. At first it may be best to repeat this thought over and over. It may be necessary to repeat it aloud.

4. As you acquire proficiency at reaching your Supraconscious, you will find that you can suggest to yourself any positive thought, silently and a single time.

IV

Rediscovering Your Supersense

You have, perhaps often, used one of the greatest powers of your mind.

You have used it and have perhaps wondered a little about it. Or you have thanked good fortune for having shown you the way, and not bothered to think about it.

What is this power? Why have you not used it more often? Can you now utilize it to its fullest extent?

The answer to the last question is: Yes, as often as you want—when you learn what it is and how you can use it.

You have undoubtedly done things on a "hunch" at some time or other and later discovered that you were correct in following this unexplained direction.

Perhaps you have at some time had a "feeling"—a "feeling" that led you to take the correct action in some activity, a "feeling" that you later probably called a "sixth sense."

Perhaps you may have been sitting at your telephone and thinking, "So-and-so ought to call me—I have something very important to tell him and I can't reach him"; then within minutes have the person in question telephone you!

Perhaps you have been on your way home when for no apparent reason you stopped to buy a particular article. Then upon arrival home you have been told that had you telephoned you would have been asked to stop to buy that very article.

Maybe you have been at a gathering when suddenly you went to find the person you came with and said, "You want to go home now, don't you?" and discovered your impression was correct.

You called them "hunches" or attributed them to a "sixth sense." You may perhaps sneer when someone talks about "mental telepathy." Yet your so-called hunches or impressions resulting from your so-called sixth sense are no more incredulous than mental telepathy.

What you perhaps fail to realize is that in addition to the five senses of the conscious level—seeing, hearing, feeling, tasting and smelling—there is a sense belonging to the Supraconscious level of the mind.

It is a form of communication you are not familiar with. You encounter it infrequently. You notice it only in such rare instances as have been listed above.

Yet it apparently is functioning even more thoroughly than the five senses of the conscious level. From what little is known of it, the Supraconscious sense, unlike the five senses, never rests.

It is the Supersense.

From what little can be garnered of dead civilizations, the Supersense is nothing new to man's knowledge. It apparently was known—and used—in ages past. Why science is only now setting about rediscovering the Supersense is something that may never be explained.

The Supersense is in reality a double sense: it has all the powers of mental "television" in addition to all the powers of mental "radio."

Telepathy, the telegraph of the Supersense, is not abnormal. Eileen J. Garrett, writing in *Telepathy, In Search of a Lost Faculty*, says telepathy "is part of the creative faculty."

Further substantiating the theory that the Supersense—and the Supraconscious—can help you mold a new life for yourself, Mrs. Garrett writes:

"If you grant it is within your power to improve yourself in any way, then you are able to achieve that improvement in self-expression by developing telepathic, clairvoyant and clairaudient powers."

You see therefore that within you lies the power to make for yourself a regenerated life. There lies before you, when you tap this power potential of the Supraconscious, the ability to help yourself live a longer, healthier and more useful life. In your hands rests the ability to create for yourself new power of wealth and new concepts of happiness.

Can you see yourself adding years to your life?

Can you picture yourself a newer, healthier person—untroubled by the degenerative diseases of aging?

Can you see yourself moving ahead in business, creating new ventures, making wise investments?

Can you see yourself doing all the things you have dreamed of doing but felt incapable of accomplishing?

Can you see a future with unlimited opportunity opening up in all aspects of living?

These are no "pipe dreams," they are not "castles in the

air." They are reality within your reach if you are willing to learn to understand the powers of the Supraconscious.

The Supraconscious level of the mind—like the conscious level—has means of communicating with the same level in other persons. As the conscious mind developed, man developed his ability to communicate by speaking. But in so doing, it appears he lost the faculty of utilizing the communication-level of the Supraconscious.

It seems highly plausible that before ancient man began to make distinguishable sounds—talk—with his vocal chords, he communicated by sense—or rather, Supersense.

The Supraconscious is an entity unto itself with many powers. Not only does it store vast amounts of information, rapidly and accurately, but it has the powers to transmit to, and receive information from, the Supraconscious of other persons. Just how this works, no one has yet discovered.

Whether the psychologist or the neurosurgeon will first come on the secret and supply mankind with the answer is a question to which only time can reply.

It has long been known, however, that the electrochemical processes we call "thought" create vibrations. These thought vibrations have been electrically recorded.

It appears that these thought vibrations, utilizing the power of the Supraconscious level, act much the same as radio waves —under certain ideal circumstances.

Thought transmission is little different from radio transmission. The Supraconscious acts in much the same manner as a radio transmitter. In order to transmit messages—or "broadcast"—the modulation frequency of radio must be increased to the pitch of sound waves in the ether. And in order to have these messages audible to the human ear at the receiving end, they must be reduced again to a lower frequency. What happens in mental thought transmission is identical. The rate of thought vibration is increased to be transmittable.

The power to transmit the message comes, as well, from the Supraconscious. It has been said that the Supraconscious is not only the brain's memory storehouse, it is also the brain's powerhouse. The source of the brain's "hidden power" is emotion. The stronger the emotion, the more powerful the transmission of the thought patterns from the Supraconscious —and the conscious level.

One of the most unusual experiences I have had in the reception of a telepathic message from another person illustrates vividly how the emotional powerhouse is responsible for the energizing of the transmission ability of the mind.

As an inspector of the police department in charge of crime prevention at Saginaw, Michigan, I was interviewing a local business woman one day not too many years ago regarding a theft. She was relating to me at considerable length, and in some unnecessary detail, the circumstances surrounding the theft of money from her purse.

The boy whom she suspected of the larceny was well known to me in similar circumstances. I felt certain he was guilty of this theft. Because of this fact I did not listen too attentively to the long recital the woman was making in relating the circumstances of this latest of his petty thieveries.

I allowed my mind to concentrate subjectively while I pondered certain peculiar aspects of her facial expressions. I began to sense that something more than the theft of the money was bothering this woman.

I wondered what the trouble could be when suddenly I was possessed with an irresistible urge to talk to her about the most unusual idea that had flashed through to my conscious mind. The thought seemed fantastic and irrational to my reason. But the urge was so unmistakably in the same category I had had—and other people had had—in the field of extrasensory perception, I felt I had to do something about it.

I decided to chance telling the woman of the extraordinary impressions that had flashed across the threshold of my consciousness as I studied the perplexing signs of deep mental stress and anxiety showing on her face as she talked to me.

"I think I know who took the five dollars from your pocketbook," I said to her. Then I added, a little more cautiously:

"But I would like to talk to you about a more serious matter, if you don't mind."

She looked at me with the sort of expectancy which indicated to me that she sensed the impact of my deep feeling of sympathy for her perturbed mental state. She only muttered quickly: "Of course not, go ahead." Then she appeared almost breathless as she waited for the words she must have felt were ominous.

"You have been contemplating suicide."

My voice was quiet and, in comparison, her exclamation seemed to tear through the room.

"My God! How do you know that?"

She turned deathly pale.

I explained quite frankly that I did not know how I came to know the fact that she planned self-destruction. I told her, however, that I suspected it was the so-far-unexplained phenomenon called telepathy. This seemed to stabilize her wits, and we were able to discuss her situation quite calmly and objectively.

The misunderstanding responsible for her terrible obsession was easy to point out to her as we openly discussed the circumstances of her family discord without hiding or distorting any facts.

I feel sure that our conversation released the nervous tension underlying this good woman's mental disturbance—but that is something I wish to discuss later on.

While I have not seen this woman since her visit to my office in the 1940s—though she still lives in Saginaw and would corroborate my story—perhaps it is not assuming too much to believe that this incident of my Supersense at work may have saved her life.

So we come upon evidence of the correctness of the sixth proposition of the working hypothesis: the Supraconscious has the power to communicate by means other than the recognized channels of the five senses.

All of my telepathic experiences have been spontaneous ones. I have not ever attempted to use my Supersense for such communication. But I feel certain that the Supersense is a vital part of the Golden Gift. I will tell you later how I discovered the constant functioning of the Supersense in mass communication with all persons without the awareness of the conscious level.

In each of the telepathic experiences I have had, I have been aware of deep emotional stirring, usually in a sympathetic attitude of helpfulness for someone. I therefore believe that the phenomenon of telepathy takes place when the human nervous system attains a certain intensity of mutual frequency which permits the transference of thoughts from one person to another at the subjective level of consciousness.

The emotional stirring I have experienced—providing the necessary power for the transmission of thoughts from the Supraconscious—is an experience everyone has had at some time or other. The experience of telepathy, as a result, is also an experience common to most people at some time. Most have not been sufficiently interested in taking more than passing notice of the unusual manifestations.

In my own case, the over-all problem of the work in which

I was involved, gave my emotional nature a certain responsive fluidity which the average person does not have the opportunity to acquire and develop. For many years I have done research into the problem of juvenile delinquency. I have sought a workable solution to the behavior difficulties of young people who get into trouble with the law. This aroused my interest in many phases of human nature with which a person ordinarily does not come in contact.

The conditioning of my emotional reactions has come from handling thousands of problem children. They were always handled with sympathy and understanding of the erring youngster and his unsolved problems.

This sensitizing of my Supersense led me to the discoveries I have made in the realm of the Supersense and the Supraconscious. Yet my discoveries took me further into the fields of telepathy and like phenomena. They astonished me when I discovered it was well established that telepathy is known as the means of communication between minds beyond the conscious level—that is, between the Supraconscious levels of the human brain.

And the communication of the Supersense is a never-ending function. It is a constant stream of telegraphy going from mind to mind—despite the fact that the "conscious" knows nothing of this occurrence.

Your Supraconscious, as you now know, is a vast storehouse of knowledge. Where this knowledge comes from is apparent. The Supersense-radio is constantly receiving communications from the minds of people all around you. Your Supraconscious is constantly accumulating new stores of knowledge through this telepathic communication.

Perhaps the most amazing case on record of such accumulation of knowledge by the Supraconscious mind is that of Edgar Cayce, the so-called "Miracle Man of Virginia Beach." There are many stories of the powers of Cayce was able to utilize after he discovered that he could use them—and some of these I will discuss later.

First I want to tell you how he performed phenomena that were called in his time—and today would be, too—"miracles." Yet they were, by the words of his own Supraconscious mind, only the use of the accumulated knowledge within that level of the Golden Gift.

Edgar Cayce as a boy of twelve first experienced phenomena that were termed psychic. He discovered then, unwittingly—

though by means of clairvoyance—the powers of the Supra-conscious.

But his use of the accumulated knowledge of the Supra-conscious—and the "collective unconscious"—did not come until he was grown to manhood. Through chance, and a misfortune, Cayce and scientific researchers discovered his ability to call on powers which startled the world.

Edgar Cayce had worked as a salesman. When he lost the use of his voice, he returned to his home at Hopkinsville, Kentucky, where he took a job as a photographer's apprentice. An entertainer, known as Hart the Laugh King, was booked into the town opera house, where he was to give an exhibition of hypnotism.

Virtually all of the townspeople in Hopkinsville went to Holland's Opera House to watch the fun. Hart entertained the people in the usual fashion, putting members of the audience into hypnotic trance and having them do all manner of amusing things for the enjoyment of their friends and relatives.

Someone spoke to Hart about Cayce's condition. While the hypnotist was not a therapist, he was interested in the results of posthypnotic suggestion and thought he might be able to help the young man. While in a hypnotic trance, Cayce was able to speak quite normally. Awakened, he could speak only in a hoarse whisper, and the posthypnotic suggestion apparently failed.

Hart tried a second time, but the posthypnotic suggestion again did not succeed with Cayce. However, Dr. John P. Quackenboss, a New York physician, later heard of the matter directly from Professor William Girao of the psychology department at South Kentucky College.

Dr. Quackenboss had great faith in the possibility of curing illness by hypnotism. It was his belief that in posthypnotic suggestion a patient could be healed by directing the mind to remove the cause of the illness.

Dr. Quackenboss tried his skill on Cayce but he, too, failed. Later, however, Dr. Quackenboss wrote to the South Kentucky professor with the theory that Cayce failed to respond to the posthypnotic suggestion because Cayce's own Supraconscious took charge while in the hypnotic state—not the mind of the hypnotist. Dr. Quackenboss based his theory on reports of similar occurrences in France some years earlier. The French cases showed that the patients had had the power of clairvoyance while under hypnosis. Dr. Quackenboss suggested that

Edgar Cayce should be put into hypnotic spell and asked about his own illness.

Cayce was told about this suggestion and he offered to put himself to sleep—in the same way he had done as a boy when studying. As a boy Cayce had found that if he slept on his schoolbooks he was able to absorb their contents with facility and did not need to study further.

Thomas Sugrue describes the experiment in his book *There Is a River*.

"Edgar lay down on the family couch, a horsehair sofa that had been part of his grandmother Cayce's wedding suite. He put himself to sleep.

"Al C. Layne [a local hypnotist], watching, saw the breathing deepen. There was a long sigh, then the body seemed to sleep. The squire sat in a chair near by. His wife, nervous, stood up. Layne began to talk in a low, soothing voice, suggesting that Edgar see his body and describe the trouble in the throat. He suggested that Edgar speak in a normal tone of voice.

"In a few minutes Edgar began to mumble. Then he cleared his throat and began to speak in a clear, unafflicted voice.

" 'Yes,' he said, 'we can see the body.'

" 'Take it down!' Layne said to the squire [Cayce's father].

"The squire looked at him helplessly. The nearest pencil was in the kitchen, tied to the grocery list.

" 'In the normal state,' Edgar went on, 'this body is unable to speak, due to a partial paralysis of the inferior muscles of the vocal cords, produced by nerve strain. This is a psychological condition producing a physical effect. This may be removed by increasing the circulation to the affected parts by suggestion while in this unconscious condition.'

" 'The circulation to the affected parts will now increase,' Layne said, 'and the condition will be removed.'

"Edgar was silent. They watched his throat. The squire leaned over and further loosened his son's shirt. Gradually the upper part of the chest, then the throat, turned pink. The pink deepened to rose, the rose became a violent red. Ten, fifteen, twenty minutes passed.

"Edgar cleared his throat again.

" 'It is all right now,' he said. 'The condition is removed. Make the suggestion that the circulation return to normal, and after that the body awaken.'

" 'The circulation will return to normal,' Layne said. 'The body will then awaken.'

"They watched while the red faded back through rose to pink. The skin resumed its normal color. Edgar wakened, sat up, and reached for his handkerchief. He coughed and spat blood.

" 'Hello,' he said tentatively.

"Then he grinned.

" 'Hey,' he said, 'I can talk! I'm all right!'

"His mother wept. His father seized his hand and shook it again and again."

The inevitable result was the suggestion that as Cayce had been able to diagnose his own ailment, perhaps under the same conditions, he could do so for others. Edgar was willing to try—and his success was phenomenal.

While he actually knew nothing about physiology, biology, anatomy or medicine, this humble man was able in a hypnotic trance to diagnose all manner of afflictions and ailments. In addition he was able to prescribe a wide variety of medicine and methods of treatment that invariably effected cures.

But Edgar Cayce did not understand how he did this. Despite the many successes he had, he was confused and fearful of the ability he possessed. Often he would read and read again stenographic transcripts of what he said while in a hypnotic spell, hoping to discover some explanation in his own words of the strange power he possessed.

He was amazed at the technical language he used. He was astounded at the scientific knowledge he displayed. Each session's transcripts left him more confused—but he went on with the miraculous successes. But though he continued to search in the transcripts of his own words for some explanation of his power, it never occurred to him to have questions asked of him about the power while he was in his trance state.

This method of probing into the discovery of the use of Edgar Cayce's Golden Gift did, however, occur to Dr. Wesley H. Ketchum, a young homeopathic physician who had opened an office in Hopkinsville and became vitally interested in Cayce's "gift." Dr. Ketchum posed the question to Cayce while in a hypnotic state. Cayce's answer was included in a published report given before a meeting of the American Society of Clinical Research at Boston in September, 1910.

Dr. Ketchum told the gathering of his curiosity in this direction and said that Cayce answered the question in the third person. Part of the paper read by Dr. Ketchum follows:

"When asked the source of his knowledge, he (Cayce) stated: 'Edgar Cayce's mind is amenable to suggestion, the same as all other subconscious minds, but in addition thereto it has the power to interpret to the objective mind of others what it acquires from the subconscious mind of other individuals of the same kind.

" 'The subconscious mind forgets nothing. The conscious mind receives the impression from without and transfers all thought to the subconscious, where it remains even though the conscious is destroyed.' "

Thus it was that Edgar Cayce described to the world for the first time what we have come to discover is the Supraconscious level of the mind. He used the terminology current in that day. But although he did not recognize the fact that he had uncovered the key to the Golden Gift, that is exactly what he had done.

The medical men and scientists who worked with him and who read of his work, too, failed to realize that they had in Edgar Cayce the key to the wondrous treasure of the Divine Plan of Infinite Intelligence.

Cayce in his hypnotic state—that is, in the control of his Supraconscious—knew that this level of his mind was in direct communication with the same level of mind in other persons. He knew, too, that the Supraconscious was capable of interpreting through his objective mind and imparting the impressions received to other objective minds. In this way he gathered all the knowledge possessed by countless millions of minds through the communications means of the Supraconscious.

Time and space mean nothing to the scope of the Supraconscious. It appears obvious that the communications system of the Supraconscious can reach out for information from the tremendous storehouse of memory of the Supraconscious of other minds no matter where they may be.

Edgar Cayce was never satisfied with the "why" of his power. He was able to understand the "how." This he learned from his own explanations while in hypnosis. He knew absolutely nothing of the laws governing human nature. Consequently he did not realize that the powers that made him different were the fruits of his own efforts. They were the attributes of the deeper consciousness from which the essence and substance of spirituality is nurtured through individual conscious effort.

These great powers are possessed by all humans. But they are undeveloped. Edgar Cayce did not know this. In him the development of these powers of the Golden Gift was the end result of his having spent countless hours in his childhood in reading the Bible and meditating on the spiritual aspects of what he read.

It is the cause-and-effect manifestation of the Law of Use to which this parable refers:

"For unto everyone that hath shall be given, and he shall have abundance; but from him that hath not shall be taken away even that which he hath."

In its most simple language it means that God gives help to those who seek to help themselves.

The power of thought transference is not one in which the conscious level necessarily participates. That is to say that which is being communicated from one Supraconscious to another is not necessarily something about which either person is consciously thinking.

Usually there is no connection whatever with the conscious thoughts of either of the persons involved in the transcommunication on the Supraconscious level. A message of the utmost importance may therefore never reach the threshold of the percipient's consciousness, or even be consciously sent by the agent.

You see, therefore, that with this telepathic communication possible—going on virtually at all times—and with development of the Supersense and controlled tapping of this additional power by the conscious, there are unlimited horizons open for you to explore, utilize and profit by.

With the power of the Supersense untapped consciously, it appears that those persons who are able to utilize this system of communications are developed to some degree psychically. It obviously requires an extraordinary degree of development of psychic power for one to tap the telegraph of the Supraconscious as a man such as Joseph Dunninger, the popular magician and "mentalist," purports to do. (Dunninger's demonstrations are authentic, but he requires a large audience in which to communicate on the Supraconscious level with minds tuned to the same emotional frequency as his.)

The one great beauty of the power of the Supraconscious means of telecommunication is that the "message" is never lost. It is not necessary for the conscious level of the mind to tap the power of the Supersense in receiving a message at the moment it is received.

The great storehouse of memory called the Supraconscious assures that the message received—and all such messages which apparently are being received at a constant rate—is permanently filed in the bins of knowledge of the Golden Gift.

Failure to become objectively conscious of the reception of the message delivered to the Supraconscious intelligence, does not mean, therefore, that the subjectively communicated matter is lost.

The recipient of the message may not belong in the class of "sensitives" able to elevate their subjective impressions to the level of the conscious. But hypnosis and other psychic experiments have proved that the information thus received by the Supraconscious is stored at that level indefinitely.

The mere fact that all this intelligence remains latent in the Supraconscious storehouse means that every individual has within his own power the ability to do things far beyond the reach of his own conscious imagination.

Your Supraconscious is receiving, at a constant rate, great amounts of information daily. The thoughts of persons everywhere are being projected by their Supraconscious telecommunication systems to yours. Similarly, your Supraconscious is sending out to all the fruit of your thoughts.

It remains with you, then, to learn to tap this system and bring its message to the conscious level. It is within your power to search through the great memory storehouse of the Supraconscious and pick out the knowledge that you require at any given time for any given task.

Achieving liaison between the conscious and the Supraconscious levels—between objective and subjective thought—is a matter of how "sensitive" you are at any given moment. The "sensitivity" is a quality which you can and you should develop.

Unlike the Supraconscious and the Supersense, both of which you have been born with, emotional sensitivity is a power you must develop. It can be developed to a level of great intensity—and thus bring you vast treasures.

Many creative persons have unwittingly credited this development for the works they have done. We know of the stories told by such men as Edison, Ford and Marconi about themselves. There are countless other instances of this utilization of the power.

"Happy ideas come unexpectedly," said the great German scientist Hermann von Helmholtz. "They have never come to me when my mind was fatigued or when I was at my working table."

Other scientists claim that creative ideas usually flash to them while they are engaged in other activities—the conscious mind then being most receptive to communication with the higher level of the Supraconscious.

In the field of the arts the same is true. Great musicians have recorded their impressions of this great Supraconscious power. Wolfgang Mozart said the process of composition "is like a vivid dream," referring to the mental activity going on beyond the conscious level of his mind. Peter Tschaikowsky said: "The germ of a future composition comes suddenly and unexpectedly."

Fontaine Fox, the famous cartoonist of "Toonerville Folks," recently recalled, shortly before he "retired" at the young age of seventy, that he started to run out of ideas for his comic strip the second day he started drawing the antics of the Toonerville gang:

"So I followed some early advice of my father's. I went for a long walk. I got an idea and started for the office . . . I've been rolling ever since on the same theory."

The great untapped wealth of the Supraconscious is yours, too, to develop and use.

The telecommunication of the Supraconscious takes other forms. Some investigators are inclined to disbelieve the phenomenon of mental "television"—clairvoyance. They believe that this phenomenon belongs in the same category as telepathy. It is their contention that the power to "see" through the Supraconscious is strictly thought-transference from the Supraconscious of one person to that of another.

A classic example is that of Emanuel Swedenborg's vision of the great Stockholm fire in the summer of 1759. Swedenborg was in Gothenburg at the time, three hundred miles from his home in Stockholm.

Suddenly he became perturbed and announced that there was a big fire in Stockholm. He added that a friend's house had been destroyed by the flames and his own home was in danger of being destroyed by fire.

There was no means of rapid communication or travel in those days, of course, and so nothing could be done to confirm or contradict the picture seen by Swedenborg in his mind's eye.

Two hours after his first "vision" and announcement,

Swedenborg said suddenly that the fire had been brought under control only a few doors from his residence.

Two days later messengers brought the news of the conflagration to Gothenburg, confirming the philosopher's vision in exact detail.

This historical incident has all the earmarks of being a case of mental "television" of the Supraconscious. Those investigators who believe that the power of clairvoyance is the same as that of telepathy state that it is possible that the information was subjectively communicated through the emotionally excited mind of one of Swedenborg's friends who witnessed the fire—possibly the very person whose house he had "seen" burn at the time his own abode was threatened.

Swedenborg naturally believed he was Divinely inspired. He was nearer right than he suspected when he said:

"There appertains to every man an internal man, a rational man, and an external man, which is properly called the natural man."

Scientists still debate the reality of telepathy, clairvoyance and clairaudience—the mental "radio" I mentioned before. I know from personal experience they are real.

Perhaps the most vivid experience I have had with mental "television" as a power of the Supraconscious occurred some years ago. It involved a boy—now a married man with four children of his own, still living in Saginaw—who then lived on the outskirts of that city.

His mother used to bring him to my office regularly every Friday morning for several months. One particular day I saw the boy carrying a large paper bag. I thought nothing of that fact, other than that he and his mother had probably been shopping before visiting me.

When the youth did not seat himself in his customary place, and with the first step he took in my direction, I sensed that he had brought me a gift. Not realizing it, I suddenly said:

"You have brought me two quarts of home-grown strawberries!"

The boy stopped in his tracks. He was frightened and confused and turned instinctively toward his mother. His own power of reasoning was stunned by incredulity and confusion.

The surprised mother asked in astonishment:

"How did you know that?"

It was my turn to express surprise along with that of my visitors. My frank reply at the moment was:

"I really don't know!"

What happened in effect, I realized later, was that I actually "saw" the strawberries. I saw them, despite the fact they were hidden from my sight and other ordinary senses of perception, quite securely in a heavy brown paper bag.

The skeptical investigator may say it was a demonstration of telepathy—not clairvoyance. Perhaps there was some sort of unusual contact between the boy's mind and mine at that particular moment.

Be that as it may, I know that a deep feeling of gratitude was the emotional trigger that caused some particular part of my brain—in the Supraconscious level—to flash into action and provide the "sight" of the gift.

I cannot see this incident as being anything else than the power of the Supraconscious to receive pictures, as well as thoughts and sound.

Edgar Cayce's first contact with his Supraconscious powers of perception was in the form of clairvoyance. As I said before, Cayce was deeply religious, and this spiritual aptitude appeared early in childhood. He delighted in attending Bible meetings and was so impressed by what he heard that by the time he was ten years old he decided to read the Holy Bible through once for every year of his life.

With ten years to catch up, all the boy's spare time was spent in reading the Bible and thinking about God. Little wonder that his imagination should dip deeply into the spiritual contents of his "collective unconscious."

One day at the age of twelve, while meditating on things he had read in the Bible, he suddenly "saw" a lady who looked like his mother. She asked him what he wanted most out of life. His greatest desire, he said, was to help others, especially children when they were sick.

Young Edgar, though not a dull boy, was uninterested in his schoolwork, and after this incident he became even less interested in school. His original disinterest started immediately after his first year in school. His teacher then was a pretty, soft-spoken, gentle woman who loved children and was loved in return. Under this woman's tutelage, Edgar learned quickly. He liked her and therefore he was able to please her in this manner. But when she left the school a year later, Edgar's incentive to study was gone. He became listless and could not keep his mind on his work.

When he discovered his liking for the Bible, his father—disappointed in the boy's schoolwork—encouraged him by buying a Bible for his son. When not occupied with chores, Edgar read the Bible on his self-appointed task—but never once would he touch homework from school.

Reading the Bible became an obsession with the boy and thus he activated the inherent faculties of his Supraconscious that normally remain comparatively dormant while the mental development is confined solely to objective learning.

Why the appearance of the "lady" to his mind's eye had anything to do with the boy's increased lack of interest in schoolwork is not known. But by this time his teacher—an uncle, as it happened—complained to the boy's father.

The elder Cayce decided to take a hand in the affair and told the boy that his stupidity was a disgrace to the family. He would learn his lessons from then on—or else!

The first study period set by his father was a long and painful evening for the distraught lad. Time and again his father would hear his spelling lesson. The answers were always wrong. Finally the father slapped the boy off his chair with the threat of terrible things if he failed again.

Young Edgar was tired and sleepy. He remained on the floor where he had been knocked by his father. Suddenly he heard a "voice." He recognized it as the "voice" of the "lady" he had seen earlier. The "voice" told him to put the spelling book under his head and go to sleep.

The boy closed the book, used it as a pillow and went to sleep. (This marked the first instance of Edgar Cayce's long series of experiences in self-hypnosis about which you have already read.) When his father returned, he was fast asleep. The exasperated parent snatched the book from under his head and no sooner had the boy opened his eyes than the father gave him words to spell. To the amazement of the elder Cayce, the boy spelled every word of the lesson correctly.

Young Edgar gleefully informed his father that he could spell every word in the book. The astonished father found this to be correct and accused the boy of having played dumb. In school, Edgar was brilliant in spelling from that day—but he was as dumb as ever in his other studies.

He took his other books home with him one day and put them under his head when he went to bed. Then he thought of the "lady" of his vision and prayed to her until he fell asleep. Again the wondrous miracle occurred! He awakened to find that he knew the contents of all the books in a single night.

Thus it was a phenomenon of clairvoyance—of mental

77

"television"—which led Edgar Cayce to discovering the great powers of the Supraconscious.

To those who have never experienced a psychic phenomenon such "visions" seem inexplicable—except in a "supernatural" sense. Visions, clairvoyancy, or, as I prefer to term it, mental "television" are not to be construed as "heaven sent." They are a medium of Divine guidance that stems from the level beyond the conscious nurturing spirituality.

To those persons who have had occasion to meditate for long periods or to concentrate their thoughts on a single quest —as I have in my long search for a solution to the problem of juvenile delinquency—these "visions" are recognized as symbolic expressions of the reactions of the Supersense in the Supraconscious level of the mind.

An example of mental "television" that I experienced in connection with my research will illustrate the point. I am indebted to the *Catholic Weekly,* which printed this experience in its April 8, 1951, edition for permission to retell it here.

I was at the time trying to reconcile the theory of evolution, as developed in the study of anthropology, with the story of the Garden of Eden which I had been taught by the good Sisters of St. Mary's. That issue was highly controversial in my conscious thinking—and that is the reason I had difficulty in comprehending the true meaning of the clairvoyant thought I had.

Upon awakening from a sound sleep one night, I "saw" the image of a weighing scale. On one of the balance trays were the words "Garden of Eden Story," on the other were the words "Theory of Evolution." It seemed strange to me at the time that the trays on the scale appeared to be in perfect balance.

And all the while an inexplicable feeling of peace and serenity, such as I never before or since had, permeated my entire being.

This experience occurred during the early 1940s when my eldest son was attending the University of Michigan. When he came home to visit the next weekend, I told him of my mental "television" experience.

"Perhaps," he offered me his opinion, "the balance of the scales indicates that one theory is as good as the other."

He insisted that I consult a local priest. Although I felt reluctant at the time to talk about my strange experience, for fear others might think me odd or even conclude that I was losing my sanity, I finally decided to ask one of the older priests if he believed in the theory of evolution.

Much to my own surprise, I discovered that he did. Furthermore, he told me that all informed persons now accept the theory as a fact.

I concluded then that my son's interpretation of my clairvoyant experience was correct.

Later I realized that though the controversial aspects of the two theories would ordinarily have caused me to have experienced some mental confusion and the resulting upset of my nervous system would have created mental stress and physical discomfort, I was at the time of the experience at complete peace and harmony, as I described earlier.

The third power of the Supersense is that of mental "radio" —clairaudience. This is a faculty that is much more rarely developed than the two previously discussed.

One dictionary definition of clairaudience is "the act or power of hearing in a mesmeric trance sounds which are not audible to the ear in the natural waking condition." I would define it as the faculty of human intelligence that enables the conscious level of one's mind to receive communications by means of the spoken word from the Supraconscious level of one's own mind or the mind of another person.

The power is by no means confined to persons in "mesmeric trance." But it seems quite likely that for best results one should be in a partially subjective state, such as deep concentration or reverie, to enable oneself to hear clairaudiently his own thoughts of the Supraconscious which are frequently communicated to him subjectively by others.

The "sounds"—if one can use that term for something that does not cause atmospheric vibrations—are quite distinct to the conscious of the hearer. They are, however, not at all perceptible to others who may be near the hearer and in a normal state.

Although clairaudience (or mental "radio") is an entirely different sort of phenomenon from either telepathy (mental "telegraphy") and clairvoyance (mental "television"), it is frequently tied in with some telepathic message from the Supraconscious. The following illustration may serve as an example:

One evening in February, 1941, another of my sons, who was then eleven years old, was listening to the radio while I was deeply engrossed in some reading in connection with research I was doing.

I was totally unaware of the nature of the radio program to

which my son was listening. But suddenly something within me seemed to say:

"That's what you're interested in!"

I turned my attention from the book to the radio in time to hear a speaker talk about some article which had been published in the March issue of *The Reader's Digest*. I missed hearing what the article concerned. I went back to my reading, but later went to the library to see the issue about which I had heard on the program.

I read through the index on the cover seeking some title that I hoped would lead me to the article I sought—though actually I had no idea what the article was about. I did not associate any of the titles in the index with what I was interested in at the time.

The next step, then, was to read the magazine from cover to cover. No one article seemed to give me any enlightenment on the feeling I had had a few days earlier about the "unknown" article being discussed. One piece, however—"Prayer Is Power" by Dr. Alexis Carrel—did intrigue me and I re-read it several times.

It was only after several readings that I noticed in fine print an editorial reference to Dr. Carrel's book *Man, the Unknown*—a best seller in 1935. I borrowed this book from the library and found in reading it something in which indeed I was most interested.

I have been convinced for many years that the negative attitude held by many leading scientists in regard to so-called extrasensory perception has been a definite block to human progress. These learned men have been reluctant to apply scientific study to this virtually unexplored field. They have instead relegated all such experiences to the category of abnormal psychology.

I decided therefore to write an article for the purpose of stimulating discussion with a view to doing something about this feeling of the scientists. Being a public servant at the time, I was a little hesitant to offer for publication the article—"Mind and Behavior."

You will realize my reluctance. I had absolutely nothing to support the conclusions I had reached. And these conclusions were all contrary to accepted academic opinion.

All I had was the strength of my own convictions in the value of certain hypotheses of what I call "sleep thinking." These were confirmed only by my own experiences and observations. And I was not a scientist and therefore might be ridiculed as a "crackpot." Not that I minded the ridicule, but I felt that my only hope in getting anyone interested was in getting some sort of confirmation for my beliefs. In that way, I felt, I could make even the most skeptical scientific reader sit up and take at least a little notice.

Obviously it would have been unwise to attempt publication of my "unorthodox" views without some substantiation. I felt therefore that the incident of discovering the Dr. Carrel book by the roundabout means of reading the *Digest* article—led to it by my clairaudient message—put me on to a most valuable piece of supporting information.

In his book Dr. Carrel wrote:

"At the present time, scientists who are concerned solely in the physical and chemical aspects of physiological process still look upon telepathy and other metaphysical phenomena as illusions.

"Evident facts having an unorthodox appearance are suppressed.

"By reason of these difficulties, the inventory of the things which could lead us to better understanding of the human being, has been left incomplete."

There are numerous accounts of mental "radio" in recorded history. Even the Bible bears out this phenomenon.

Plato records that Socrates, the wisest man of all Greece when that country was in its cultural glory, heard a "voice" from childhood on. This great Greek philosopher, who ranks with the keenest intellects ever produced by the human race, was told of the coming of good and bad by this "voice." And, Plato adds, the "voice" sometimes warned Socrates not to do certain things that he had been contemplating, warnings which Socrates obeyed.

Aristophanes, too, mentions Socrates' extrasensory powers. In his great comedy *The Birds* the playwright has Socrates conducting a séance. Plato tells us that Socrates was sent into a sort of trance state at times. During one of these, it is recorded, the philosopher stood motionless for twenty-four hours. This "motionless" condition you will easily recognize as a form of "suspended animation" produced by self-induced hypnosis.

This man whose wisdom is accepted as unquestioned throughout the world today was one of the unfortunate individuals with great psychic powers whom the ignorant of that day put to death for "the practice of religious novelties." The same taboo on the so-called "occult" which brought death to one of the world's greatest thinkers more than twenty-three centuries ago still prevails against honest investigators today.

In these past twenty-three centuries—and in even earlier times, no doubt—how many geniuses have been put to death for being "witches," "wizards" and "dealers with the devil" by those persons who would eliminate evidence rather than investigate it scientifically, as the late Dr. Carrel admonished.

You and your neighbor feel, and to a great extent rightly, that you live today in an enlightened age. You pride yourselves on the fact that mentally ill persons are no longer put to death because it is believed they are "in league with the devil."

Yet so many scientists today, in not discriminating between what is destructive and what is constructive—that is to say between the abnormal and the extranormal—are actually being a hindrance to human progress. They are no different in their own way from the thinkers of past ages who decried the "magic" of the early philosophers and healers.

The late Dr. Morton Prince, specialist in nervous diseases, once said:

"The biographies of saints like Catherine of Siena, and Francis, the founder of the Franciscan Order, and of leaders of religious thought like George Fox the Quaker, John Bunyan, and Savonarola, to say nothing of minor lights like Savonarola's follower, Fra Silvestre, are replete with accounts of visions and internal voices which once upon a time were interpreted as visitations or supernatural messages of one kind or another.

"The researchers of recent years in abnormal psychology enable us to understand the genesis of these sensory automatons, even if we cannot explain their exact psychological mechanism. In the light of this knowledge, it becomes clear that they are due to the autogenic influence of the subjects' own thoughts, conscious and subconscious." (That is, thoughts on the conscious and Supraconscious levels).

Admitting that these phenomena might be due to the autogenic influence of the subjects' thoughts on the Supraconscious level, Dr. Prince covered more territory than he seemingly realized. He was not aware of the exchange of thoughts at the Supraconscious level of human intelligence.

Dr. Prince made the same mistakes that many others do in assuming that all sensory automatons are hallucinations. Classifying all extrasensory perceptions as abnormal is as ignorant of the true facts as believing that extranormal manifestations come directly from a supernatural source.

One of the best illustrations of the "inner voice" or mental "radio" which people for centuries have mistakenly connected directly with the "supernatural" (and which scientists now call abnormal), is to be found in a published conversation G. Lloyd Preacher, of Atlanta, Georgia, architect and inventor, had with his life-long friend Thomas Alva Edison.

In this conversation Edison said:

"Don't give me so much credit for my work. The credit is not all mine. I mean only that I am merely the instrument through which a Supreme Intelligence carries on His work. I am pioneering in undiscovered country and have been from the first.

"When I began this work I knew nothing of electrical or mechanical science. My schooling covered little more than a year. If I had not worked under the direction of a Supreme Intelligence, the work would never have been done at all."

Edison worked days and nights with little sleep. He was, he claimed, sustained by the Supreme Intelligence. He was once asked how and where he was first aware of Divine direction.

"It began when I was a telegraph operator in a lonely mountain town," he replied.

"I became aware of messages or directions coming clearly into my mind as I sat there through the long nights, and began the work which I was directed to do!"

"But why," he was then asked, "have you kept this to yourself?"

"Because my work alone was important," Edison replied. "The world would have said, 'Edison is crazy!' or, 'Edison has got religion!'

"What they said afterward does not matter."

Although Edison may nor may not have recognized the phenomenon as mental "radio" and not the "voice" of God, he was nevertheless quite correct in stating that he was the instrument through which Supreme Intelligence carried on His work.

Are we not all?

Edison did not say in so many words, as did the late Dr. George Washington Carver, that he heard God speak to him. Edison merely stated that he became aware of messages or directions coming clearly into his mind while he sat through the long night as a telegraph operator in a lonely little mountain town.

The great inventor was indeed fortunate to have had the solitude of this mountain town in combination with a job that required him to spend long lonely nights as a telegraph operator. That combination of factors left him alone with his own thoughts.

Roger W. Babson, the famed economist, recommends this very combination of factors—seclusion and solitude—as a basis for making important decisions.

In his helpful book *Before Making Important Decisions,* Babson says the seclusion of a quiet church is the place to think over one's problems prior to coming to an important decision.

The quiet of the long nights in the seclusion of a telegraph room in a lonely mountain town added together two ideal circumstances for Edison's temperament and mentality. He was a deep thinker who could completely absorb his "inner self" in research work to the exclusion of both the awareness of time and surroundings.

Edison admitted that he feared other people would say he was crazy. It is generally believed that mentally ill persons hear "voices"—and that is exactly what Edison experienced. But the inventor did not lose the use of his reason during his periods of deep concentration.

Instead, he found his real self and, by placing his conscious awareness in a state of temporary abeyance (during concentration), he was able to make use of the vastly greater store of intelligence and ability of the Supraconscious level of his mind.

This deeper consciousness is much like a self-induced hypnotic state. It simply means placing consciousness in a neutral state of inactivity while the greater resources of the Supraconscious are brought into play.

The successes of a man such as Edison are no great mystery or secret. Edison did not hesitate to admit that had he not worked under the direction of a Supreme Intelligence, the work he did would never have been done at all.

Had Edison not recognized that the Supreme Intelligence was within his own being, he certainly would not have stated that his formula for success was simply:

"Ninety-nine per cent perspiration and one per cent inspiration."

When Edison said that he worked under the direction of a Supreme Intelligence, he probably had in mind the fact that few people ever learn how to think as God intended that we should.

That is our fault, not His.

No one is born without the illimitable resources of the Supra-conscious.

Medical science has shown in recent years that clairvoy-ance and clairaudience—mental "television" and "radio"—are mechanisms of the human brain. We are told now that these phenomena have no "supernatural" significance—other than in the sense that God works His wonders through the medium of His handiwork, of which the human organism is perhaps His greatest exhibit.

By probing the exposed surface of the human brain with an electrical impulse, researchers have found that memory centers can be activated when electric currents are established.

One subject "heard" the voices of members of his family in a conversation that took place during his early youth. Another "saw" the scene of a childhood episode in minute detail.

The findings of these scientific experiments are obvious. Among many other hypotheses, they confirm the belief that the forces that make the human organism tick are electro-chemical vibrations. It is this electrical force that makes telepathy, clairvoyance and clairaudience possible—much in the same way as wireless telegraphy, television and radio work.

It has often been noted that persons who never develop beyond the stage of idiocy, or who have become afflicted with certain forms of insanity, have great ability to tame and subdue animals. In such persons the activity of the conscious level of the mind—or the sense of reason—either is wholly or partially in abeyance (if, indeed, it has been developed at all).

In these persons, then, the Supraconscious level of the mind is proportionately more active. (Could this explain the "voices" that insane persons hear?)

Apparently a telepathic "meeting of minds" on the subjective animal level of intelligence unconsciously provides some basis for mutual understanding and friendliness between man and beast. At any rate, the immunity of many idiots (and so-called Holy Men, it may be noted) from harm by animals, however ferocious, is proverbial.

So numerous are the facts showing the power of the Supra-conscious of mankind over the "minds" of animals, that volumes could be written on the subject. But enough is generally known to realize that the power exists. Under certain well-defined conditions, this power can be exercised by any person of ordinary intelligence.

There is, for example, the tradition of Daniel. Of course Daniel was not an ordinary, run-of-the-mine individual. He was a prophet, a seer. In this modern age he would be known in some circles as a spiritual medium, in others as a mind reader, in yet others as a clairvoyant—all according to the particular conception of each individual as to his powers. (The skeptics would, of course, proclaim him a fake.)

It is the belief of many people, of course, that Daniel was saved from being torn to shreds and eaten by the lions by the power of God. To that I add, "Amen!" But I wish to offer this one opinion:

Daniel, being a man possessed of great subjective power, his own "animal" brain and those of the lions had enough in common to render him immune from harm. This, simply because his presence did not excite fear or anger in the beasts.

For the still skeptical, let me cite an experiment made in Paris shortly after the turn of the century. It is interesting and should be illuminating in this instance.

A young lady was hypnotized and placed in a cage of lions. The object of the experiment is not now known—but its results make that object unimportant in comparison. Just as was Daniel, the young lady was not touched. She showed—and had —no conscious fear of the king of the beasts, and the lions in turn paid not the slightest attention to her.

The adepts of India, and even the "inferior priests" of the Buddhist faith, often display their powers by entering jungles so infested by man-eating tigers that an ordinary person would not remain alive an hour. Yet they remain there through the night with no weapons of defense other than the God-given powers of their subjective mental attitudes.

The explanation is simple. The subjective powers of primitive man were undoubtedly far superior to any now possessed by anyone save, perhaps, the East Indian adepts and such persons. Before the development of objective means of communication, in the form of speech, primitive man conveyed his ideas to his fellow man by telepathic means. Hence the definition of this power as "the lost faculty."

As man developed the use of speech through countless generations, he ceased to use—and finally lost—his primitive power to communicate telepathically. Yet, despite this fact, among certain primitive tribes the use of communication on the Supraconscious level still is in use, much to the amazement of scientific investigators and the consternation of others who stubbornly deny the existence of extrasensory powers of perception.

It is written in the Bible that God gave man dominion over the beast of the fields and the fowl of the air. In his prehistoric state, primitive man was destitute of effective weapons of offense or defense such as were evolved during the long ages of later civilizations. Yet man was surrounded by monstrous beasts and reptiles, capable of annihilating the present race of civilized people—were the monsters suddenly resurrected and turned loose in their old haunts and numbers and were we weaponless.

Considering this, then, what was the power of our primitive ancestor to assert and maintain his God-decreed dominion over the monsters of his day? It must have been the same power that is exercised now and then by partial or total displacement of objective intelligence.

Georgi Ivanovitch Gurdjieff summoned up his spiritual philosophy in five simple words: "the harmonious development of man." Man, the Russian philosopher said, is an unfinished product. Nature had evolved him up to a certain stage. Then man was left to his own devices, to struggle to a higher level of consciousness or to remain as he was, an incomplete being.

The question remains for us to answer then: Can modern man utilize more of the "hidden power" of his natural heritage? Can man bring into play the full powers of the Golden Gift of the Great Creative Force?

I say he can. Through intellectual and spiritual development —by eliminating the destructive effect of the many negative feeling-attitudes which stem from primitive fear and anger—it can be accomplished.

The Golden Gift is yours. God has granted it for your use. Within the Supraconscious there lies the Supersense—for you to use and utilize, for you to "spend" in positive production for the benefit of yourself and mankind.

The "hidden power" need not be hidden to you. You have read how to unlock it. You have seen how it can be used for the positive good. You have been shown how you can benefit by it.

And yet this treasure that has been granted you by the power of Infinite Intelligence is not one for which you have to wait to use. It is within your grasp now. Its benefits can be reaped now. Its beauties are apparent now.

All that is asked of you is understanding of the greatness and immensity of the Golden Gift.

You must meditate. You must send yourself into the open

space of deeper consciousness. You must search out the power within yourself.

Then, all that is becomes yours.

DEVELOPING THE USE OF YOUR SUPERSENSE

There are three components of the Supersense: "radio" (or clairaudience), "telegraphy" (or telepathy), and "television" (or clairvoyance).

All three parts of this gift you can put to use if you follow these simple rules:

1. Never disregard any single thought of the "hunch" or "sixth sense" variety. Note it well when it makes itself known to you.

2. Write down all such thoughts on a small note pad which you should keep with you at all times.

3. Before going to sleep at night, turn to the thought—or possibly thoughts—that you had during the day.

4. Meditate on them. Allow them to be retransmitted by your conscious to your Supraconscious.

5. In the morning reread the thought, or thoughts, again.

6. Meditate in silence until your conscious mind brings to you the answer giving the worth of this matter as evaluated by your Supraconscious.

7. Don't hesitate to use the wealth of this knowledge, immediately and to the fullest.

V

Your Incredible Memory
and What It Can Do

Your Supraconscious puts the proverbial elephant to shame!

The elephant, or so they say, never forgets. But the poor elephant is limited. He can only remember those things that he has encountered.

The Supraconscious is so vast a storehouse of memory that it staggers the imagination to realize how much knowledge is recorded in that small mass of matter that we call the brain.

The Supraconscious is a huge, though compact, library of facts. How many facts are stored there is impossible to count. The source of these facts seems to range all the way back through the ages of our ancestry—for our very way of life bases itself on the patterns developed in centuries past.

In recent years we have been astounded by newspaper and magazine stories about electric "brains." We have marveled at the vast amounts of knowledge stored in them and at the speed with which they can be made to utilize this learning. And yet, while man's brain may never match the speed of these mechanical giants, it is the product of man's knowledge that makes possible technological development.

Every fact down to the smallest detail has been laboriously placed in these electrical brains. They can "think" of nothing other than what has been inserted in them. We can watch with wonderment at how a problem is "fed" to the giant "brain"— often filling two large rooms—and how it rumbles out an answer within a matter of minutes.

It is truly wonderful. For man has, with the power of his brain, developed a "brain" that can speed up man's own deductive processes and thus aid civilization and mankind.

But place the human brain—a little more than three pounds of it—beside the tons of electric "brain" and realize that the tiny lump of gray matter holds in it a millionfold more information than the hulking monster of its creation. Then you know the meaning of wonder.

In that fifty ounces of living matter is recorded more information, more knowledge than it seems likely a person could record in the space of a lifetime.

Your brain is the possessor of a memory the scope of which is virtually impossible to explain, let alone imagine. And added to all that, this memory—an integral part of the Supraconscious—is constantly being added to by direct communication with the memories of every other Supraconscious.

How often have you had occasion to say to yourself:

"Where did I hear that before?" Or:

"I've seen that somewhere!" Or:

"How do I happen to know that?"

There is no doubt you've had such experiences many times and in many ways. Some fact, some statement, some place, some thing, will be completely familiar to you. Yet consciously you were positive that until that very moment you had never encountered it previously. And it was familiar! Why?

Is it that the conscious memory often fails us and forgets things it has experienced? That is partially so. But the conscious, if we jog it sufficiently, will bring back memories of all things it has known.

Or is the answer that the Supraconscious suddenly relays to the conscious level of our brain the memory of something we have not actually experienced, either consciously or actually in our lifetime?

Although it seems impossible to measure the powers of the Supraconscious, we can safely say that the Supraconscious level of the brain is greater than the conscious level in much the same way the universe is greater than our planet.

And look at the greatness of the conscious. Look at the incredibly immense powers of the conscious brain's five senses. How often have you marveled at man's inventions of the radio, or television, or telegraphy and its various facets which speed communications? But we take for granted the powers of sight, smell, taste, touch and hearing.

These powers of the conscious are fabulous wonders. With the powers of invention, man has only been able to duplicate two of the senses—machines that "see" and those that "hear." Man still has not been able to duplicate God's wonders of the senses of smell, taste and touch.

And man's failure to realize the powers he has been given by Divine gift has led him to depths rather than to heights. When you accept the fact that within you there is the power of all-doing, you can rise to the peaks of good-doing.

For years one of the things I tried to impress on the young

people with whom I came in contact after they had come into conflict with the law was the wondrousness of the brain. I tried to explain to each and every youth the powers of the delicate instrument they carried in their skulls.

I would tell them how the impressions of their five senses are conveyed to the brain by the complicated "wiring" network in the body—the nervous system.

And, more incredible still, the fact that this nervous system is so sensitive and effective that every detail of things seen, heard, tasted, touched or smelled is completely and permanently registered in the memory storehouse of the Supraconscious.

The conscious level of the memory records only such details in which you are interested. But your Supraconscious memory constantly collects all information and indelibly imprints it within itself.

As a practical illustration of the difference in functioning of the conscious and Supraconscious memories, I would ask each of the boys I was interviewing to tell me how many holes there were in the perforated soundproof ceiling of my office. Obviously they were far too numerous to count.

Each boy reacted the same way. He looked up to the ceiling for the first time and a look of perplexity appeared on his face. When I explained that his sense of sight had actually made a count of the number of holes and this was recorded by his Supraconscious, the little grin that usually followed the first conscious glance at the ceiling turned to an expression of incredulity.

Long before I started my research studies, I often found myself wondering where or when I had encountered some thing or fact before. Prod my memory as I would—and no doubt you have done the same thing—there was no conscious recollection of the source of this information.

Especially in dealing with youngsters who had gone astray of the law—and their parents—I found myself often giving advice the source of which I had no idea. And I was offering this advice with the confidence and belief equal to the inborn faith of my religion.

Finally late in 1939 I decided to write an article on my therapy methods for these young people in the hope that it might be used elsewhere to help humanity.

As I wrote the words "How does science know these things?" I realized that if I could not remember where or how I had come to learn of these mysteries of the mind, certainly I could not hope to prove the existence of the Supraconscious level of the mind, much less promote public confidence in its deeper consciousness and its hyperintelligence.

Some months earlier I had come upon an old book, *Increasing Personal Efficiency: The Psychology of Personal Progress,* by Donald A. Laird, which I had read many years before. More recently, on discovering that book again, I happened to open it at a picture the caption of which read:

"What the Mental Iceberg is capable of doing. This is a drawing made by automatic writing; the person who drew it did not know she was drawing."

I had been using that picture and the discussion pertaining to it as I talked to the boys whom I dealt with in my capacity in the police department as I tried to explain to them the wondrous powers of the Supraconscious.

I had read to them:

"The mental underworld also thinks while we are unaware of this thinking. Posthypnotic suggestion shows in an interesting way how the thinking takes place unbeknown to one—in his mental basement, as it were—and later breaks through the barriers and comes upstairs to modify conscious thoughts.

"These underworld ideas break through into consciousness and modify our daily thoughts and actions. . . ."

Apparently all that I had been telling them met the need of the occasion.

But when the greater need of proving statements presented itself, then the amazing thing that is the Supraconscious reached down into the "collective unconscious" for the answer.

Had I simply "remembered" having read these things in that book, this explanation would be quite commonplace—as you have seen that the memory of the Supraconscious level is perfect. But the psychic reaction was much more complicated than that.

There was something that seemed to "tell" me to get that book from its untouched place on the bookshelf and read the two pages preceding the illustration on "automatic writing."

I read:

"To understand fully your own and other personalities, you must know about a mental underworld. When a person is hypnotized, it is found that the eyes have been seeing and the mind has kept an accurate record of countless thousands of events and features that the upper world of the mind has never known about. . . ."

At this point in the book the author listed two experiments

that proved the unusual powers of the Supraconscious. Then his text continued:

"There is the eye of the subconscious mind for you! Just as it sees, so it hears, and tastes and feels. Things that we do not sense, it senses. Events that we forget, it remembers."

The power of intuitive perception has long been known to scientists as a faculty of the Supraconscious. Many persons, even to this day, think of intuition—which has manifested itself many times to most everyone in what people commonly call "hunches"—as the sixth sense, or as I term it, the Supersense.

Robert Collier in his remarkable book *Riches Within Your Reach* says that to develop intuitive consciousness you must cultivate a dominant desire for this higher consciousness which comes only as the result of a tremendous yearning for spiritual truth, and a hunger and thirst after things of the spirit.

The understanding of the power in you is a necessary condition to this development, he says. And the vital key to mastering this understanding is the knowledge that no matter how little or how much education you have received—or been exposed to, as some educators choose to put it—there is this power in you.

Regardless of who you are, what you are, where you are, what you do, you are the possessor of this great power—this same power which directs and animates all of the universe.

Call it what you will: your good genie, your unconscious, your subconscious, the Supraconscious—it is there, in you.

It is yours to turn failure into success. Yours to create prosperity, not penury. Yours to achieve progress instead of fostering frustration. Yours to encourage growth and keep you from stagnation.

Your mental and emotional activity in connection with the Supraconscious cannot be measured in terms of measurements as you know them. But that does not mean that these activities are not real. They are definite and concrete things. A thought expressed or projected becomes an enduring part of the personality that has created it.

The mind is a creative organ and its activity provides the power for the attainment of those things which the mind creates. You know full well from experience that you can only do what you think you can do, and attain what you think you can attain.

The whole of your life is the result of thought.

Therefore it lies with you to attain what you wish, to progress, to develop, to acquire health and happiness by using your emotional and mental activity in a constructive fashion.

What is the vision of the artist? It is the development of his creative thought.

What is the inspiration of the writer, or the discovery of the scientist? It is the constructive creation of his intuitive consciousness at work.

Ask almost any great author and he will tell you that he does not "work out" his plot situations and dialogues. They just "come" to him. As simple as that!

"The key to successful methods comes right out of the air," are the words of the late Thomas Alva Edison. "A real new thing like a general idea, a beautiful melody, is pulled out of space—a fact which is inexplicable."

And while it was unexplainable to Edison, today the explanation is simple. The Supraconscious is constantly alert and alive. It needs only the powerful emotional direction of constructive thinking to activate its machinery.

But an alert and alive Supraconscious is not the whole answer to the development of this power and its use. The conscious level of the mind must also be alive to what the Supraconscious is pushing into the area of the conscious thinking.

G. C. Suite, General Electric's Director of Research, said once: "Be on the alert for hunches and whenever you find one hovering on the threshold of your consciousness, welcome it with open arms.

"Aim to keep an open mind. Don't rely too much on logic. Try to locate the treasure chest of ideas which lies hidden in your brain."

The flash of inspiration does not come without hard work. The Supraconscious and the conscious have to prepare the way for the emotional power of the Supraconscious to create. Louis Pasteur once observed: "Intuition is given only to him who has undergone long preparation for receiving it."

And despite the hard groundwork, the plowing of the fertile field, intuition may strike when you least expect it. That is why you have to "welcome it with open arms." It might all too easily escape you.

Mr. Suite tells how General Electric scientists have had ideas pop into their heads. One, he relates, discovered a prize-winning idea emerging from his Supraconscious while he was chopping ice from his front steps. Another man told of a discovery occurring to him in the midst of shaving.

"In my own work," Mr. Suite says, ". . . my hunches come

to me most frequently in bed, in a plane, or while staring out of a Pullman window."

Such flashes from the Supraconscious should be recorded quickly. For often they pass before the conscious level of the mind and quickly disappear. Most persons who have discovered the power that they are endowed with keep a pad and pencil by the bedside nightly and a pocket memo book with them at other times.

One young man I know whose creative endeavor takes him into many artistic fields rarely passes a night that his bedside pad does not get used. A note about a book he is writing, a memo about a projected magazine story, a few notes of a theme for some music, an idea for a radio or television program—all these come to him either before falling asleep or upon waking, when his conscious mind is most receptive to the suggestions passed to it from his Supraconscious.

Robert Louis Stevenson pointed the way when he told how he worked out the plot for *Dr. Jekyll and Mr. Hyde*.

"My Brownies, God bless them!" he said. "They do half of my work for me when I am fast asleep and in all human likelihood do the rest for me as well when I am wide awake and foolishly suppose that I do it myself.

"I had long been wanting to write a book on man's double being. For two days I went about racking my brains for a plot of any sort, and on the second night I dreamt the scene in *Dr. Jekyll and Mr. Hyde* at the window, and a scene afterwards split in two, in which Hyde, pursued, took the powder and underwent the change in the presence of his pursuer."

Theron Q. Dumont, writing in *The Master Mind*, used Stevenson's "Brownies" to explain his theory:

"There are many ways of setting the Brownies to work. Nearly everyone has had some experience, more or less, in the matter, although it is produced almost unconsciously, and without purpose and intent.

"Perhaps the best way for the average person, or rather the majority of persons, to get the desired results is for one to get as clear an idea of what one really wants to know—as clear an idea or mental image of the question you wish answered, as you have of the result you want.

"Then after rolling it around in your mind, mentally chewing it, as it were, giving it a high degree of voluntary attention, you can pass it on to your Subconscious Mentality with the mental command: 'Attend to this for me—work out the answer!' or some such similar order. This command may be given silently, or spoken aloud; either will do."

Dumont suggested that you speak to your Supraconscious "or its little workers"—the "Brownies" of Stevenson—just as you would speak to persons in your employ, "kindly but firmly."

"Talk to the little workers and firmly command them to do your work," he said. "And then forget all about the matter—throw it off your conscious mind, and attend to your other tasks."

In due time, he stated, you will have the answer to your problem flashed to your conscious.

Dumont remarks, too, as have others who have noted this phenomenon in connection with the powers of the "collective unconscious" at the Supraconscious level, that most often the "answer" you require will not be flashed to your conscious mind until the very moment when you must decide the matter in question or need the information.

If you have your "Brownies" well trained, Dumont said, you may give them orders "to report at such and such a time, just as you do when you tell them to awaken you at a certain time in the morning so as to catch the early train, or just as they remind you of the hour of your appointment, if you have them all well trained."

The learned minds of past ages, who discovered the vast powers and great wisdom that the brain possesses, tried vainly to explain the phenomena of the Golden Gift. Failing to comprehend the mechanism of mind, they resorted to all sorts of metaphorical figures of speech as they attempted to describe these psychic reactions.

As well as attributing this great power to "supernatural" origins, many thinkers have generally located the Supraconscious in the solar plexus, as you learned in Chapter I, "The Magic In Your Mind." Other thinkers did not give it structural identity but were content with conveying the vague impression that the Supraconscious is some sort of mystical entity.

Evidence we have today, however, shows almost conclusively that the thalamus (the central section of nuclear cells within the brain) is the seat of the Supraconscious and its memory storehouse, the "collective unconscious."

It is possible to determine the approximate number of brain cells in the cerebrum, the mental structure of the conscious mind. "The figure is so stupendous," says Dr. C. Judson Herrick, formerly of the University of Chicago, "that astronomical figures dealing in hundreds of millions of light years become insignificant by comparison. It has been determined that there are from ten to fourteen billion nerve cells in the human cerebral cortex, and we know that these are arranged in definite patterns. These arrangements are not haphazard. They are orderly. Recently developed methods of electro-physiology draw off action currents from very precisely located cells, or fibers with micro-electrodes, amplify them with radio tubes, and record potential differences to a millionth of a volt."

But the brain cells of the thalamus, the seat of the "collective unconscious," are so tightly packed through countless years of cumulated inheritive growth that they cannot be counted by the usual laboratory process of dissection.

The conclusion is therefore reasonable that the "collective unconscious"—the memory storehouse of the Supraconscious—contains all the accumulated experiences of life since the crack of dawn.

The significance of this staggers the imagination!

Yet there is no reason why you should not recognize the fundamental truth that the potential power and the intelligence of the human brain have never been fully realized. This is so because man's progressive evolution in intellectual and spiritual areas has not been sufficient for the average person to recognize, much less utilize, the constructive resources that Christ apparently had in mind when He said:

"He that believeth on me, the works that I do shall he do also; and greater works than these shall he do. . . ."

You must learn how to think as God intended you should.

You must eliminate from your daily life thoughts and conduct that are the projected effects of primitive greed, fear and anger. Until you do this you will not be able to benefit fully from the constructive elements of your "collective unconscious."

A few persons get a glimpse of the power of the Supraconscious and the "collective unconscious" from time to time, through what we commonly call intuition, telepathy, clairvoyance, clairaudience or some such other extrasensory perception which is the commonplace of the Supraconscious and the "to-be-marveled-at phenomenon" of the conscious.

Every human is a composite continuity of an almost endless array of ancestors. This has been graphically illustrated by the late Dr. Louis Berman, a noted specialist on disturbances of the glands of internal secretion and the biochemistry of health and disease.

Dr. Berman pointed out the very basic facts of numbers in parenthood and ancestry. A man's parents are two; his grandparents number four; his great grandparents eight, and so forth. Within five generations—about a century—a person is the development of thirty-two persons. Another five generations, counting back about two hundred years, a man has more than one thousand ancestors who have contributed their protoplasm to one particular individual.

By this same method, it is evident that counting back less than six hundred years one man's ancestors total 536,870,912 —an impossible situation, as that is much more than the entire population of the world was at the time.

We therefore cannot conclude otherwise than to realize that each one of us today has in his make-up something of everyone who has lived in the past. Every human who ever existed has gone in some way or fashion into making up every one who exists today.

The same holds true for future generations. Less than seven hundreds years from now, some part of every one of us alive today will conceivably be a part and share in the constitution of every personality then alive. For in that time every person will have had more than two billion ancestors living in this decade.

So it is that generations fuse incessantly in one flux of life. The personality of this generation, the individual of today, is no more than a condensation in the current of the living and he will be redistilled into a tremendously greater and ever swelling tide of life. And as humans are linked one with the other, so human life is linked in turn with all of Divine creation.

As an individual, you, then, are a constituent part of the great synthesis of physical protoplasm. And it is therefore so much truer that your thoughts and wills, your emotions and decisions, your memories and achievements, are tributary to that greater inclusive psychic movement that is the life personality.

For you are but an interval in the larger duration of being— the single pulsation of a heartbeat in time. All so-called individualities are only tiny droplets from an immense vat of memory into which every thought and every effort of all mankind as well as of all the beings of Divine creation have funneled their experience.

Manifestations of the "psychic movement that is life personality" frequently are so strangely phenomenal that they sometimes are erroneously thought of in terms of spiritual or supernatural origin.

A startling example of this is one of the busiest and best amateur painters in Britain. This woman honestly admits she knows nothing about painting. Her name is Anne Wiltha, and she is as baffled as the critics at the great quantity—and strange quality—of the canvases she has created.

"I have never been one to believe in ghosts," Mrs. Wiltha said, "but since 1941, when I first felt the urge to paint, someone, or something—I call it my spiritual guide for want of a better phrase—has been directing my hands."

Mrs. Wiltha had never taken an art lesson in her life, but at some time during that year she sensed that she had to try painting. Her hand fairly itched to put brush to canvas.

"I felt silly when I went to the art store with my two children. I had no idea what equipment I needed and the clerk looked at me as though I were just another foolish matron wasting her good money on a useless fling at a difficult profession."

A few days after she had purchased her equipment, she says, the strange impulse to paint struck her again. She set up her easel in her living room, put a canvas panel on it and spread out the paints she had bought.

"I had no idea what I wanted to paint, but I stood at the easel waiting.

"Suddenly lines, like the shadowy pattern on an X-ray film, began to spread themselves over the canvas—and I saw it was a simple landscape. All I did was paint over the lines of this ghostly tracing."

That first effort amazed the woman's friends in Windermere, the town in which she lives. But the result of that afternoon frightened Mrs. Wiltha. There was, she said, something uncanny about the way the task was accomplished.

A week later the "command," as she terms it, came again and she set up another blank canvas on her easel. This time the subject was a portrait—the smiling face of a young girl.

Again the undertaking was completed in virtually an automatic fashion. Mrs. Wiltha said she just laid color on the pattern which seemed to glow mysteriously before her astounded eyes.

In the more than dozen years since that time she has done many pictures. Some have been in oil, others in watercolor. They are by no means masterpieces—but they are good. Many a competent critic of the arts has said so.

"I am no longer scared at what some people call my talent. But I can't explain it so that it makes sense.

"Every now and then the inspiration to do a picture hits me and I go to work," she says. "I never know what the subject is going to be until it appears X-ray-like on the blank canvas."

Mrs. Wiltha's work includes portraits, landscapes, animals and designs. Some of them are highly original and, as her painting skill has improved over the years, they are worth hanging with the work of recognized experts.

No one who has talked with Mrs. Wiltha, or has watched her work, has questioned the honesty of her statements. They have found her a person of normal intelligence and of becoming honesty. She has no yearning for the limelight.

"I'm always a little afraid," she says, "that people think I'm a crackpot.

"I know I have improved in technique and the brushes no longer feel awkward in my hand. But it always embarrasses me to have people compliment me on work I have never felt is mine."

This is no "ghost story." It is just one of the many manifestations of the strange power that at times emanates spontaneously from the vast memory storehouse of the "collective unconscious."

It probably is an unusually intense expression of a deep unconscious yearning that we call, academically, "aptitude." The shadowy pattern on Mrs. Wiltha's easel could have been a projection of what she was seeing with her mind's eye on the Supraconscious level. This is no different from the psychic imagery commonly called "visions."

In *The Egyptian Miracle*, F. H. Wood reports another such intriguing case. It concerns an English girl who spoke a strange language when in a trancelike sleep.

At first what she said was so unlike any known language that it was believed she was just babbling senselessly. But then it was decided to make phonograph recordings of her speech to determine whether the sounds could be decoded. These recordings were turned over to linguists and cryptographers for an attempt at translation. The cryptographers, experts at decoding any sort of message, finally began to make some sense of what the girl was saying.

By "breaking the code," these men discovered that the girl was speaking ancient Egyptian, a language which has been extinct for several thousands of years. Once the translations could be made it was discovered, moreover, that her messages were historically accurate with regard to the few known facts about the extinct civilization.

Her messages completed missing gaps for historians. And archeologists, by studying the language she spoke, were able to decipher some hitherto meaningless writings on stone tablets that had been unearthed in Egypt.

Understanding the principle of the "collective unconscious" makes many of these otherwise inexplicable phenomena of the composite-life personality far less mystifying.

The existence of many conflicting subpersonalities within the same individual is simply demonstrated by hypnosis. Many different personalities exist in every individual. They are bound up in invisible strands of protoplasmic and psychic continuity by virtue of the progressive evolution of immortal man.

The primitive concept considered this transformation of human personality as either diabolical or Divine, both in origin and in meaning. We know now, of course, that there is no more "supernatural" significance in the split personality of man than there is such significance in thunder and lightning (which man once believe signified the wrath of God).

Yet it was not until the end of the nineteenth century, when scientific study of the unconscious started making headway, that these particular manifestations of human nature were properly evaluated. But superstition is deeply imbedded in the mind of mankind. It is an integral part of our biological constitution. Many people therefore still associate the phenomena of the split personality with what is called the "supernatural."

When Stevenson dramatized the scientific discovery of the dual personality in his famous dual character, Dr. Jekyll and Mr. Hyde, he created a figure of modern folklore. Dr. Jekyll, the kind, generous, honorable physician, beloved by all for his philanthropic labors, could, by means of potions he had discovered, turn himself into a loathsome and criminal individual who called himself Hyde. And Hyde, by means of the antidote potion, could turn himself back into his older, socialized self.

The conflict of the two characters in the same body has become symbolic of the universally recognized problem of every individual: the reconciliation and co-ordination of clashing motives and instincts in his composite make-up—perhaps due to unresolved emotional conflicts of long standing within the memory storehouse of the "collective unconscious."

These clashing motives and instincts within the "collective unconscious" may be more than dual. Numerous divisions of the personality may exist at the same time. These sub-personalities may emerge from the unconscious into the conscious only in certain "dream" states, in periods of reverie, in the trance state, or they may erupt in outbreaks of irrational conduct.

Amnesia often results from these unconscious personality conflicts. This development occurs when the individual forgets who he has been all his past life and lives the life of one of the personalities which temporarily takes possession of the conscious level.

One of the more famous of many such cases was that of Ansel Bourne, a Baptist clergyman who suddenly disappeared from his Rhode Island home. Every effort was made to find him, without avail. At the end of two months he returned to his home. It appeared that the two-month interval was filled with an experience of the strangest nature for him.

An investigation conducted on the behalf of the London Society for Physical Research showed that the Reverend Bourne lost normal consciousness soon after leaving home. He wandered around in several different towns and cities and finally reached Norristown, Pennsylvania, where he rented a store. He stocked the store with small wares and carried on a successful business there for six weeks under the name of A. J. Brown.

To the citizens of Norristown he appeared to be a perfectly normal person, conducting his business properly, contracting no unnecessary debts, and always paying promptly. At the end of his six-week mercantile career he suddenly regained his normal consciousness and remembered nothing whatsoever of his experiences in Norristown as a merchant.

Another typical illustration of a split personality is the widely known case of "Patience Worth." This case was given much publicity in 1916 by Casper W. Yost of the *St. Louis Post-Dispatch* as "A Psychic Mystery."

The normal personality was that of Mrs. John H. Curran. She lived in St. Louis, Missouri. She was a middle-class young woman with rather limited advantages, having enjoyed no travel and few literary contacts.

"Patience Worth" was Mrs. Curran's other personality, the author of many books which earned Mrs. Curran a considerable amount in royalties. "Patience Worth" also composed poetry with amazing ease and skill when in a trance state.

The Sorry Tale was regarded by most critics as her master-piece. *A Story of the Time of Christ* was published in 1917 and was followed a year later by *Hope Trueblood*, a lengthy novel set some centuries earlier, which deals rather senti-mentally with the complications of village life in the England of that period. *The Pot Upon the Wheel*, another of her novels, is an allegory of life.

The dual personality of Mrs. Curran seemingly could live in the century of her choice by simply drawing from the memory storehouse of her "collective unconscious." While in a trance she would describe people and places of former generations just as though the scenes were taking place at the moment. As Mrs. Curran, she could hardly rhyme two lines—but as "Patience Worth" she composed poetry by the volume.

She demonstrated these phenomena in public appearances in some parts of the country. A lecture tour was booked for her but was abandoned after an appearance in Detroit because it was the consensus of the large audience who came to see her there that she was "possessed by the devil."

Somnambulism, or "sleep walking," is the mechanism used by the Supraconscious to get rid of a reprehensible impulse or criminal tendency of which the conscious level is not aware. In reality, sleepwalkers are not walking in their sleep. They are the victims of split personalities. Persons who are gentle and orderly in their normal lives are often argumentative, hostile and dangerous in the personality that comes to the fore in their sleep walking escapades.

There is the well-known case of the postal employee who reported for work at midnight. There was only one other clerk on duty at night. The postal employee in question received a registered package at two o'clock one morning. The package contained a large sum of money, government bonds and jewelry for which the employee gave a receipt.

On turning over the mail to the other clerk, he was asked about registered mail and told the other clerk specifically that there was none. He left work at seven o'clock. Six hours later he sent a telegram to the proper authorities reporting the pouch of registered mail as missing.

When he was questioned later by postal inspectors, he claimed that he had no recollection of what had happened. A search of his car, however, revealed more than $1,500 in currency. At the local jail, when an official heard the young clerk's story of his discharge from the Marine Corps five years earlier for sleep walking, it was suggested that the clerk go to sleep and try to remember what had happened.

Two hours later the clerk fell asleep and soon offered to direct officials to the stolen articles. He then led them to his mother's farm and showed them the spot where he had buried the contents of the package.

In all cases of split personality certain characteristics constantly reappear. The new personality is always consistent with itself. That is to say, it is always the same whenever it reappears.

The new personality's normal characterisics are sometimes in marked contrast to the lifelong character developed in the normal state. But the new personality never varies from one time to another. If a dozen different personalities should be assumed at different times, each would always be consistent with the other version of the new personality.

The incidents occurring during one interval of the split personality will always be remembered whenever the same personality reappears. In that way, the existence of the new personality, when it reappears with frequency, is practically continuous. The intervals of normal consciousness usually do not seem to be remembered.

The split personality does sometimes remember the existence of the normal one. But this memory is always that of remembering another person, upon whom it often looks and of whom it often speaks with pitying contempt. In the case where two or more new personalities are assumed, what generally happens is that each of the personalities remembers all the others but regards each as a different individual having no connection whatever with itself.

On the other hand, the normal personality never remembers what occurred during the abnormal, or paranormal, interval.

The late Dr. Morton Prince, famed Boston specialist in diseases of the nervous system, reported a case of multiple personalities within one person that is amazing in the wide differentiation between the personalities.

Dr. Prince told of a young woman who came to him one day and complained of suffering from a nervous disorder. The woman, Dr. Prince recorded, was quite pale and appeared nervous. She appeared to have all the symptoms that accompany hysteria—she could not sleep and her general health was very poor.

In order to relieve the young woman quickly of some of her troubles, Dr. Prince hypnotized her. In the hypnotic trance, he noted a remarkable change. In most cases a hypnotized patient awakens from the trance in much the same state as he was before the hypnosis. But in this woman's case the trancelike sleep seemed to change her character entirely.

In the place of the quiet, reserved woman with a seemingly infinite capacity for suffering, with the ideals and aspirations of a saint, there appeared an entirely different young woman. This personality was a breezy, slangy, "modern" young woman who looked as if she might have stepped out of the cover photograph of one of the currently popular magazines.

The same body sat before Dr. Prince, but an entirely different person inhabited that body.

The two personalities that belonged to the one body differed in every way imaginable, other than in outward appearance. The personalities were unlike in vivacity and even in facial expression. The second personality was far less intelligent, less matured and considerably healthier than the personality that Dr. Prince first encountered in his patient.

The "second" young woman was of a relentlessly, heedlessly selfish turn of mind. She enjoyed books and persons very different from those her "first" counterpart enjoyed.

While the "first" woman had had a college education and was fluent in French, the "second" personality was entirely lost in that language. This was a factor that later became of the greatest use to Dr. Prince. For by using French for his conversations with the "first" woman he was assured that he could convey to her things that Miss "Second" could not possibly understand.

Dr. Prince was intrigued by these strange occurrences. But as he continued his experiments further, he was even more astounded. It was not too long afterward that a third personality appeared. And then a fourth. Finally Dr. Prince came to speak of the many personalities inhabiting the woman's body as "the family."

While the "third" person was not as distinct a personality as the original saintly and reserved woman who had first come to the physician nor as the mischievous and selfish "second" personality, the "fourth" was another strong personality. Miss "Fourth" was a strong and rebellious woman.

All four personalities were distinguishable one from the other. Each called the "self" by a different name. And all shared the one body.

There are countless cases on record of such "split personalities." They often are explained by the theory of "reincarnation" or "spiritism." Yet it appears obvious that this phenomenon is best explained in the theorem of the "collective unconscious." These personalities are part of the immense vat of memory.

Whether one chooses to interpret the scope of this "immense vat of memory" as within or without the human mind, the fact remains that each of us has access to these illimitable resources that God has provided in his Divine Plan for the progressive process of intellectual and spiritual evolution.

This pertinent speculation was made by Joseph Sadony, writing in a recent issue of his privately printed journal, *The Valley Caravel:*

"You may think that you can remember only your own childhood. But there is a state of consciousness in which one can remember the childhood of others, too—things that even they have forgotten.

"This I have proved and can prove again. We all have flashes of it; and if this reminder helps you open that one little gate of your mind which admits that extension of your consciousness, you will feel that inner sense of identity whereby when you say 'I' and when I say 'I' it is the same 'I.' And you will comprehend the continuity of life and consciousness which links memories of all your forebears with your own.

"You may think that your great-grandfather is no more; but he still lives and breathes in YOU, even if the mortal consciousness of the body bearing his name has been divided. You still think with part of his life and thoughts as your own."

Consider the significance of this further piece of evidence of the power of the "collective unconscious." Dr. Charles Bernstein, superintendent of a school for the feeble-minded, tells of an inmate who was unable to read or write, never saw a calendar, and whose mental age was that of a six-year-old child.

This inmate, however, was able to name the day of the week of any date, past or future, without a moment's hesitation.

There is also recorded the case of a Slovakian boy, John Popelka, who, when but five years old, could be told the time of any person's birth and without a moment's thought could state exactly the time which had elapsed to the minute.

While unable to read or write, Alex Buchanan of Henderson, North Carolina, can tell the day of the week of any date and in addition can instantly subtract or multiply the most intricate of arithmetical fractions.

Willis Dysart of Tift County, Georgia, was fourteen years old when he discovered that by glancing at a list of figures as many as seventy-three in number for seven seconds, he could give their total.

Every automobile license he has ever seen and every telephone number he has ever heard can be repeated by Charles Welch of Bloomfield, Mississippi.

Are these people "freaks"? Do you wish to disregard such phenomena by categorizing their possessors so? Do you wish to place these persons in the class of being "circus material"?

Or is it not more logical to assume that these unusual mental faculties are made available by some special canalization between the conscious level and the Supraconscious level? For these people are users of the immense memory storehouse of the "collective unconscious."

Why these persons have been able to utilize this wonderful power, we cannot yet answer. But it is most reasonable to presume that the vast potentialities of the Supraconscious, of the "collective unconscious" and its mental library of encyclopedias is there to be made available to all mankind.

Man apparently has progressed far enough along the time-track of intellectual and spiritual evolution to make use of this power. Man now seems to be on the threshold of discovering the key which will allow him into the sanctum of the Divine Plan's memory storehouse.

You must move forward by means of individual and collective self-help to find this key and to achieve the greatness that the Divine Plan has set out for mankind.

You must help fight the present trend toward retrogression. God's Divine Plan of evolution will not tolerate your standing still.

You can do either of two things. You can progress, or you can retrogress.

The answer lies within you.

The answer is yours to give, yours to discover, yours to benefit by.

Knowledge of self is essential to intellectual and spiritual development. It is the only means of accomplishing human progress. It is the only possible way to save civilization.

You have the power. You will achieve the glory.

Within you lies the greatest storehouse of knowledge: a collection outside the comprehension of your own conscious reasoning, beyond the scope of your conscious imagining, and with the power to do all things that are good.

This knowledge is the knowledge of all times, of all peoples, of all things.

By eliminating from your daily life thoughts and conduct that only reflect man's primitive greed, fear and anger, you are thinking as God intended you should. Then you will benefit fully from the constructive elements of your "collective unconscious."

This is God's Divine Plan for mankind. Its fruits await only your discovery and utilization of them.

MAKING THE MOST OF YOUR MEMORY

You already have near you at all times a small note pad on which you record the results of your Supersense thinking. This pad now will prove to have a second use.

In this pad you are going to record the results of your Supraconscious memory—the results of tapping your "collective unconscious."

Your note pad should already be at your bedside for perusal after you awaken of all of your thoughts of the day previous, so upon awakening:

1. Think deeply to reveal to yourself any ideas that have pushed to the conscious surface during your sleep hours.

2. Write them down. This need not be a thorough exposition of the thought. A catch phrase is probably best, especially if there has been more than one thought to record so that lengthy writing of any one will fade the others from the conscious memory of the moment.

3. After you have eaten breakfast, reread what you have written.

4. Apply the creativeness of your memory, as recorded in your note pad, to your problems of the day.

5. Don't hesitate to use your note pad all through the day— or even upon awakening during your sleeping hours—to register the results of your memory as they flash to your conscious.

VI

Your Mind Can Control Matter

The power of the Supraconscious is so great that it affects your very being.

Uncontrolled, however, it usually has an adverse effect on you. The many feelings of "ill" which you consciously bury because you know they are wrong are unfortunately buried in the level of the mind that is the Supraconscious.

All the hates you repress, the dislikes you fail to express, the ill-feelings you hide—these imprint themselves on the grasping Supraconscious. At first they make only the tiniest impression. But soon, when they are repeated and continually pushed to the background, the impression becomes more intense and clearer.

It takes but a little time for some action to trigger the feeling that has been recorded in the Supraconscious to become overt and express itself on your organic being.

The whole science of psychosomatic medicine is based on this knowledge. Not that the theory behind psychosomatic medicine is new. The country doctor of a half-century ago practiced a somewhat similar sort of treatment because he really knew his patients personally.

The old country practitioner was more than a doctor to his patients. He was a confidant of their feelings, their hopes, their failures, their repressions, their despairs. He saw how these feelings had effect on their organic well-being and he treated them correspondingly in understanding fashion.

With this practitioner grew the usage of the placebo—the "sugar pill" given because the patient felt better after being given some "medicine" rather than being told to go home and not worry because nothing was wrong.

True, nothing was organically wrong. What was wrong was an organic expression of a mental anxiety. But the theories of psychiatry were little known then and the analyst's practice had not yet come into being. The country doctor practiced some real down-to-earth psychiatry with his "sugar pill."

"This is just the thing to cure your ill, Mrs. Doe," said the kindly old fellow. And like as not, it did. All Mrs. Doe wanted was someone to tell her troubles to, someone who would sympathize silently, someone who would "understand."

"Your pills sure worked the trick, Doctor!" was the invariable comment in weeks that passed. And old Dr. Countryman was a great physician—he had the cure to a million diseases.

Today this very theory has been utilized in the school of psychosomatic medicine. What is psychosomatic medicine? It is exactly what its name implies. The study of the psyche, or mind, in its relationship to the soma, or body.

In other words, medicine has realized the great effect that the Supraconscious has on the organic body. It is the modern study of the old platitude of "mind over matter."

Generally the Supraconscious' control over the body has been allowed to grow wild. Consequently its effect are too often adverse. The ill that you have repressed within you is expressed in unhealthy fashion. Is it not an incontrovertible truth, then, that the good that you store up within you can be used in healthy fashion?

And therefore it follows that the more good that you can store up within your Supraconscious, the greater good will its accumulated effects be on you yourself.

Just as you unconsciously build a "file" of ills within you, so you can create and fill to overflowing "files" of good. These goodnesses should be made to tax the illimitable capacities of the memory's storehouse.

The Golden Gift is much like a young girl's hope chest. It does not come filled, and, while much of that which is put into it comes from other sources (the "collective unconscious"), it still rests with you to fill as you desire. The most wondrous thing about it is that you need never stop filling it—it has "infinite capacity."

What you put into it pays you back with compounded interest. Place *good* in the Supraconscious and the cumulative "capital" and "interest" will give you a Life Limitless.

Does the sound of the words "Life Limitless" frighten you? Does the idea of being able to control your destinies, your very living, bring fear into your conscious thoughts? Undoubtedly not—for it is an idea you probably have thought about in many a moment of deep consideration as well as in reverie.

The control of the self has been man's eternal aim. Yet he has so seldom achieved it. Only a few individuals have discovered the whole secret of the Golden Gift. Man has been too taken up with things external and material to ponder the self and learn about it.

Those who have done so are the people who have made possible the great accomplishments of mankind. Now the power to achieve the same things is being shown to you. It rests only with you to accomplish.

At all times within you, as within all persons, the universal Law of Suggestion is at work. It influences your life and thoughts. Whether an idea originates within your own mind or is transmitted there from without—from some other person or agency—matters little to the over-all scheme.

The neurological process remains the same no matter where the suggestion comes from. The idea is submitted to your Supraconscious. There it is either acted upon, if such action is called for at the moment, or it is stored away for future use. The future use may not even come within your own life span. It may be for the use of posterity.

In autosuggestion you have seen how the individual selects the ideas he desires the all-powerful Supraconscious to transform into reality or to make a part of his active life.

In the case of the unconscious suggestion, the individual may not be aware of the fact that he is being influenced by the idea or the condition. This is particularly true of negative "emotional thinking" where one's sense of reason fails to check the powerful emotional forces that so frequently impair health and destroy happiness.

The destructive influences of negative suggestion are strikingly shown by the new psychosomatic approach to the entire problem of disease in the human. The study of the emotional forces present in physical ailments has cast new light on the causes underlying such common ailments as heart disease, high blood pressure, arthritis, diabetes, stomach ulcers, pneumonia, asthma, colitis and other ills which plague mankind.

Chronic fear (anxiety) and anger (resentment) are the basic emotional forces that disrupt bodily functions and cause ailments. The particular type of psychosomatic ailment is determined by the nature of the suppressed emotions starting as far back as a person's infancy or early childhood.

Suppressed emotions create mental irritation. This in turn makes a person highly susceptible to chronic anxiety or resentment. Just how you can repel this basic attack on your own system and acquire the ability to extend your own life span will be discussed in a later chapter.

Unconscious feeling-attitudes too frequently work havoc on the human organism. It is with this in mind that the study of psychosomatic medicine has grown. The practitioners of this type of medicine realize that a general understanding of a patient's mental health is necessary in preventing disease.

Self-help in overcoming crippling ailments that are created and encouraged by mental anxieties *is* possible. And it is entirely practical. You must understand the basis of this newest approach to medical aid and apply the knowledge to your own everyday living.

The theory upon which psychosomatic medicine is based is a simple one. Its proponents say that medical science in the past century has studied the immediate cause of disease too closely and neglected to study the patient. As a result, the medical man of the past learned a great many useful facts about what happens to a patient after he has contracted a disease. But the important questions of why the patient contracted the disease and why he was susceptible to it were neglected.

Medicine was too slow in realizing that where persons were equally exposed to the same infections only some of them contracted the disease. No inquiry, for example, was made into the cases of husbands and wives, both eating the same meals and sharing the same habits, when one would suffer from peptic ulcers and the other not.

The clue to the mystery of why we become ill is offered by a better understanding of the human and his emotions.

Emotions in the human cause physiological changes. Take a simple emotion such as embarrassment. A situation causes you to become embarrassed and the physiology of the body causes your blood to rush to your cheeks—you blush.

Or you suddenly become frightened. Your body reacts physically by shivering and your skin becomes raised and bumpy—we call it "goose flesh."

Or you become angry and a whole complex series of changes occur in the body. Your glands increase the output of adrenalin. The heart therefore beats more quickly and the sugar content of the blood increases.

So you see how conscious emotion can bring about bodily changes which you can recognize easily.

But emotion is not always conscious. There is in each of us desires and longings that are buried simply because we are ashamed to admit them ourselves. But they are there; they are real forces and drives which must find an outlet.

112

The neighbor of yours who seems so gentle and harmless on the surface may be hiding a violent resentment against a world that he believes treated him harshly when he was a child. But he has been taught that hatred is an "evil thing." So he has bottled it up. He even refuses to admit to himself that he has hostile feelings.

These feelings will at some time or other express themselves —even against his own will. If he does not burst through the dam of repression and commit mayhem (as so many murderers have done in the past), he will burst within himself. The result will often express itself in the form of heart disease.

Sometimes the relationship between emotion and illness is quite clear. Take this simple case of this woman with boils:

The patient was a young married woman who admitted that she felt deeply ashamed of her inability to like her husband's family. She would not admit, even to herself, how much she resented her mother-in-law. Whenever a conscious hatred of the older woman presented itself to her thinking, she repressed it.

This young woman was very conscientious and she had a vague feeling that she must be punished for having these feelings of hostility. She sensed this even though most of the time she managed to forget that such a thing as hatred had ever crossed her mind.

Eventually her punishment came. Every time her mother-in-law visited, the young woman developed a virulent attack of boils which the doctor's report said "resisted all treatment."

In spite of medical care, they always lasted to the exact day of her mother-in-law's departure. That day they promptly began to disappear. The connection between the boils and the mother-in-law never occurred to the young woman until a psychiatrist showed her how her resentment and the need for self-punishment were finding expression in a physical malady.

Wise physicians have always had an intuitive knowledge of some such relations between emotion and disease. Contemporaries of the great British statesman Benjamin Disraeli mentioned his famous "diplomatic colds." These were real enough, but they always occurred when an uncongenial meeting had been arranged. And they cleared up as soon as the dreaded date had passed.

The advent of psychosomatic medicine has made it possible to substitute exact, scientific findings for the vague intuition of the doctor of yesteryear. Psychosomatic medicine has found definite proof that such specific ailments as arthritis, diabetes, heart disease, high blood pressure, peptic ulcers—and even bone fractures as well as their inability to heal—usually are found in persons whose life situations are such that strong, unconscious feelings seek expression through these illnesses.

Elaborate studies have been made during the past two decades on the connection between emotion and disease. In one thorough investigation of the influence played by emotional problems, a study was made of two specific maladies—heart disease and diabetes.

The researchers arranged to study the psychological life pattern of all patients suffering from either of these maladies admitted to a particular hospital. Wishing to compare the two groups with another class of patients—those in whose illnesses they figured emotion would play no part—they decided to select as the comparison group patients admitted with fractures.

The results were amazing. Over a five-year period, during which they also studied other diseases with relation to emotional background, they examined sixteen hundred patients. In all diseases, the psychological examinations showed that no fewer than fifty per cent of any group of persons with one illness expressed through that illness an emotion which was denied expression in other ways.

For some illnesses, the proportion for whom the malady was an expression of an emotional upset ranged as high as ninety per cent. And most amazing of all to the researchers, their check group—the fracture patients—were found to have as large a psychological incentive toward the accidents that brought them to the hospital as the other groups.

Among the fracture patients the researchers found that the unconscious desire to escape responsibility sometimes caused a "proneness" to accident. In other cases a desire to fight against something that the patient knew he could not fight openly had the same result.

There were even clues that a continuation of this emotional state resulted in the patients' failing to recover as quickly as deemed likely and in numerous relapses of one type or another.

A typical example was that of a professional dancer who in twelve years of being tossed about by her dancing partners never had had a mishap. But at three different times she broke her leg while hurrying to leave her home after having quarreled with her parents.

The insurance company that carried the dancer's policy, requiring them to pay each time she was incapacitated, decided to have a psychiatrist investigate the case. Without telling her his profession, the psychiatrist made friends with the dancer. He soon found out that her unhappy home life was causing deep emotional disturbances within the woman.

The conflicting emotions of an inborn love for her parents and her raging fury at their interference with her life outside the home formed the cause of her having accidents, he found. Each time she broke her leg and went to the hospital for a long stay, everyone—but the psychiatrist—was surprised by her cheerfulness as a patient.

It was only when it became time for her to return to her home from the hospital that she became gloomy.

"There's some jinx waiting for me outside!" she said to her friend (the insurance company psychiatrist).

"The jinx is an unconscious habit you've formed," he told her. "Whenever things at home are more than you can stand, you break a leg.

"You think it is an accident. Well, you'll have the same kind of accidents as long as you're suffering from the tension of the same emotional conflicts."

Soon after that she married, set up a home of her own—and never broke a limb again.

Let us examine the high-blood-pressure patients. If the theories of psychosomatic medicine are correct, we should find that almost all the persons suffering from this ailment would have similar life problems and ways of solving them.

They have!

In their childhood they all were secretive and "too good." They learned to "swallow" their emotions, instead of expressing them freely. Few of them had strict religious upbringing. The demands they made on themselves were self-created and extremely severe.

All of them became men and women with a "need to be perfect." As a result, they tended to work at jobs beneath their abilities. In this way they could do their jobs without fear of failure. Anything more ambitious would bring them failure or criticism, things they dreaded.

These high-blood-pressure sufferers all bear signs of anxiety in their faces. They admit difficulty in making decisions. Occasionally their conflicting emotions break out in a violent and explosive form. But for the most part they appear to be shy, gentle and considerate.

In many cases the onset of the malady has been associated with the death or separation of a much-loved person or with acute financial strain.

The emotional strain of persons who develop high blood pressure has been obvious to the psychological researcher. Studies have shown that these persons live constantly with fear: fear of themselves, of what might happen if they once "let the lid off," of choosing wrongly or making a mistake.

Fear is an emotion. It is a dangerous emotion, and if you do not express it, it will find its own devious ways out of your system. This result often causes physical damage. You must avoid living with the phantasmagoria of fear.

Remember, fear is not the only emotion that can do you harm if repressed. Any and all of your emotions can have the same ill effect on you. They must not be bottled up within you. They must not be given the chance to imprint themselves too heavily on the Supraconscious.

In the case of the high-blood-pressure victim, the way in which fear has escaped from within the Supraconscious is easy to understand. Increased blood pressure is one of the body's normal methods by which every healthy person prepares himself to meet danger. In this case the danger is "fear."

The phantasmagoria of fear is a constant companion. It is with you day and night, and it does not take long for the body to recognize a danger signal. To the danger signal of "fear," the body's physical response is the fast onrushing of blood through the arteries and veins.

This reaction to fear is a useful one when the reason for your fear comes from some outside danger. For then you must be prepared to flee or fight, and the increased pressure of your blood puts you into instant trim to take action.

But the constant reaction to the ever-present fear created by self-made anxiety soon wears out your body's mechanism by mere continual repetition over a long period. The result: high blood pressure.

Nervous tension also seeks expression through bodily symptoms. These, called medically "dissociated conversions," most commonly take the form of paralysis of the limbs, inability to feel, or see, hear, speak, walk or remember. These symptoms are sometimes called symbolic symptoms. That is to say, the physical disability is a symbolic expression of some distressing or emotionally disturbing experience from which the sufferer has "dissociated" himself by means of some alleged physical disability.

There are countless examples of such symbolic conversions. Yet, common as the "disease" is, it is futile to try to convince the "sufferers" that there is nothing organically wrong with them. The conversion symptoms are real to them because they actually feel the sensations which the physical ailment would produce.

Take the case of the young woman whose symptom from such a cause developed into blindness. She had witnessed an automobile accident in which her fiancé was killed. The loss of eyesight was a conversion symptom. By that means she unconsciously tried to blank out the distressing "sight" of the shocking calamity that had befallen her.

A middle-aged married woman developed the symptoms of paralysis of the legs. After several months in hospital she regained the use of her limbs. But when her physician told her she could then return home, the paralysis returned. It was finally discovered through psychoanalysis that her condition was an unconscious expression of her dislike for her husband.

There is the case of a newly-wed husband who walked out of his home in a huff after a violent quarrel with his bride. The young woman committed suicide. When her widowed husband heard of what had happened, he symbolically expressed his deep remorse over the quarrel in a conversion symptom of muteness.

These are extreme examples. There are milder ones that are no less real to the sufferer. There are cases of persons who have developed various illnesses to avoid going to a job which was distasteful to them. It even is found in cases of children, in which sickness develops when a child has to go to school to face a teacher whom he does not like or does not get along with.

The human is unconsciously capable of finding many ways to avoid facing realities that consciously he does not want to face. When strong, unconscious impulses cannot find a direct outlet in action or speech or thought, they often seek what is termed an "organ language" symptom.

Some of our most common everyday phrases have unconsciously recognized that the body can play a kind of charade. We say such things as: "I can't swallow her!" or "I can't stomach him!" And often, surprisingly enough, an attack of indigestion will follow a scene with that hated person.

Or we may say someone "gives me a pain in the neck." Such pains have been known to develop organically.

"Oh my aching back!" expressed over a situation may result in a backache when that situation recurs, thus relieving the "sufferer" from facing the unwanted or unliked.

There are countless other such expressions: "Sick of life"; "lost appetite for living"; "thin-skinned"; "heartsick"; "heavy-hearted"—too many to list and explain. In any event, this is quite unnecessary, for their meaning becomes obvious to you as soon as you see one or think of another.

These phrases show that there has long been some inkling of the fact that unhappy people become ill more easily than happy ones. You speak, for instance, of a consumptive person's "wasting away" with more wisdom than you realize.

Every person harbors the tubercular bacillus—but only few contract tuberculosis and fewer still die of the disease. In many instances, however, the flight into a tubercular ill-ness is a way to satisfy the death instinct—indeed a form of human "waste."

But you may well ask, "Why does one person need to flee from his problems into tuberculosis while another, who may have more apparent worries, remains well?"

Some light has been shed on this question, but no pat an-swer is yet available. The life story of each and every patient must be slowly drawn out before any understanding of the destruction pattern is achieved. The illness may be trying to express any of a number of complaints the patient has. Careful psychotherapeutic study is required before discovery of what protest the patient is trying to make by having unconsciously willed the malady to develop.

One married woman developed insomnia, indigestion and mental depression. Why? The psychiatrist discovered that her husband was cold and unromantic and her life was filled with financial worries. She lived in an uncongenial neighbor-hood. The simple fact that this woman was actually living a life stripped of most of its good things gave her a real sense of anxiety. This she expressed through the symptoms she developed.

The root of the trouble, however, doesn't necessarily ac-count for what the symptoms will be. Take the case of an-other woman, happily married to a devoted husband, who developed the same illness as the unloved woman.

Why should this be? This second woman had no apparent worries. But a psychotherapist discovered that this woman, the oldest of eleven children, had had a great deal of respon-sibility forced on her at an early age in looking after and taking care of her younger brothers and sisters. She had been deprived of the normal amount of motherly attention. Her childhood hunger for attention, then, manifested itself in later years in the form of illness.

The roots of both cases were far from the same. The fruit, however, was the same—resentment. In each case the resentment sought expression through the symptoms the body could provide—organic ones.

Another common ingrown feeling of inadequacy is found among persons suffering from asthma. Asthmatic patients typically do not cry when they are unhappy. Most of them boast of not having shed a tear "in years." Of course they haven't. They have pretended to themselves and others that they were too "grown up" to ever need the help of anyone else. The opposite is, of course, truer.

Crying occurs in the infant when it is first separated from the mother in the process of birth. Later the infant cries to express its helplessness and need of its mother's care. The adult who refuses to cry often wants to cry far more than the rest of us. Else he would not be so ashamed of this simple everyday reaction.

Analysis of a large number of asthmatic patients has shown this to be true. The asthmatic was often "pushed out of the nest" too soon. He was too often weighed down with the burden of independence at too young an age. As a child, the asthmatic patient most often was forced to live far beyond its own emotional means.

This person then developed a great, unconfessed longing for security and shelter. But he learned to conceal this as a shameful and "babyish" feeling. Unfortunately a concealed emotion does not cease to exist or demand expression. The Supraconscious level of the mind has taken cognizance of the need. The organic symptom then develops to take the place of the required outlet.

In this case asthma is a perverted form of having "a good cry." And when, under psychiatric treatment, some of these factors become clear to the patient, he often abandons his asthma and sheds the first "real" tears he has had through the many years of strain and loneliness.

The physicians who specialize in this approach to disease believe that they can often trace the physiological routes through which hidden emotions give rise to nearly every form of physical disease.

How do you "catch" cold? One simple way is that used by a man who suffered from numerous colds each winter.

He had been spoiled as a child by an overindulgent mother. He suffered a strong, unconscious resentment against the world that did not continue to gratify all of his whims.

Whenever he was frustrated by someone who opposed him in adult life, he would have frightening dreams about this person. The dreams were always the same—he would attack his opponent by biting him.

His wife noticed that he often ground his teeth while sleeping. This habit was checked and it correlated with the man's dreams. As a result of his "biting" dreams and the physical action of teeth grinding in the night, this man would awaken with sore jaws, gums and throat. He was subject to any infection that he would ordinarily have fought off without difficulty. Dental researchers have recently discovered that this grinding action is a major cause of tooth damage in persons past forty.

The psychosomatists have not discarded the classic methods of treatment by means of medicines, rest and surgery. They merely supplement such physical efforts to restore the damaged body by a psychological study of the emotions that set the disease in motion.

Psychiatrists and psychotherapists are not "faith healers." They accept all the knowledge of medical science and add to it the knowledge of psychology and psychiatry. In this way they try to help the patient find healthier expression for unconscious longings that actually make them ill.

An oft-quoted case of such therapy is that of a nineteen-year-old girl who had suffered a severe loss of weight. She "could not eat" and was down to seventy-four pounds. She was given every physical remedy possible. Psychological treatment was started.

It was discovered that this girl had no friends. Whenever an acquaintance threatened to develop into intimacy, she broke it off. She had a distinct fear of marriage and was outspoken about her reluctance ever to bear children. She not only starved herself physically but she had starved herself emotionally as well.

Simply adding a few pounds to this patient by means of forced feeding or other artificial means would have only been a temporary measure. As soon as the girl left the hospital and met another emotional situation she could not cope with, she would again reject food just as she tried to reject life.

Instead, her emotions were brought out into the light where

she, with the aid of her psychiatrist, was able to examine them —and re-educate them. When she recovered an ability to "taste life," she was eager to "taste food" as well.

The whole field of nutritional disease, and those focused in the gastro-intestinal tract, have been of great interest to the doctors in this new field of medicine. A majority of gastric cases, it has been found, are the result of a strong unconscious longing to get love and care.

On the surface such sufferers are usually the active go-getting type. This is the cloak they wear to show the world: "I am an efficient, active, productive person. I give to everybody, support many people, help many people, assume responsibilities and enjoy having people depend on me."

Yet underneath is the need of help for themselves. There is a gnawing hunger for affection very like the infant's desire to be cared for, caressed, loved and fed by its mother. Such repressed hunger—which was first associated with nutrition at the suckling stage—may serve as a constant stimulus to the stomach. It is quite independent of the hunger or repletion demand of the grown person.

Under this constant stimulation the stomach apparently behaves throughout the day as it should behave during digestion. The result may be the development of any number of gastric disturbances, including ulcers.

"Most forms of indigestion are due to emotional upsets," a doctor has stated. "Indeed so are most forms of heart disease, uterine disease, kidney disease or disease of every other organ you can name.

"Of course there are such things as organic diseases—such as cancer, gallstones, measles—and they can and must be treated with organic remedies.

"But most adult patients are sick partly or wholly because they think they are sick. Nine-tenths of any doctor's practice is made up of this group. If he treats them entirely from the organic standpoint, he fails."

The psychosomatic specialists make no claims of miraculous cures. They recognize, as all doctors do, that there are some irreversible stages of disease, when the tissue or bone destruction has gone too far for Nature's processes to repair. But they do believe that a psychological approach, added to the usual physical treatment, can often arrest the progress of a disease even when it has reached an irreversible stage.

If a malady has been caught early enough, of course, the irreversible stage may never be reached.

The psychosomatist talks less of infectious agents than do other doctors, simply because he feels that medicine has neglected the psychic factor in disease and stressed the physical alone. But both the physical and the psychological must be understood if the greatest number of persons is to be helped.

Even when disease seems to spring from the "feelings" alone and has no ascertainable physical cause, it cannot be laughed off as being "imaginary." Pain in the abdomen caused by anxiety is no less painful and no more imaginary than the pain caused by an infected appendix.

Thus it is that your Supraconscious must not be allowed uncontrolled interpretation of your emotions. For in that way your emotions express themselves in physical illness.

Sooner or later these repressed emotions are going to be triggered into physical action. The sufferer will be you. The causer will be you—unless you learn to understand your emotions and channel them to useful and good ends, rather than repress them and allow them to be channeled into ends that can cause you actual bodily harm.

Life Limitless—a life of health and happiness, of growing older without senility and sickness—is within your own making.

The control of self has been man's eternal aim—now it is yours to achieve.

By placing those thoughts into your Supraconscious that are going to affect it in ways to your advantage, you are going to control matter with mind.

The "good" you store up within you is going to be used by the Supraconscious in healthy fashion.

The more "good" you store up, the greater "good" is accumulated. The more you accumulate, the greater the effect on you—and this is something over which you have sole control.

Empty the "file" of ills within your Supraconscious.

Create a "file" of "good" and fill it to overflowing.

Tax the illimitable capacities of the memory's storehouse by stocking it with "good." It will pay you back a millionfold. It will give you happy life, long life and healthy life.

THE MATTER OF "MIND OVER MATTER"

The key to controlling your own body is the practice of making all your thoughts positive ones.

Think of your brain as a warehouse of thoughts. You are the "stock-keeper." You have the responsibility of "ordering" and keeping in good supply the positive thoughts necessary for running your "plant," the body.

Think over every emotion twice before allowing it to register on your Supraconscious:

1a. If it is a positive thought—a constructive, purposive, healthy thought—then think it again and meditate on it.

b. Allow it to "soak in" so that you can store it for future help to you.

2a. If it is a negative thought—an "ill," bad, evil, destructive thought—recognize it as the result of anxiety and fear.

b. Go to the root of that fear, recognize the immaturity of having such a fear, and laugh at your own self for having been tricked into such an anxiety.

c. Now meditate until you reverse the negative emotional thought into one of positive and constructive value.

d. Once you have made your negative thought into a positive one, follow the procedure as outlined above in step 1.

VII

Live Longer and Love It

Did it ever occur to you that you are cheating yourself?

"Cheating myself?" you ask. "Of what?"

Of three simple things—simple if you have them, but complex if they are missing. And, wonderfully, three things simple for you to achieve once you know how. They are:

Health, happiness and . . . longevity!

Sure, people have told me, you can perhaps control to a great extent your health and your happiness, but longevity?

"Do you mean I can live longer if I want to?" I was asked by one man.

The answer is YES.

You can live longer, and do so without senility. That means that, despite your increasing years, you will be healthier; not the other way around. And naturally, being healthier, you will be happier.

Actually, the truth of the matter is that by being happier, you will be healthier. It is a double-barrelled process. One accomplishment brings the other—either way. And, fortunately, both are achieved in the identical way.

You go on living day by day without really living, so to speak. You exist. Living implies a knowledge of all the things that are about you, within you and concern you. Yet you may feel that you have no time to bother with these things.

If you are a follower of this philosophy, you are cheating yourself.

Have you ever stopped to think about the prominent role your feelings play in your everyday reactions to the situations of your life?

Has it ever occurred to you that the three processes of your nervous system that are called thoughts, words and deeds are greatly affected by the emotional reactions you have to the everyday things in life? Perhaps the question would be better put were I to ask if you realize just how greatly your emotions affect your normal processes of being and doing?

Without your consciously knowing it, or even realizing it most times, the basic urges for survival dominate the unconscious forces that keep you functioning as a human. Throughout the ages of man's development, the Supraconscious level of the mind has been dominated by three primary instincts of survival. These are self-preservation, reproduction and protection of our offspring.

It is these instincts which cause you—without your realizing it consciously—to seek pleasures and avoid pain. That is to say, you seek (and require) security and shy away from insecurity. So it is that conditions and events that make you "feel good" by enhancing your sense of security are conducive to the three goals of better living: health, happiness and longevity. Those things that arouse a sense of insecurity will induce deep anxiety and stir feelings of resentment.

Have you ever noticed, for instance, how if you worry about something a great deal you literally become sick? The phrase is a common enough one—"worry yourself sick." That is what actually happens!

The same thing occurs when resentment grows too deep within you. You upset your entire system and bring on unhealthy conditions—even premature death. How often have you found that men in their prime who have died of heart disease are the ones who bore some deep resentment about something or other in their life? Much, much too often!

Worry or resentment allowed to grow within yourself is almost like signing your own death certificate in advance. If your inner thoughts are dominated by "gripe" and "groan," if you are a consistent "bellyacher" or "worrier," you are shortening the years of your life just as surely as you are growing older by the day.

But the mere fact that you are aging daily needn't mean that the days remaining are fewer. It should mean that by increasing your happiness each day you are assuring yourself more and more days to live.

The truth is that you are undoubtedly cheating yourself of the very things in life you want! Look around you and see how many of your friends and acquaintances already are suffering from the degenerative diseases that are becoming the earmarks of this age.

Negative "emotional thinking" is the one reason so many persons die of heart disease at their peak years, or are afflicted by high blood pressure, arthritis, diabetes or any of the other degenerative diseases we all know so well. Negative thinking is depriving people of their natural birthright of health. It is the prime cause in shortening the lives of so many of us.

And yet it is so simple to live a healthier, longer—and so much happier—life. We have only to recognize how God works His wonders through laws governing nature and "human nature."

That is the secret! It has been yours to know if you had sought it. If you did not know it before, if you had not sought it—here it is. There is no price to pay, unless you consider happiness for yourself a price.

It is not a complex secret to understand. It is simple, yet possesses all the depth of simplicity.

Before you can correct your faults, you must face them!

That is a basic law of nature. And it is a basic law of "human nature."

You must look into yourself and see how and why negative attitudes or feeling are destructive to you. You must discover how and why these negativisms disrupt harmonious functioning of the human organism and therefore cause you mental as well as physical ills.

From birth to death, no matter how long this life is, the human organism is undergoing constant change. Look how great the change has been since the beginning of life-matter. Man has achieved his present state of development from that jellylike cell that scientists call the amoeba. The amoeba is so called because "amoibe" is the word for "change" in Greek. This cell is capable of changing itself in many ways.

So we see that animate life from the very beginnings has had the automatic property of effecting changes in itself. These changes were necessary to protect life against conditions that threatened its existence. The ability to change is the "secret spark" with which God endowed human life. For without this "secret spark," without this adaptiveness to all form of environment and all sorts of problems, the human form of life would hardly have survived.

This "secret spark" for change is still a part of the human. After countless centuries of progressive evolution in man, changes in environmental conditions are still met by the activity of this traditional physiological mechanism that is known as the adaptive function.

This adaptive function, this "secret spark," is controlled not by the conscious level of the mind, but by the Supraconscious. Man is consciously aware that the function exists, he is consciously aware of what it has accomplished, but he is not consciously in control of the power.

His conscious level can only transmit to the Supraconscious

the need for the adaptive function to be brought into play. The Supraconscious relays to the various organs, nerves and blood cells the need for ways and means to meet new situations. The Supraconscious aids the organs of the body in improvising ways to meet these problems.

The adaptive function operates by means of "chemical messengers"—the hormones—which are secreted directly into the blood stream by the various endocrine glands.

Dr. Hans Selye, Director of the Institute of Experimental Medicine and Surgery at the University of Montreal, calls this adaptive function "the body's unified Department of Defence." Working harmoniously, the body's defensive setup knows when to give battle to dangerous germ life and when to ignore the harmless—and helpful—microscopic life within your system.

This network of alarm and protection knows when to protect you from cold and exhaustion, from high-pressure work and emotional tension. But if any of these "enemies" reach proportions of unbalance with the defensive mechanism, your body and your mind succumb to stress, or the system reacts so violently that it injures itself.

This line of defense against attack by internal enemies is the very answer to the question at the start of this chapter.

The very means by which you can live longer is this adaptive function of the body. This is the key to Life Limitless. Scientific study has shown that life is not limited to the proverbial three score and ten years. Man should be able to live to the century mark and more. The Bible makes reference to such life spans, but misinterpretation or misinformation has led us to believe that these were exceptional or unusual. Perhaps they were, but the exceptionality of these long lives is only that those who lived them had obviously found the clue to the "secret spark"—and had used it to achieve Life Limitless.

By knowing how the body inflicts upon itself degenerative diseases—"diseases of adaptation" as Dr. Selye calls them—you can learn the secret of extending the span of your life to beyond the limits of a century.

Man's status, like his present mode of living, was not developed in the course of a single lifetime. The gradual transition from the savage state of life to the present state of civilization accounts for man's highly developed external environment and his relative internal decline. In the so-called uncivilized state, man, the savage creature, maintained a well-balanced co-ordination of his mental instincts and physical faculties compatible with his wild environment. This creature was concerned solely with the task of obtaining food for his existence and with living from day to day in competition with the many other creatures around him that were intent on destroying him. His main objective in life was survival.

To cope successfully with the wildness of his surroundings, his physical development reached a high state of perfection and coordination. Man's environment during the savage state of his development endowed him with instinctive qualities equal to the animal life about him with which he had to compete if his quest for existence was to be successful.

During the savage era of his evolution, man developed instinctive functioning of his physical powers by means of Supraconscious direction. Because of the regular routine of his daily activities, the savage man required no higher mental processes than this Supraconscious guidance of his highly developed instincts and emotions.

To illustrate how instincts and emotions served to meet the needs of primitive man, let us consider briefly the psychophysical action that took place when he was faced with danger and it was necessary to escape or give battle, the first flight or fight reaction of "human nature."

When he was faced with an adversary too powerful to overcome, the instinctive urge for survival within the Supraconscious caused the emotional impulse of fear to be transmitted to the pituitary gland (attached to the lower base of the brain). Hormones from the pituitary caused excitation of the adrenal glands—the glands of combat, as they sometimes are called— one of which is attached to each kidney.

Hormones from the adrenal glands caused the liver to discharge its sugar into the blood stream for use by the muscles. The lungs reacted with rapid, deep breathing. This quickened the supply of oxygen and the elimination of carbon dioxide from the system. The heart then beat more rapidly and strongly. The blood pressure thus increased drove blood to the muscles of the legs to enable our primitive man to escape from the danger that threatened him by the simple process of running away.

On the other hand, when there was a need to "fight for dear life," the same instinctive urge for survival caused the emotion of anger to arouse identical physical action—the same bellowing of the lungs, acceleration of the heart beat, increased blood pressure, and so on. But the energy from the blood's sugar, instead of going to the lower extremities, was directed by the Supraconscious to the muscles of the arms so that fight rather than flight was possible.

You know from actual experience that you can run much faster when danger threatens and you are scared. You know likewise from personal experience how anger will intensify your combative attitudes. This instinctive mechanism was of great value to man's primitive ancestors. But man today is civilized. He does not leap upon his enemy and battle ferociously in ordinary social contacts, nor does he run for miles to escape danger.

Quite likely, if man did these things today, there would be vastly fewer deaths from heart disease as well as a much smaller percentage of degenerative diseases. The stresses you undergo by not reacting as your primitive ancestors did make for wear and tear on the body and the mind far worse than the wear of the physical action of running or fighting.

The primitive instincts, however, that were developed in the human brain through man's daily competition with wild animals and fellow men through countless generations of uncivilized existence are still active in the Supraconscious. Too frequently modern man is caused by these instincts to use his emotions destructively, simply because he does not always find suitable outlets available for the release of the emergency energy.

Fear and anger are instinctive emotions that were designed by God for the preservation of the species. It is indeed a sad commentary in this age of enlightenment that more and more persons are literally destroying themselves in body, mind and soul with the very same primary emotional forces that were designed for the perpetuation of the human race.

This trend toward retrogression is a serious one. But it can be checked, and simply. All that is necessary is better understanding of the self and compliance with the laws governing "human nature."

Why do you worry? You worry because you "fear" that someone or something has threatened your security in some way. This fear may conceivably not be a conscious fear. It may very well be an unconscious fear. But, nonetheless, it causes worry. And if you work up resentment at the situation, anger is aroused.

These are negativisms. These negativisms and other forms of negative emotion—and there are so many that it would be impossible to list them all here—are offshoots of your primary emotions of fear and anger.

If you are to allow fear and anger, and/or any of their off-shoots, to become chronic, they will eventually unbalance your body. The result will be an unfailing culmination in some degenerative disease.

When negative emotions become chronic, the adrenal glands are almost constantly pouring adrenalin into the blood stream. The muscles become tense, energy is wasted, the heart overworked, the liver strained in an effort to supply the excesses of sugar called for—and all this is in response to the primordial urge for survival. But, paradoxically, this urge for survival under these negativistic circumstances results in functional disorders of the body and mind.

The excesses of sugar frequently cause diabetes, the overworking of the liver leads to many complications, the overstraining of the heart brings general deterioration and frequently premature death.

We see therefore that fear is the most destructive of all the emotions. And as it is the chief emotional component of worry, fear is active in the daily living of nearly all of us at some time or other.

You probably have not thought of worry as being fear. The simple fact is, however, that if you were not afraid, you would not worry.

Fear does to some extent serve a useful purpose. It excites the adrenal glands to stimulate mind and body to meet emergency situations necessary to the preservation of the organism's equilibrium and stability.

But despite this usefulness, you must not be lulled into believing that prolonged worry will therefore not affect your body. You must know the ill effects that continual or lengthy worry has upon you. You certainly would not voluntarily tolerate any physical state that depletes and exhausts your vitality! Yet many persons do allow a mental state to exist that does this very thing—for that is precisely what happens when you permit worry to dominate your mind.

If you are an average person, you are prone to rationalize your own weaknesses. It is a human failing. You probably are thinking at this minute that a state of prolonged worry and consequent breakdown can't happen to you.

After all, your thoughts are probably running, I don't worry —at least not enough to injure myself!

Let a celebrated professor of psychiatry answer you. In his book *Emotional Maturity*, J. B. Saul says:

"Few persons, indeed, realize how hostile they are, and our

ignorance does not help us in attacking the problem of this inner force which menaces humanity today as it has throughout history.

"For men treat moralistically, heatedly, vindictively, an emotional force whch they repress and do not wish to see in its full intensity within themselves—rather than facing it frankly, objectively, and scientifically like a disease or any other force of nature.

"It is obvious that so intricate, fundamental and universal a reaction as this quick mobilization for flight or fight must play a fateful role in human life and human affairs. Many are the frustrations and irritations of everyday life, even in peacetime, hence there are few people who do not endure constant frustration, constant irritation and hence constant anger.

"As Thoreau once said, 'The mass of men lead lives of quiet desperation.' The irritation may be physical or psychologic, internal or external, real or imagined. It may arise from a decayed tooth, or a miscarriage of justice, from feelings of inadequacy due to prolonged and excessive dependence on one's parents, to an unhappy home life, or to years of mistreatment during childhood, from loss of a button, or loss of a friend, from living under a leaky roof, from an uneasy conscience, or from exposure to battle conditions.

"Whatever the irritation, man fights it by trying to attack and destroy the source, or by escaping; and his feelings are anger and anxiety."

A great many people pride themselves on having the good sense not to worry, at least not about unessential things. Perhaps you do not worry too much during your waking hours. Most of us are much too busy earning our livelihoods to worry while we work.

But how many of us lie down to sleep at night without our worries creeping into the forefront of our minds? Like the camel, most of us retire for the night with our packs still on our backs.

Too many become slaves of night worry. You fall into the habit of thinking over the affairs of the day after you have retired for the night. The thinking habit at bedtime is a wonderful habit to cultivate—but it must be used for thoughts of pleasant and cheerful things. This thinking period must be positive and constructive. You must think about your desires and yearnings and about ways to constructively gain them. But this is something I will deal with at greater length in a later chapter.

131

The first proposition of the working hypothesis I have discussed earlier makes it clear that the Supraconscious is constantly amenable to control by suggestion. And the fifth proposition points out that the Supraconscious has absolute control of the functions and conditions of the body. Therefore, if you fall asleep entertaining positive thoughts—cheerful and constructive ideas—your mind and body will be the benefactors of your thinking during your sleeping hours. And your sleep, you will find, will always be sound and refreshing.

But, if you lie down to sleep with your mind troubled by the trials, pettinesses and stresses of your workaday existence, have you any reason to wonder why you awake in the morning feeling tired and listless?

You have seen how worry will sap vitality and destroy health. So it is that taking your troubles with you to bed at night will surely make you grow old prematurely. A troubled sleep is not one that will benefit you. An untroubled, peaceful and sound sleep is one in which the body's recuperative powers have a chance to work. It is such sleep which can be made amenable to suggestion of added rebuilding and regeneration of the body's tissues and cells.

Going to sleep in a cheerful mood will always mean awakening refreshed and vigorous, simply because your body has had a chance to replenish itself, to grow, to build. Going to sleep in an ugly mood or in a state of depression or worry will only cause you to forfeit the natural benefit of sleep. In addition you will harm your health, shorten your life, destroy your happiness and quite conceivably bring to reality all the disagreeable things about which you thought at bedtime.

Worry is a thief in the night. It robs you of your natural heritage of health, happiness and longevity.

The problem you must solve is "How do I stop worrying?"

The answer is given in five simple words:

"Cultivate a well-balanced mind!"

How? Simply by replacing every negative thought with a positive one. Do you remember the popular song of not so many years ago—"Accentuate the Positive"? The positive must dominate, the negative must be quelled.

Your mental process that produces the phenomenon called thinking is caused by the interaction of the "feeling" attitudes and your "reasoning" conclusions. But your feelings must not dominate your reason, for feelings can be negative and domination under these circumstances is the making of your downfall.

Learn to test the "reasonableness" of each thought or contemplated act before you indulge in it. Learn to ask yourself: "Is this right or wrong?" Constant testing consciously will lead you to constant testing unconsciously, so that eventually your mind will tell you right or wrong without a moment's hesitation.

In the beginning, when you test consciously, if your sense of reason tells you that you are wrong, do not rationalize the desire or feeling-attitude by attempting to make black appear to be white, as it were. Instantly dismiss the entire idea from your mind by deliberately thinking about something else.

The simple reason this technique is such a practical one is that your conscious level cannot think of more than one thing at a time. It is therefore quite easy to dismiss any "bad" or undesirable thought from consciousness by simply thinking about something else. In due time the process will become automatic. You will instantly dismiss those thoughts or actions that are classified as negativisms. You will start living a positive life and will reap the benefits of "good" living.

The value of this technique depends upon the diligence and persistence with which you practice this mental exercise.

You must learn to do it once today, and twice tomorrow. The day after tomorrow you must do it three times and continue to increase it by one time each day so that your *positive* thinking will become automatic.

You will find after practice that right thinking will be a conditioned reflex of your mind. It will be a habit resulting in a noticeably rapid mental and physical improvement.

So you now have a concrete example of how you can use the Golden Gift for one of the many powers it was intended. By this practical and simple method you will be able to train your own Supraconscious to be a good servant rather than an unconsciously bad one.

The involuntary functions of your body can be brought under conscious control by this simple technique, if you persevere.

BUT YOU MUST PERSEVERE!

It is not sufficient to remember one day and forget on others—and then try to catch up with what you carelessly missed by forgetting. Conscious perseverance in this pursuit is of the same necessity as constant practice is for any athletic pastime or mental exercise if perfection is to be achieved.

Before you go on, reread the fundamental principles of this therapeutic phenomenon:

1. The Supraconscious exercises complete control over the functions and conditions of the body.

2. The Supraconscious is amenable to control by suggestion of the conscious mind.

3. These two propositions of the working hypothesis lead then to the unchallenged conclusion that the functions and conditions of the body can be controlled by suggestions of the conscious mind.

It will take only a little practice before you find to your surprise how quickly and completely you can change your mental habits so that you will automatically review the happenings of each day with constructive mental attitudes before you fall asleep each night.

You will find how wonderfully serene, calm, refreshed and completely rejuvenated you will be when you awake each morning.

You will find how easy it will be to start the day with cheerfulness for all and malice toward none.

On the other hand, if you go to bed in a sour mood, ill-humored, or permitting your conscious mind to dwell on negative thoughts, your Supraconscious will continue to entertain disturbing thoughts while you sleep. This will be a constant strain on your nervous system and cause malfunctioning of your bodily organs.

It must become a fixed rule for you to set your mental house in good order upon retiring each night.

Within short days you will become much healthier and happier than you ever were.

By properly preparing your mind for sleep you hold the power of building for yourself a healthier body and a happier and longer life.

Each night at bedtime you must visualize as vividly as possible constructive mental pictures of what you would like to be, or what you would like to possess, or what you would like to have happen to you.

It will amaze you when you discover how the creative forces of the Supraconscious can be put to work in refashioning your mental, physical, spiritual and material life. But you must train this "genie" of your mind in positive "emotional thinking" while you sleep. For if you allow negative suggestions to weave themselves into the fabric of life's reality, you will be doing the very thing you seek to avoid—giving the mind the fears and worries so many people have, caused mostly by imaginary things.

Edward van Duyne of Rochester, New York, has a short recipe for a long life: "Don't worry!" Isn't that a wonderful plan to follow; and isn't it a simple one once you know how. Mr. van Duyne should know what he is talking about. When he disclosed this recipe for longevity not too long ago, he was one hundred and six years old.

A Rochester psychiatrist, Dr. Daniel B. Schuster, described Mr. van Duyne as "amazingly alert." There is no senility here, no breakdown of the mental processes due to unnecessary worry and fear. This man at the age of one hundred and six recorded an intelligence quotient of 126—an IQ-reading well into the "superior" category.

His alert brain is up to the minute on current affairs in all fields. He is active in his lodge and other organizations and loves to spend evenings playing cards with younger cronies. He drinks beer frequently and smokes six cigars a day.

This is no exceptional phenomenon; this can be the rule for everyone. Dr. Schuster has offered the case of Mr. van Duyne as evidence to support the scientific theory that there is "not necessarily" a direct relationship between age and breakdown of intellectual functions.

Dr. William Brady, whose syndicated newspaper column is widely read, has given us this sound advice:

"You should endeavor to learn more about life, physical life, biology, physiology, growth, development, maturity and degeneration, physical degeneration. With an intelligent view of these vital processes, your attitude toward life in all these phases will become less squeamish, more philosophical and conducive to peace of mind.

"Knowledge is the antidote to fear."

This is probably what Dr. A. P. Merrill of St. Barnabas Hospital in New York City meant when he said recently that it might be possible for man to live to be one hundred and fifteen years old if chronic diseases were to be wiped out.

"Some day," he said, "it may be possible to go to the death-bed of a man of sixty-five and tell him, 'There has been a mistake; you have another fifty years to live.'

"This miracle will come to pass only after chronic disease —the nation's number one health problem—has been put to rout."

My good friend Jacques Romano, in New York, claims that people could live to be one hundred and twenty years old if they would learn to think sanely and live wisely. Jacques is more than ninety-two now, and his mental and physical condition is like that of a perfectly healthy person of thirty-five.

Through persistent practice and conscious control of his emotional life, this amazing man has proved that even the involuntary functions of the human body can be consciously controlled.

"The mental faculty of stopping the pulse, stopping the blood circulation in parts of my body, stopping and starting digestion, raising and lowering the blood pressure, has come with practice," he has said. "It has nothing to do with religious beliefs or 'soul development.'

"Learn to understand with humility instead of superiority. Hate is a confession of fear and lack of confidence. Avoid those who spread propaganda of hate, regardless of what religion they profess or what position they hold.

"The true Christian does not degrade the teachings of the Master by stooping to hate, bigotry or bloodshed.

"True development rises from one's mental attitudes. Self-discipline, self-control and self-mastery are the basic principles of self-development. Only when you have attained these can you experience the exaltation of what the Great Master meant by saying, 'Peace be with you.'

"As for health—my mind does not permit my body to recognize the proverbial three score and ten. With neither worry, envy, hate nor malice toward anyone, my physical structure is beyond disorder."

Such men as Mr. van Duyne and Mr. Romano have learned how to meet life's stresses with perfect tranquility. The formula they use is an old one—but it has never failed.

And this formula will work for you, if only you conform to the laws governing "human nature."

This formula recognizes that the primary emotions of fear and rage are the biological roots from which all destructive emotional reactions stem. The antithesis of these destructive reactions is the feeling-attitude of love.

The great modern "mystic" Joseph Sadony has made this pertinent statement:

"We started our 'Scientific Investigation of God' with Pope's famous warning ringing in our ears:

"'Know then thyself, presume not God to scan.
The proper study of mankind is man.'
"But we soon found an answer to it:
"'Seek thou within: seek not for God above!
The proper name for God in man is Love!' "

No less an authority than the late Dr. Alexis Carrel pointed out the basic similarity of the rules of mental hygiene and the moral law as expounded by Christ when one of the Pharisees asked: "Master, which is the greatest commandment in the law?"

Jesus said to him:

"Thou shalt love the Lord thy God with all thy heart, and with all thy soul, and with all thy mind.

"This is the first and great commandment.

"And the second is like unto it. Thou shalt love thy neighbor as thyself.

"On these two commandments hang all the Law and the prophets."

If you wish to witness the greatest of all miracles—the operation in your own life of the great law that governs human nature—just use the formula of love. This formula is the most effective means of attaining perfect tranquility—the basis of health, happiness and longevity.

As of this very moment start loving your fellow men—every one of them. Pour out the love of your heart to your spouse, your children, your relatives, your neighbors, your associates. Above all, this outpouring of love, this feeling-attitude that will bring you the perfection of tranquility, must be lavished on those persons about whom up to this minute you care least.

And don't feel that your love must be confined only to your fellow man. You can, and must, love everything that God has created—the trees, the flowers, the birds; everything, all that is about you.

You must strive to increase your love each and every day.

Aging is a disease. The technique of bestowing love upon everyone and everything will slow down this process of aging. It will bring you health. It will bring you happiness. It will bring you a long and fruitful life.

It has worked for others. It will work for you.

It is there for you to try: Learn to love and you will live!

But today—not "tomorrow"—is the day to start!

FIGHTING THE AGE-DISEASE

Love is the all-curing medicine that conquers the dreaded disease known as old age.

Age is a relative thing. The number of years you have lived is only an arithmetical symbol.

The happiness you have spread, and have thus yourself had, during that time is the true determinant of your youth.

Learn to use the formula of love.

At least once each night before you fall asleep—and again at least once each day, preferably in the morning before the strain of the day's work is upon you—repeat either or both of the following thoughts:

"The proper name for God in man is Love!"

and

"Thou shalt love the Lord thy God with all thy heart, and with all thy soul, and with all thy mind. Thou shalt love thy neighbor as thyself."

The best active use of the formula of love will come at any time during a period of stress or strain in any day.

At such times you must repeat this thought (inserting in the blank space the word or phrase signifying that which has caused the moment of grief):

"I love ——————— as I do myself!"

VIII

How to Generate
Prayer Power

We hear a great deal these days about what prayer can do.

"The trouble is," said the late Dr. George Washington Carver, "people don't know how to pray.

"Their prayers don't even reach the ceiling."

A psychologist, speaking of prayer, said: "The trouble is that most prayers are neither honest to God nor to one's self.

"Too many folks pray with malice still in their hearts. Greed, resentment, envy, jealousy and lust dissipate the power their prayers would have if they had real love for God and their neighbor in their heart."

What is prayer?

The dictionary defines it broadly as "a request." The average person feels that one does not pray unless one has something specific being sought.

This undoubtedly is a purpose of prayer—but it is not the prime purpose. Prayer, as Fyodor Dostoyevsky wrote in his great novel *The Brothers Karamazov,* is an education.

The poet Samuel Coleridge once said, "He prayeth best who *loveth* best." The emphasis is mine. For here you see the necessity of tying in the formula of love—love for all things— with the need of prayer.

You must learn the *real* meaning of prayer—not the commonly understood dictionary definition. When you do find that meaning, you will find that what really counts is not what you are, but what you may become.

Despite a general misunderstanding as to the real meaning of prayer, no intelligent person will deny its value in any progressive plan of life.

Prayer enlivens the spirit of man by stimulating constructive excitation of the human emotions.

Prayer has a stabilizing effect upon the human organism.

It tends to harmonize the interaction of thalamic "feeling" impulses and cortical "reasoning" attitudes.

In essence, prayer subdues the turbulence of the mental conflicts within the Supraconscious and effects a state of harmony in the entire consciousness. Eventually that state of harmony is reflected throughout the whole human organism.

This peaceful and harmonious state of mind will result in a healthier condition of the body. For the body then comes under the positive influence of constructive thinking that characterizes sincere prayer.

It has been the belief since time immemorial that prayer derives its extraordinary power from a "supernatural" source. In effect, this is true. But it is true in only the same sense that the force of gravity or other such laws of nature derive their power from God.

Dr. Alexis Carrel, in an article in *The Reader's Digest* published in 1941, said: "Prayer is not only worship; it is also an invisible emanation of man's worshipping spirit—the most powerful form of energy that one can generate.

"The influence of prayer on the human mind and body is as demonstrable as that of secreting glands. Its results can be measured in terms of increased physical buoyancy, greater intellectual vigor, moral stamina, and a deeper understanding of the realities underlying human relationships."

"All this," some skeptic may ask, "from a little thing like a prayer? After all, isn't prayer something you are taught as a child to help you develop a worshipful respect for God? What good can prayer really do?"

The skeptic who asks these questions certainly doesn't understand the basic value of prayer to the individual. In the first place he fails even to understand what prayer is. Prayer is not necessarily saying words; it more often is just meditating quietly. "Thinking about God," is the way Norman Vincent Peale put it in his book *The Power of Positive Thinking*.

Try thinking about God; make it your prayer until such time as you have developed the power to pray. For unless you develop the power to pray, you will never be able to utilize the power of prayer.

Try to pray when you are alone, where it is quiet. Until you are able to utilize the power of prayer, try to choose a spot conducive to a receptive mood. You may find that, once you have developed this great and wonderful power, you will always return to such a spot—for freedom from distracting thoughts is an essential in good prayer.

Next, try to free yourself from negative emotions. These, as I have repeatedly pointed out up to this time, are destructive. Your mind cannot function properly if it is filled with feelings of worry and fear, of self-pity or hatred or jealousy.

Finally, the main rule of prayer is to relax. Let yourself go, as the once-popular song said. Let yourself go, both physically and mentally. Dr. Albert E. Cliffe put it this way: "Let go and let God."

When Dr. Carrel referred to the realities underlying human relationships, what did he mean?

It is a generally accepted fact that the laws of nature—the cosmic forces, if you will—govern inanimate life. Under God, there are immutable laws that likewise govern "human nature."

It has been said that the ideal state of being for the human is one of peace and poise. This implies complete union with the all-pervading spirit. The obvious relationship between the psyche that is the soul-of-the-mind and the psyche that is the mind-of-the-body is proof of how negative thinking can produce an ill soul.

Psychosomatic ills, as it has been pointed out, are the end products of some malfunctioning of the human nervous system. They are states of the mind-of-the-body produced by negative thinking at either the conscious or the Supraconscious level—or both.

The "collective unconscious" of the Supraconscious mind's level is a veritable jungle of conflicting memories. With the psychic self bound to a negative state, the redeeming function of prayer becomes obvious.

Elevating conscious thoughts to a higher power alleviates the disturbances of negative "emotional thinking." It sublimates emotional conflicts which are the irritating causes that underlie psychosomatic ills and human aberrations.

One of the most effective means of substituting positive conscious thoughts for the negative "emotional thinking," which destroys us, is prayer. In the words of psychological-organ language, which I have mentioned before, we say: "To lift one's heart in prayer."

And that is almost exactly what happens—the heart, as the pump of life, beats more quickly in response to the greatness of good. The heart is virtually "lifted" with prayer.

The effect of prayer is to remove the burden of troublesome feeling-attitudes from the Supraconscious mind. The resultant harmony brings peace of mind. Peace of mind is true happiness.

141

This peace, this poise, this power of the integrated whole consciousness constitutes the invisible emanation of man's worshipping spirit. And that spirit of man's is the most powerful form of energy that can be generated in the human.

That Mahatma Gandhi, the great prophet of India, recognized this practical aspect of prayer is obvious. "Prayer," he said, "can work miracles, but it should not be considered only in terms of miracles.

"And let us not think that it is concerned solely with spiritual salvation. That is a common error, perhaps the commonest, and if we fall into it we have lost a good part of the meaning that prayer should have for us.

"It brings us an awareness of God, yes, but also it nourishes the one who prays, both mentally and physically."

The holy men of the ages, the savants, the sages, and the prophets, all did discover that there is a "hidden power" within man that has a constructive, as well as a destructive, force. They didn't know how it worked. But that wasn't important as long as they knew enough to abolish negative states of mind by stimulating positive emotional forces through the power of prayer.

In this day of enlightenment, of rapid communication of scientific fact and education, there are many people who are not content with knowing simply that "right thinking" will be beneficial. These people have experienced the effect. Now they want to comprehend fully the cause of this phenomenon.

The late Dr. Carrel spent much time at Lourdes, in France, studying the "miracles" in healing that were claimed there. He saw a cancerous sore shrivel to a scar before his own eyes. The only condition that Dr. Carrel believed to be indispensable to the occurrence of extraordinary rapid acceleration of the process of bodily repair, or "miraculous healing," is prayer.

In his book *Man, the Unknown* Dr. Carrel wrote:

"Generally, the patient who is cured is not praying for himself, but for another. Such a type of prayer demands a complete renunciation—that is a higher form of asceticism.

"The modest, the ignorant and the poor are more capable of this self-denial than the rich and the intellectual. When it possesses such characteristics, prayer may set in motion a strange phenomenon—the miracle.

"The process of healing changes little from one individual to another. Often there is an acute pain. Then a sudden sensation of being cured.

"In a few seconds, a few minutes, at the most a few hours

the wounds are cicatrized, pathological symptoms disappear, appetite returns. Sometimes functional disorders vanish before the anatomical lesions are repaired. The skeletal deformations of Pott's disease, the cancerous glands, may still persist two or three days after the healing of the main lesions.

"The miracle is chiefly characterized by an extreme acceleration of the processes of organic repair. There is not a doubt that the rate of cicatrization of the anatomical defects is much greater than the normal one ...

"But there is no need for the patient himself to pray, or even to have any religious faith. It is sufficient that someone around him be in a state of prayer. Such facts are of profound significance. They show the reality of certain relations, of still unknown nature, between psychological and organic processes. They prove the objective importance of the spiritual activities, which hygienists, physicians, educators and sociologists have always neglected to study. They open to man a new world ...

"Miraculous cures seldom occur, but despite their small number, they prove the existence of organic and mental processes that we do not know. They show that certain mystic states, such as that of prayer, have definite effects. They are stubborn, irreducible facts, which must be taken into account."

So we see that two elements are necessary to produce the phenomenon of "miraculous healing." First there is the deep, subjective faith. Secondly, there is extreme acceleration of the processes of organic repair.

There is a great deal of evidence throughout the ages that faith is the one essential prerequisite to the successful exercise of the catalytic power of the Supraconscious. It is recorded that Christ Himself did not hesitate to acknowledge His inability to heal the sick in the absence of that favorable mental attitude called faith.

His reproof to His followers when they returned to Him and announced any failure of their powers to heal the sick was that they lacked faith. In this way He offered the greatest proof that He Himself regarded faith as an essential element of success, not only in the patient, but in the therapist.

What is this essential element called faith which appears to be the key to so many powers that the human can call upon? How can we best define this great "hidden power" of "human nature?" The dictionary definition is a cold one, too brief, too terse, too unmeaning—"reliance; trust in; belief founded on authority." Scripture provides much better the enlightenment we seek. After Jesus cured the "lunatic," the disciples inquired why they had failed in this task.

"And Jesus said unto them, Because of your unbelief: for verily I say unto you, If ye have faith as a grain of mustard seed, ye shall say unto this mountain, Remove hence to yonder place; and it shall remove; and nothing shall be impossible unto you."

Again when the disciples saw Jesus walking toward them on the sea, they were troubled and frightened, saying: "It is a spirit." But He admonished them not to be afraid. He even reassured them by telling Peter to come to Him.

It is recorded in Matthew how Peter "walked on the water, to go to Jesus.

"But when he saw the wind boisterous, he was afraid; and beginning to sink, he cried, saying, Lord, save me.

"And immediately Jesus stretched forth his hand, and caught him, and said unto him, O thou of little faith, wherefore didst thou doubt?"

Here we have the authority of Christ Himself that faith is belief.

Fear and doubt destroy the positive feeling-attitudes of faith. And fear and doubt are all about us. They must be overcome, for doubt leads to increased fear and fear leads to disbelief and complete stagnation. Having thoughts of fear, having thoughts of doubt sets up negative thoughts within you and breaks down the powers that the Supraconscious gives us all.

You are well advised to work at your own religion if cultivation of a deep subjective faith is desired. It is only in this way, be assured, that you can enjoy the many benefits of the healing power of faith and the ability it gives you to improve yourself in every way conceivable.

It is not necessary—nor is it even advisable—to change your religious convictions or your church affiliations. The church is man's greatest invention for his own self-help. It has been quite properly named "the House of God," for if you are sincere in your desire to make use of this implement of religion to worship God and employ the facilities that your own church provides, you will have no great difficulty in communicating with God's Infinite Intelligence.

It is easy enough to explain the mechanics of the positive feeling-attitude that we call faith. But explanation of any subject does not necessarily mean that you can employ or utilize it. Faith is something, once it has been explained to you, you and only you can make work.

Many persons have found that the mystical rituals of their own religion have been helpful. To me, personally, these rituals have become indispensable ever since I learned, through biological knowledge-of-self, how inseparable are the physical, mental and spiritual aspects of human nature.

To deny the power of prayer, or even to pray without deep feeling and conviction, dissipates the value of faith—and such petitions, as Dr. Carver said, "don't even reach the ceiling."

I have been asked: "Why is it that belief has anything to do with the miraculous results that can be obtained through prayer, meditation and other constructive means of arousing the catalytic force of human emotions?"

My only reply, and the only one there is, is that the creative power of "human nature" is controlled by the positive emotional forces of the Supraconscious. This power simply will not function constructively when mental attitudes are negative. It will not function when doubt, or prejudice, or intolerance, or bigotry, or fear—any of these negative millstones of mankind—dominates the mind.

You may find it hard to concentrate on the thoughts that are constructive, the thoughts that give you positive emotional powers.

You may find it hard to hold your mind to the constructive thoughts of prayer, to keep out other distracting—and destructive—thoughts and ideas.

If that is so, perhaps you will be benefited by these five simple rules:

1. Pray when you are by yourself.
2. Pray in a quiet place.
3. Free yourself from destructive emotions.
4. Relax physically and emotionally.
5. Concentrate on a simple truth and do not wander from it.

You will find it so much easier to set about concentrating on positive and constructive thoughts if you are in a place that is conducive to a receptive mood.

Remember, too, that if your mind is preoccupied with feelings of worry, fear, self-pity, hatred and jealousy, there is no place for constructive thoughts. Negative thoughts, the destructive ones, tend to be like elephants—they are too big to allow for even a flea in the same space.

Don't let them be there!

And—as I pointed out before in using the words "Let yourself go!"—there must be no tenseness in you. If you are relaxed physically, there is a greater chance that you will relax mentally. Once relaxed, you are free to allow the powers of prayer to seep into your system and go to work.

Choose a basic truth upon which to practice concentration with care. Perhaps the words of Coleridge that I quoted before: "He prayeth best who loveth best." Or from the Psalms: "The Lord is my shepherd." Whatever you choose, do not let yourself wander from your chosen affirmation. Allow it to become deeply engraved on your mind.

If other thoughts tend to intrude on your meditation, push them back and return to your own positive thoughts. You will soon begin to feel that you are a part of the great Divine Plan. Calm, quiet and peace will follow.

You will find that prayer will become more natural every day. You will discover that you, too, have the power to concentrate and touch deep into the powers of the mind. You will find the way to use the Golden Gift.

The primary purpose of prayer is to fill your mind with such constructive mental images that you will change your attitude from a discordant one to a harmonious one.

Your life will first change inwardly. Then, as the inward changes take place, you will yourself be able to change outward conditions.

Prayer is the means of letting loose the hidden power of the Golden Gift. Prayer is the essential agent in bringing to yourself the required insight to the Divine Plan.

Prayer is the master power that will help you to develop the powers of the Supraconscious, powers which were meant to be yours.

Don't expect miracles overnight. You must practice how to pray. When you have acquired the technique of praying, you must practice praying so that you may generate the power it has.

Remember the rules of praying:

Pray when you are by yourself; pray in a quiet place; free yourself from destructive emotions; relax physically and emotionally; and concentrate on a simple truth.

One of the hardest daily tasks is waiting patiently, being content with one small step at a time on the road to a cherished goal.

Patient waiting is a part of life.

Prayer will give you patience while it prepares to generate power.

SETTING YOUR PRAYER-POWER GENERATOR IN MOTION

In order to use the power of your Supraconscious, you must learn to set this power in motion.

To accomplish this, there are five easy rules. These rules must be memorized and used constantly. With them you can concentrate on all the constructive aspects you seek in life. Without them you will constantly flounder along a winding and bumpy road that most often ends right back where you started from.

1. You must pray when you are by yourself.
2. You must find a place of quiet in which to pray.
3. You must free yourself from all destructive emotions.
4. You must relax yourself both physically and emotionally.
5. You must concentrate on a simple truth and never wander from it.

IX

How To Use Your Faith
For Accomplishment

Faith, says the dictionary simply, is belief.

And the great key to happiness, to betterment, to achievement is faith—faith in yourself. That is to say, you must believe in yourself!

Without this self-belief, this faith, your power of accomplishment is limited immeasurably.

"Believe in yourself! Have faith in your abilities! Without a humble but reasonable confidence in your own powers you cannot be successful or happy." These two dozen words, directly put, are the opening words of Norman Vincent Peale's great best-selling book, *The Power of Positive Thinking*.

Success depends upon self-confidence. You must not have a poor opinion of yourself, although you should recognize that you are not perfect. The imperfections, though, are slight. They are trivial and you need only give them passing notice.

Instead of dwelling on the minor things you feel are imperfections, count up the major things in your favor. Don't underestimate the things you have taken for granted in the passing years of your life. List all the assets you know of; restore your faith in yourself. Faith will sweep away your doubts.

Doubts themselves are great revivers of faith. Robert Browning in his poem *Bishop Blougram's Apology*, the central character of which is said to have been modeled after the great Cardinal Wiseman, wrote:

"I show you doubt, to prove that faith exists.
The more of doubt, the stronger faith. . . ."

I have heard people say, "It's easy to talk of faith, but it's hard to practice."

How easily fooled were these people. I do not know what they conceived faith to be. Perhaps they believed it to be some great "supernatural" gift, a package from God that only a few of the chosen have. Well, it is a gift but it does not belong to any chosen few.

Faith is a gift that you have always owned. It is another of

148

the great gifts that the Divine Plan has placed within your grasp. It is a gift that can carry you successfully on any road you choose.

The gift you possess, the great helper-to-do which you own and can use, is the faith factor.

The faith factor is a part of everyone, but too few people realize it, recognize it and make use of it.

By failing to use your faith factor, you are failing to give yourself all the opportunities that the Divine Plan has in store for you.

The faith factor is much like an efficient vehicle—it can get you there! Without faith, that is, if you fail to use your faith factor, you are going nowhere.

Faith-factor failure is as much a stumbling block to your success and happiness as negative thinking.

Of course it is easy to talk faith, you may say. But, remember this, it is just as easy to practice faith. It is just as simple to have faith in yourself as it is to say the word "faith."

There is no doubt that "faith" has become a vastly overworked and overused word. We are too easily inclined to gloss over it so that, while we see it and hear it and use it, it makes little impression on us.

Think of what Henry Ford once said: "Few people realize what a substantial thing faith is."

Yes, faith is substantial. How substantial it is can be seen by how faith has helped countless thousands in their work, their beliefs, their thoughts and their plans. If your faith factor is being put to use and helps you—keeps on helping you—it is genuine.

The trick of using the faith factor is by acting it. Elmer Wheeler, author, lecturer and business consultant, in his book *The Wealth Within You,* says: "You must act as if you knew your success were already assured." That, he says, is faith.

The faith factor is not a mysterious thing. Having faith is not a matter of feeling it, it is a matter of acting it. You must act as though faith is working for you. That will put the faith factor in working order and it will begin to run of its own accord.

Don't fall into negative thinking that the faith factor will prove a substitute for work. Nor is it a substitute for preparation. The faith factor is a necessary part of both these vital aspects of your life.

Elmer Wheeler points out that "the man who says he has

faith he can do something and then does nothing has never known faith."

Belief in anything, that is faith in anything, will produce results—any results—you desire, provided you plan and work for those results.

Do you sincerely feel you cannot believe? I doubt that, but let us assume for a moment that this is true. Let us pretend that you are a person who feels he cannot believe, cannot have faith in himself.

Now let me pose another question: Have you any superstitions? Your answer is unquestionably: "Yes!" Then you have refuted your own first statement. Superstition is much the same as belief.

Faith and superstition produce the same phenomena.

If you actually believe anything, that is, if you have faith in it, even though it is generally thought by other persons to be mere superstition, your mental attitude toward this belief will produce the desired result. What is superstition to some is faith to others.

In an operative sense the same instrument that one person uses successfully to arouse the catalytic force of the God-power within his own being, may be scoffed at by others as pure superstition. In reality, the only difference is the quality of the mental attitude. In the first instance, the individual's feeling-attitude is positive. In the latter case, the other person's "emotional thinking" is negative.

How pure superstition can arouse the same "magical" power that true faith can, is depicted by the machinations of the so-called "witch doctors" of Africa.

All African wizards are not evildoers as is sometimes popularly supposed. In fact, most are practically harmless, and their activities are not wholly medicinal.

Their trafficking in spells, charms and general quackery is the reason that they have been thought of in the light of roguery and crime. When one realizes that, among the African tribes, sickness and death, except in cases of extreme old age, are looked upon as being unnatural and due to the malignant spells of some enemy or evil spirit, it is easy to see how fertile a field the witch doctor has.

After being called to attend a patient, the witch doctor always performs a lot of mumbo jumbo to impress the client with his ability to attempt a cure. In the case of simple ailments, the wizard often prescribes some basic medicinal formula that *is* curative.

But the witch doctor is careful to point out, always, that the "trouble" is the work of an ill-wisher—either human or ghostly. This leads to his own employment so that, by way of reprisal, he may "cast evil" on the supposed enemy. This practice frequently ends in the death of the unfortunate person singled out for attack.

Poison is usually the agent employed, but often there is found a case of terrible, and unaccountable, "sinking." The victim, seemingly without the will or hope to live, merely lies down and dies. Even superstitious fears and blind belief in the potency of the wizard's charms hardly seem enough to cause the demise of a big, strong, happy-go-lucky native without any trace of some organic disease.

In some places in Africa, a comprehensive Witchcraft Ordinance is in force. And although natives are shy of invoking the white man's law in cases touching on the "supernatural," they do sometimes appeal to it.

The following recorded incident is a case in point:

There was an elderly man called Njero who possessed a bad reputation. He was originally a harmless "doctor" but as he grew older he dabbled more and more in so-called "black magic." At least two deaths were attributed to his foul play. He also levied a form of blackmail on his fellow tribesmen under the threat of sickness, or worse.

Njero had a son who went by the name of Jerogi. Jerogi had been educated at a mission. He returned to his home one day wearing a silk shirt of a vivid color. Njero at once coveted the garment and demanded it. The boy, much attached to his colorful piece of wearing apparel, refused to give it up.

Hearing this, Njero became enraged at his own son and cursed him bitterly, threatening him with tribal banishment—a very serious thing. The tribal elders were approached by Njero, but they refused to take this drastic step. So, for a time, the youth was permitted to retain his property and his clanship.

Some weeks went by when one day Njero saw his son walking with a girl. Jerogi's choice of woman pleased the old man's eyes and he ordered his son to have no more to do with her. He wanted the girl for himself, he said.

Naturally Jerogi was furious and he refused to obey his father's demand. He told his father that as he had gone to the mission school he was no longer a shenzi—that is, a savage bushman—who could be frightened by threats.

More argument followed, and again Njero threatened Jerogi and cursed him. Then, seizing a goat and killing it with a club, the old man shouted: "In the morning of the coming day your life will be as the life of this goat!"

In this tribe, such is the taboo and the horror of death that any hut in which a person has died must be immediately destroyed. And anyone believed to be near the end of his natural life is placed in the bush with a few scraps of food and some water to await death. Exposure and meat-eating hyenas soon make the matter certain.

It was in the bush the next morning that the lifeless remains of the unfortunate Jerogi were found. Only the hyenas could have told whether he had been placed there dead or dying. As it proved impossible to judge how the boy died, the bright shirt he had owned and the pretty girl he had wanted both went to his father.

Wearing the brilliant garment, Njero married the girl. But one day not long after, an elder of the tribe, named Kisingo, met Njero on a forest path and in a discussion with the witch doctor bluntly accused him of having killed Jerogi by poisoning.

For a moment old Njero made no answer. He stared at the tribal elder, who was known for his kindliness, and then in a voice charged with malice, he replied: "You are a bold man, Kisingo. If by tomorrow's sun you are able to carry out your daily duties, you will be very lucky!"

In spite of himself, Kisingo was troubled, for he was born with the deep-rooted superstitious tendencies that are inherent in all bushmen. Kisingo returned to his home and during the night suffered a stroke. By morning he was virtually helpless and very near death.

In the ordinary course of events he would have been put out into the bush to await his end. But his wife, who happened to be a strong-minded woman, went alone to the witch doctor's hut and, without any reproaches or hedging, bluntly asked Njero what he would take to remove his spell.

Njero attempted no denial of responsibility. Instead, he demanded a high fee, including native beer and two heifers. The wife agreed, returned home and sent the fee to Njero.

The tribal elder started to improve almost at the same time as the extortion fee was due to reach the witch doctor's hut. He became well rapidly and in a short time was completely fit. Instead of being cowed and thankful, however, for his narrow escape, Kisingo was furious with Njero. He made the long journey to the nearest village where the governing Europeans held

152

forth and told a magistrate the story and placed a charge against Njero.

In due course Njero was arrested and convicted. The long spell of imprisonment to which he was sentenced may or may not have caused the evildoer to mend his ways. This case is unusual inasmuch as it was settled by law.

Of a far more common type is the case that follows:

The principal was a man named Kibuti. He belonged to a tribe in what is considered the most witch-ridden part of Kenya.

His wife, Kabanja, was working on their maize patch one afternoon when a woman named M'Njeri, long suspected of witchcraft, who was working on an adjacent piece of land, approached. She said to Kabanja: "Oh, wife of Kibuti, help me with my patch for the sun journeys down the hill."

Kabanja, having quite enough to do on her own land, denied M'Njeri's request in short order. The other woman went away but soon returned with another request: "Oh, woman of Kibuti, lend me your hoe."

Kibuti's wife lost her temper: "If I lend you my hoe, might I not as well work for you? Stop pestering me, fool!"

At that M'Njeri became furious and cursed Kabanja, finishing with the ominous words:

"You, who named me fool, will soon sit among the spirits! Under the sun you refused me help, but under the moon you will give it to me. Alive you revile me, dead you will work for me!"

Knowing M'Njeri's sinister reputation, other women toiling nearby were horrified at what they heard. Kabanja, however, appeared to be stunned. Actually, it turned out later she had been quickly hypnotized. Soon Kabanja collapsed and her companions were too frightened to go to her aid. In fact, they were so scared that they did not tell Kibuti of what had happened to his wife until well after sundown.

Kibuti, on hearing the news, was torn between fear and anger. He took his bow and a quiver of poisoned arrows and went out to the maize patch with a friend. There he found his wife apparently lying dead. She was really, as we know, in a state of hypnotic coma.

Unfortunately Kibuti's friend lacked courage. And what little he did have soon deserted him and he fled. It is unfortunate, because from this point on, the story is based on the unsupported evidence of Kibuti alone.

Kibuti said he found his wife lying stiff and dead. He tried to move her, but being unable to, he decided—with considerable courage—to post himself close by and ward off any hyenas. The moon was full and he was able to see quite clearly, when, suddenly, he said, he saw M'Njeri approach. He kept out of sight as well as he could and watched. She failed to notice him and squatted down beside the prostrate body of Kabanja.

Kibuti said the woman appeared to whisper to his wife and then stood up and stared at the body. After a few minutes, to Kibuti's utter horror, he saw his wife get up, take her hoe, and with glazed and unseeing eyes follow the other woman to her maize patch.

Though he was virtually completely overcome with terror, Kibuti did not forget his mission. He fitted an arrow to his bow and fired at M'Njeri. The witch spun around with a poisoned arrow in her heart and at the very moment she crashed lifeless to the ground, his wife's body collapsed. With a wild yell of terror, Kibuti fled.

Of course Kibuti's wife was not dead. She was only in a state of trance, or suspended animation—a state I have discussed earlier in this book. This trance was brought about either by the other woman's ability to hypnotize or by her own fear-induced autosuggestion.

Suspended animation is a striking example of the fifth proposition of our working hypothesis: the Supraconscious has absolute control of the functions and conditions of the body.

There is a story, and it has been authenticated, that a famed Yogi, Haridas, was buried alive for one hundred and twenty days while in a state of self-induced catalepsy. When he was dug up, he was still clean shaven.

These phenomena explain the mystery of so-called zombies, or "living dead," who are found wherever voodoo is practiced. Evil priests, or witch doctors, often prey upon the primitive superstitions of the natives by having a zombi or two working in their fields as mute evidence of their alleged "supernatural" power.

The victim is placed into a state of suspended animation by hypnotic influence. After the "dead" man has been buried (and embalming is not practiced among African or Haitian natives), he is later dug up in the presence of relatives and friends, perhaps at the eerie hour of midnight, and placed in bondage by playing up the inherent superstition of the natives.

"I brought you back to life," says the nefarious witch doctor, "so now you belong to me."

Under a continuous hypnotic spell, the wretched victim lives in silent servitude without a mind of his own, a mute spectacle of the mystical power of the evil voodoo priest or witch doctor.

So we see how the power of suggestion frequently works its diabolical magic on the highly superstitious minds of the natives of Africa and Haiti. These graphic illustrations should make it simple for you to understand how and why faith and superstition can both produce the same results. They confirm the correctness of Paracelsus' statement that "whether the object of your faith be real or false, you will nevertheless obtain the same effects."

The cult of the Holiness Faith Healers, which has spread rapidly through the southern mining country in the United States, is another striking example of the truth of what Paracelsus said more than four hundred years ago.

Although state laws have been passed prohibiting the use of snakes in religious worship, increasing thousands of these "faith healers" continue to snuggle up against rattlesnakes and copperheads in their religious services.

To prove that they can be harmed by nothing once they have been "anointed by the Lord," as they believe, they also expose their flesh to fire and drink poison with no apparent ill effect.

The easiest way to climb to the hierarchy of the cult is to be nipped by a snake. One of the most recently raised to "sainthood" among the cult—as they term it—is a Mrs. W. M. Kleineick of Stone Creek Cove, Virginia. Mrs. Kleineick, or "Saint Mancy," as she is called, was converted to the cult when she was fifty-five years old. She was about eighty-five at this writing and had been cuddling snakes for years during the rites, singing to them with the rest of the congregation, petting them, even kissing them, but nothing happened until one day she was bitten in the hand and achieved her "sainthood."

" 'Tweren't nothin'," she said. "Didn't even know it until the next day when my hand swelled. Felt like a briar had stuck into it."

There is nothing new in the use of snakes for worship. The snake was deified by the Egyptians, the Greeks and the Romans, the Druids, the Norsemen—virtually every people of ancient times. Today the snake is venerated by the Chinese, the Japanese, the Hindu and many tribes of Africa. The American Indians in the southwest United States still hold snake festivals.

But, perhaps because of the Biblical story of the snake in

the Garden of Eden, many peoples abhor reptiles. Yet the faith healers base their rites on the Gospel of St. Mark (XVI:18):

"They shall take up serpents; and if they drink any deadly thing, it shall not hurt them; they shall lay hands on the sick, and they shall recover."

During their revival meetings, the leaders of this cult gradually work themselves into a state of near-frenzy. They pick up snakes as though they were pieces of rope, wind them about their bodies, put them on top of their heads, let the darting forked tongues touch their lips.

Mothers in the congregation bring babies forward to touch the snakes. Some babies do so gleefully. There is no record of a baby being bitten. In the fulsomeness of their zeal, the worshippers seem almost to be begging the snakes to sink their fangs—perhaps because of aspirations to what they believe is "sainthood."

Yet it is seldom that a snake makes any attempt to bite these frenzied cultists. One of their number, Paul Dodson, has been bitten nine times in seven years, and his only comment is: " 'Pears like I'm getting closer to Heaven all the time."

This dramatic illustration has been recounted to show how belief constitutes the fundamental difference between superstition and faith. It is only one of many ways in which this can be shown.

Science has shown that we can now trace the progress of the human more than one million years. During this long trek of man's progressive evolution, our primitive forebears lived in constant fear of the many dangers that threatened their very existence.

For the most part, the human instinct of self-preservation stems from a primordial environment in which the only philosophy was "kill or be killed." The more highly man developed above the wild animals with which he had to compete daily for mere existence, the more superstitious he became. This was due to an almost constant feeling of fear.

In the long road man took from savagery to civilized ways of living, our forebears, surrounded by dangers, developed the instinctive habit of appealing to their gods for protection from harm, both real and fancied. As we have seen in the case of the present-day natives of Africa, primitive people are extremely fearful of evil spirits as well as human and animal enemies.

Because of these constant fears, generation after generation through countless ages, superstition has become one of the most active forces of the "collective unconscious."

In our own time its emotional force sometimes is wisely and constructively used for the moral and spiritual uplift of human nature. Without the self-help that religion affords, enough people would revert to savagery to completely destroy all vestiges of civilized society.

Indeed, no less an authority than the late Dr. Nicholas Murray Butler, who was president of Columbia University, said in one of his annual messages that if our world is not rebuilt on a moral foundation, the end of all that has been accomplished in five thousand years will not be far away.

He traced the plight of civilization in our time to "plain immorality growing out of calloused selfishness." He went on to affirm that "the history of the world's religious philosophy, literature and science regards wisdom on the highest plane, but that wisdom has failed to control the conduct of mankind."

Dr. Butler insisted that "the force that rules the world is conduct, whether it be moral or immoral.

"If it is moral," he said, "at least there may be hope for the world; if immoral, there is no hope."

Dr. Butler called upon youth to accept the responsibility of leadership and to attack the problem that the older generation has failed to solve. He concluded with these words: "Young people will be called upon in the immediate future to determine whether mankind is intelligent and moral enough to put an end to the greater brute force and pillage which threaten to bring civilization itself to an end."

All thinking people—especially those who exercise common sense enough to control the devastating effects of such negative feeling-attitudes as prejudice, intolerance, bigotry, fear and jealousy—must subscribe to a constructive philosophy of life. This philosophy is that any and all religious convictions that help man hold in check his animal and savage tendencies are quite indispensable to further human progress through the progressive evolution of man.

As a thinking person, you should not criticize the religious beliefs of others though they may differ vastly from your own. As a thinking person, you should be completely fair-minded in conceding the logical fact that if one is sincere in the practice of his religion, he is at least displaying wisdom in utilizing man's greatest invention and implement of self-help.

Man's inherent beliefs can be used just as easily for constructive purposes as for destructive purposes. Witness the wonderful therapeutic work being done in curing habitual drunkenness on a country-wide basis by an organized group of self-admitted former drunkards who call themselves and their therapeutic technique Alcoholics Anonymous.

Three men sat around a bed of an alcoholic patient in the psychopathic ward of a large city hospital. The man in the bed, a complete stranger to them, had the drawn and slightly stupid look that inebriates get while being "de-alcoholized" after a "bender."

The only thing noteworthy about the callers, aside from the obvious contrast between their well-groomed appearance and that of the patient, was the fact that each had been through the same process many times himself. They were members of a band of ex-problem drinkers who have made it their avocation to help other alcoholics to beat the liquor habit—members of Alcoholics Anonymous.

The man in the bed was a mechanic. His visitors were a Princeton-educated salesman, a Yale-educated lawyer and a University of Pennsylvania-educated publicity man. Less than a year before, one had been in shackles in the same ward. Another had been what is known among alcoholics as a "sanitarium commuter." He had moved from place to place, bedeviling the staffs of the country's leading institutions for the treatment of alcoholics. The third had spent twenty years, all outside institution walls, making life miserable for himself, his family, his employers and sundry well-meaning relatives who had had the temerity to intervene.

These three men made it plain to the man on the bed that if he actually wanted to stop drinking, they would leave their work or get up in the middle of the night to hurry to wherever he was, whenever he required help. If he did not choose to call, however, that would be the end of it.

By nature touchy and suspicious, the alcoholic likes to be left alone to work out his puzzle. He has a convenient way of ignoring the tragedy that he inflicts upon those who are close to him. He holds desperately to a conviction that, although he has not been able to handle alcohol in the past, he will ultimately succeed in becoming a controlled drinker.

One of medicine's oddest animals, the alcoholic is as often as not an acutely intelligent person. He fences verbally with professional men and relatives who attempt to aid him and he gets a perverse satisfaction out of tripping them up in argument.

There is no plausible excuse for drinking that the trouble

shooters of Alcoholics Anonymous have not heard or used themselves. When one of their prospects offers them a rationalization of taking a drink, they match it with half a dozen of their own experiences.

This upsets the alcoholic a little and he gets defensive. He looks at their clothing and smoothly shaved faces and charges them with being "goody-goodies" who don't know what it is to struggle with drink. They reply by relating their own stories— the double Scotches and brandies before breakfast; the vague feeling of discomfort preceding a drinking bout; the awakening from a spree without being able to account for the actions of several days; and the hunting fear that possibly they had run down someone with their automobiles.

Why people become alcoholics is a question on which many authorities disagree. The consensus, however, seems to be that there is one element common to all alcoholics—emotional immaturity. No matter what may have been the external cause for the excessive drinking, if indeed there was one, the immaturity factor seems to be found in all alcoholics, very much as it is found in most persons who eat their way to excessive obesity.

Dr. Leonid Kotkin, New York physician and obesity specialist, in his book *Eat, Think and Be Slender,* says: "Eating makes the immature obese person temporarily forget his problems and unhappiness. He feels 'normal' in identically the same manner as the alcoholic finds 'normality' and comfort in alcohol, and the drug addict in morphine."

In seeking escape from some factor or combination of factors that the emotionally immature person dreads, he may immerse himself in business and drive himself twelve or fifteen hours a day. Another such immature person, to escape from off-center home atmosphere—such as one unduly cruel parent and the other overindulgent—may find outlet in excessive sports activities.

The neurotic so driven may find an outlet in an artistic field. Often the escape is in food, as Dr. Kotkin points out in his book. By the use of this theory, he has helped thousands of people to reduce.

There is also the outlet, the escape, in liquor. To alcoholics, there is no more pleasant way to escape from the hardships of life around them. The spoiled child grown to adulthood chronologically but not emotionally is often eased through the "cruelties of life" on the wings of a drink—and two, and more.

The warmth that alcohol gives helps the neurotic bolster his

159

opinion of himself. It temporarily wipes away any feeling of social inferiority he may have. Light drinking soon leads to heavy drinking. Friends and family are alienated and employers become disgusted.

The drinker smolders with resentment and wallows in self-pity. He indulges in childish rationalizations to justify the excessive drinking. A whole flock of excuses comes to mind as he tries to rationalize his actions—he has been overworking and needs to relax; his throat hurts and he needs a drink to ease the pain; he has a headache; his wife does not understand him; his nerves are jumpy; everybody is against him. On and on and on—the excuses so old they are moldy.

Unconsciously, the drinker becomes a chronic excuse-maker for himself. And all the time he is drinking, he tells himself—and those who seek to help him—that he really can control his drinking if he wants to.

To demonstrate his strength of will, he goes for weeks without taking a drop. He makes a point of calling at his favorite bar at a certain time each day and ostentatiously sipping milk or a soft drink. He does not understand that by doing this he is indulging in juvenile exhibitionism.

Thus falsely encouraged by his own belief that he can control his drinking, he shifts the routine to one drink a day. And then the old cycle, the never-ending merry-go-round, is on the way once more. One drink leads to two, and two to more. Soon he is on another first-class bender.

Oddly, the trigger that sets off the explosion again is as apt to be a stroke of success as it is to be a run of bad luck. An alcoholic can stand neither prosperity nor adversity.

How does Alcoholics Anonymous effect the cure of the habitual drinker? And what has this got to do with faith and the faith factor?

At a recent meeting of the New York State Medical Society, William G. Wilson of AA was invited to present a paper on the procedures of that organization. At the close of the session, the methods and results were discussed by a number of psychiatrists. Their reaction was one of complete approval.

The three basic elements characteristic of the principal procedures of AA have been known and practiced in a fairly loose and unorganized way by others in the treatment of alcoholism since after the First World War. The AA organization, which utilized these elements in completely organized fashion, was not founded, however, until the mid-30s.

The three basic elements are surrender, relaxation, and catharsis.

Alcoholics Anonymous was the first attempt to create an effectual set of principles for producing these reactions. Precept and example, as we have seen, are used. Group therapy as well as individual therapy is relied upon to get these principles accepted by the alcoholic.

Of the twelve steps in the program of recovery used by the AA, eight are steps of surrender, four are of catharsis.

The surrender steps are:

1 We admitted we were powerless over alcohol—that our lives had become unmanageable.

2. Came to believe that a Power greater than ourselves could restore us to sanity.

3. Made a decision to turn our will and our lives over to the care of God as we understood Him.

4. Were entirely ready to have God remove all these defects of character.

5. Humbly asked Him to remove our shortcomings.

6. Made a list of all persons we had harmed, and became willing to make amends to them all.

7. Made direct amends to such people wherever possible, except when to do so would injure them or others.

8. Sought through prayer and meditation to improve our conscious contact with God as we understood Him, praying only for knowledge of His will for us and the power to carry that out.

The steps of catharsis are:

1. Made a searching and fearless moral inventory of ourselves.

2. Admitted to God, to ourselves, and to another human being the exact nature of our wrongs.

3. Continued to take personal inventory and when we were wrong promptly admitted it.

4. Having had a spiritual awakening as the result of these steps, we tried to carry this message to alcoholics, and to practice these principles in all our affairs.

While it is not included among the twelve formulated steps, relaxation is a part of the group therapy as demonstrated by the constantly repeated phrase "Easy does it," at meetings and in conversation between members.

A wide variety of ideas, modalities, and even accidental

experiences can and do induce these states in such a way that the need for alcohol disappears. These three manifestations are found invariably in cases that show improvement. There may be others, too, but always these.

If we examine these reactions, we find that surrender is relaxation and relaxation is surrender—a giving up of tension, both physical and psychic. Catharsis is both surrender and relaxation, as those who have experienced psychiatric treatment, or Catholic confession, or the procedures of Alcoholics Anonymous, will attest.

Catharsis is the relief that comes from the removal of the burden of trouble and feeling of guilt by sharing it with another. What that "other" is makes little difference. It may be a higher power in the sense of God, or another human who acts as the therapist and in whom the subject has come to feel complete confidence and voluntary relinquishment of his own ego supremacy. This latter is the normal situation in recoveries brought about through psychiatric treatment.

The psychiatrist calls this process "transference." Its appearance invariably marks the first sign of hope, and it is only then that the hard path to a difference evaluation of the patient, by himself, can be safely explored.

All therapy, no matter of what kind, must bring the subject at least to see himself as only a part of a larger world rather than as the central figure in a world that exists primarily to serve the purpose of his inner self. The subject must then face the true picture of himself as he is, with enough insight to lower his goals and alter the emphasis of his emotions, redistributing and reorganizing them, and modifying their intensity.

The subject cannot be brought to do this until his resistance breaks down—until he surrenders, relaxes, accepts, and "tells all."

The subject will fight hard to retain his "life lie." Every imaginable pretext, excuse, alibi and rationalization will be used to protect his precious sense of grandiosity and narcotized feeling of security.

There is no way known to man to force his surrender against his own will—he must do it himself.

The therapist leaves the bait around for the patient to nibble. There is always a crisis, as in physical ailments. At this moment a single dynamic suggestion from the therapist brings the false world of the neurotic tumbling to the solid ground of common sense and factual reasoning.

The mental "ice jam" of unconscious emotional conflicts is broken and the disturbing tension released into consciousness. The effect is cataclysmic. Then comes complete surrender. It is the indispensable condition to recovery.

To repeat what I asserted before, the only demarcation between superstition and faith is one's own mental attitude.

If you BELIEVE with all your "heart" and mind anything that other people choose to call superstition, you have FAITH.

But remember, too, in order to arouse the catalytic force of human emotion—which is the instrument God has placed in your hands for literally performing miracles—your faith must be SUBJECTIVE.

It is not enough to accept the idea in your consciousness only!

At the conscious stage—which is the objective stage—the idea is merely an opinion. Not until it is accepted by the Supraconscious level of the mind and absorbed into the brain system can it change your habits of thinking and doing.

Once your thinking and doing habits are changed at the subjective level, the faith you have achieved can virtually accomplish miracles.

Don't forget the faith factor!

It can change failure to fruitfulness!

MAKING THE FAITH FACTOR FUNCTION

Faith is action. To believe, you must do.

Allow no day to begin without reading the sentence printed below. Read it aloud at first. When you realize its fullest significance has reached into your Supraconscious, you may read it silently.

But allow no day to begin without reading it:

"I can only be successful and happy if I have humble but reasonable confidence in my own powers."

Clip from the back of the book the card with this affirmation printed in it. Place it in your shaving mirror, your dressing table, the sun visor in your car, or some other place where you will see it early each and every day.

X

How To Develop the Happiness Habit

Are you happy?

That is not a silly question. Nor is it an impertinent one. It is, rather, a very pertinent question.

Without happiness, your life is virtually meaningless. No success is truly a success unless it brings with it happiness. No segment of your everyday life has true value unless happiness accompanies it.

The Greek philosopher Epictetus, who arrived at many truths during his full lifetime many centuries ago, said quite plainly: "God hath made all men to enjoy happiness and constancy of good."

But do you enjoy happiness? Not just momentary happiness, small happinesses, temporary happinesses—but full and complete happiness at all times? If you are inclined to say that such a thing is impossible, that is only a rationalization.

Happiness is possible and should always be with you. Charles Darwin, the naturalist whose theories of evolution were discussed in the first chapter of this book, was also a great philosopher. He wrote much about the hard struggle for existence, yet he also arrived at the same conclusion as Epictetus.

"All sentient things have been formed so as to enjoy, as a general rule, happiness," wrote the British thinker. And he went further to say: "Happiness decidedly prevails."

The right to be happy is yours, but I repeat the question with which I started this chapter: Are you happy?

From my experience with thousands of people in my dealings with them, as well as in just passing acquaintanceships, I have discovered that all too few people are happy. In fact, many people do not know what happiness is, for they have never experienced it.

Whose fault is it that some people have never known happiness, I asked myself. I read the philosophers, I read the teachers, I read the religionists—all agreed that man himself is responsible for his happiness.

It was Abraham Lincoln who perhaps summed it up so well when he said that people are as happy as they make up their minds to be. Yet you have only to look around you to see how people try to hide their feelings to cover up their unhappiness.

People are too often unhappy, depressed and worried. This is not as it should be. Wherein lies the trouble then? Epictetus comes to our rescue again: "If any be unhappy, let him remember that he is unhappy by reason of himself alone."

And from this truth we can come upon another—and far more important—truth. If man creates his own unhappiness, then he can create his own happiness.

To create your own happiness, you must learn a great lesson and use it often. That is, you must learn the happiness habit.

It means simply that you must say to yourself, often: "I make it a habit to be happy." In this simple statement lies a profound truth. The Book of Proverbs (XV:15) says that "he that is of a merry heart hath a continual feast."

By cultivating the happiness habit, your life can be made more enjoyable and worthwhile.

Habits are easy to cultivate. Ordinarily, we cultivate negative habits. But happiness is a positive habit. It is a habit that can bring you a happy life.

By realizing this simple truth, and by learning and utilizing the happiness habit, you can change your entire outlook on life. No longer will you face yourself in the mirror and say: "I want to be happy, but things that happen to me won't let me be."

What happens to you does not have the power to create either happiness or unhappiness. What does create the negative or positive happiness-feeling within you is how you react to circumstances.

The happiness habit will teach you the one basic philosophy of reacting to circumstances—you may not be able to do much about things that happen to you, but you can do very much about how you take them.

You cannot demand happiness. That is almost surely courting disaster. "It is one of the many paradoxes of psychology that the pursuit of happiness defeats its own purpose," said a British psychotherapist, J. Arthur Hadfield. "We find happiness only when we do not directly seek it."

The secret is not in seeking, but in expecting. Developing the happiness habit, using it unconsciously, gaining the glory of happiness from it—these things will make happiness an everyday occurrence for you. You will expect it as you expect to eat and sleep daily.

One of the first things that the use of the happiness habit will bring is the destruction of an enemy of nature—monotony. Nature abhors monotony as it abhors a vacuum. Monotony can destroy your youth and bring on age prematurely.

The truly happy person does not find life monotonous. And a life that is filled with happiness is one in which the mental faculties are not allowed to rust. So many persons who have lived beyond the century mark have admitted that they were able to do so because of one simple fact—they kept their minds young by keeping themselves busy with new interests.

For these centenarians, life was rarely monotonous. For them, life proved happy. The concepts are the two sides of a coin—happiness banishes monotony; monotony hinders happiness. Is this, then, the secret of longevity? Is the life that is filled with happiness, filled with new interests, filled with mental activity, the life that is going to be the longest and healthiest? The answer is yes!

Again I recall the complaints of persons with whom I have come in contact. How often have I heard people say that if happiness depends on such things as new interests and mental activity, it must be a difficult thing to achieve.

Nonsense! Pure and simple nonsense! Anyone can achieve happiness with little more than his own constructive reflections. This is the very basis of the therapeutic value of mystical religion.

Anyone who attains self-mastery through subjective therapy—prayer, meditation, affirmation—will never find life monotonous.

An important factor in achieving victory in the battle against monotony is knowing what I call your monotony limit.

It is virtually impossible for your entire life, every waking hour, to be constantly in a progressive phase. There are all manner of minor monotonies in life. These are the monotonies brought on by necessary repetitions of daily tasks, repeated occurrences of required duties.

These small monotonies, if allowed to accumulate without any interceding break of constructive activity and thought, can grow to a point where they will outweight the happy moments of life. Monotony tends to become top-heavy when it grows, for it develops on a small base and broadens at the top.

The first monotony limit is that point at which your monotony accumulation starts to become top-heavy. The second monotony limit is the point at which your entire psychological structure will topple due to this top-heaviness.

"Monotony, frustration and tension are the basis of much unhappiness and mental ill health," says Dr. Lawrence Kolb of the U.S. Public Health Service. "A large number of people turn in upon themselves and suffer from such conditions because they do not know how to make proper use of the native impulses and energies that they have.

"Rousing latent faculties for the appreciation of art, and promoting a wider indulgence in hobbies, in religion, will help these frustrated, tense people by giving them ease through activities that relieve tension and dispel monotony."

You have to recognize your own monotony limit. Make a small chart, on a card that you can carry in your pocket, to determine at what point your general welfare begins to break down due to undue monotony. I call this an unhappiness chart. This is how it works:

Divide the card as a chart, with divisions from left to right representing the days of the week from Sunday through Saturday, and divisions from top to bottom standing for each hour of your waking day.

For the first week, evaluate every hour as it ends. Decide whether the monotonous things you were forced to do during the hour outweighed those activities and thoughts that were not monotonous.

If your decision is that monotony filled more than twenty minutes of that hour, blacken the square with your pencil. If the hour was less than one-third filled with monotony, leave it empty.

At the end of the first week you will have a chart that resembles a checkered pattern of uncertain design—although it is possible you may at times find a very definite pattern on your card. If this is the case, it means your days follow a set formula and should be changed.

Now total the number of filled-in squares and total the number of white squares. If the white squares are not twice as many as the black, you have exceeded the first monotony limit. If the white squares are fewer than the black, you have exceeded the second monotony limit.

For example, let us say you spend sixteen waking hours a day in the seven-day week. This will give you a total of one hundred and twelve squares. If more than fifty-six are black, you are well beyond the danger limit. If more than thirty-seven are black, you have passed into the danger zone.

Keep up this unhappiness chart until your hours of excessive monotony are less than twenty-five per cent of your waking day. Work to cut the percentage daily, so that you can eventually build up your periods of happiness to ninety per cent or more of each and every week.

After the first week or two, you should be able to give up marking your chart hourly. You will find that at bedtime you will be able to recall your day quite accurately to fill in the chart. But keep on recording your unhappiness until you find you have achieved a true level of living—that is a maximum amount of happiness constantly.

Aim for ninety per cent or greater as your level of living. Accept nothing less. Work until you reach that level and work to keep it until it comes automatically—for your Supra-conscious will adjust to happiness as quickly as it adjusts to monotony.

Watch your monotony limit carefully. Don't let it crowd you out of living a happy life.

Possibly you will find, as I mentioned before, that the same hours of each day will be the black spots on your chart. If that is the case, analyze why they are there. Determine what causes these periods of general monotony at any particular time in every day.

Rooting out the cause will help you overcome the monotony of some particular boring aspect of your work, or your daily routine. Too often you do not know consciously what things are apt to grind you down. Conscious recognition will make for conscious combat, and conscious combat for ultimate victory over monotony.

Human nature is so constituted that the average person will find it difficult to enrich his life through psychological understanding of himself without spiritual growth to keep pace with the physical and mental development.

In fact, over the many years I have dealt with people and their everyday conduct, I have come to the conclusion that no method of therapy can effect permanent changes in human behavior unless it is based on a realization of the spiritual nature of man and recognition of the human personality as an instrument of God for the expression of His divine nature and the manifestation of His power and glory.

For a long time, it was thought that a human was divided into three parts, each distinct from the other: body, mind and soul. The body was believed the traditional business of the medical men; the mind was the responsibility of the educators; the soul was the preoccupation of the ecclesiastics.

We now know that, for practical therapeutic purposes, the human personality must be considered a unity of function and purpose. The human must be studied at a total organism if man is to understand himself, his relations with others in general, and his relationship with God in particular.

The trinity of man's nature makes it imperative for religion and science to abandon the negative "emotional thinking" of the past. Mutual recognition must be made—for the sake of the common welfare of humanity—of the simple truth that "spirit" manifests itself always in mental and bodily activities.

Studies in abnormal psychology have attempted to shatter the traditions of religious philosophies. Not content with labeling as merely psychopathic hysterias all the phenomena of religious conversion, the old psychology has ridiculed the visions of the great religious mystics as merely hallucinations in a self-hypnotic or traumatic state.

It has been said that humans are "ninety-nine-plus per cent a symbolic type of life." If one's interpretation of these symbols, or their reactions, is constructive, such conclusions should not be classified as abnormal. Many so-called miracles and psychic phenomena are in the symbolic category of extranormal, or what Professor J. B. Rhine of Duke University has labeled "extrasensory perception."

Be equally sure of this: religion is not without its own prejudice, intolerance and bigotry. Many ministers will not concede the value of the new psychology, preferring superstition to faith and attributing the phenomena of extra-sensory perception to supernatural causation. This preference continues despite the fact that Jesus Himself said: ". . . and greater works than these he shall do."

Will Rogers, in his straightforward philosophic way, said what we should all perhaps subscribe to, when he taked of religion:

"I have sometimes wondered if the preachers themselves have not somet ing to do with this bigotry. You hear or read a sermon nowadays and the biggest part of it is taken up by knocking or trying to prove the falseness of some other denomination.

"They say that the Catholics are damned, that the Jews' religion is all wrong, or that Christian Scientists are a fake, or that the Protestants are all out of step.

"Now just suppose, for a change, they preached to you about the Lord and not about the other fellow's church. For every man's religion is good. There is none of it bad. We are all trying to arrive at the same place according to our own conscience and teachings. It doesn't matter which road you take.

"Suppose you heard a preacher say, 'I don't care if you join my church or the other fellow's across the street. I don't claim mine is better!' Hunt out and talk about the good that is in the other fellow's church, not the bad, and you will do away with all this religious hatred you hear so much of nowadays."

This is the sort of religious philosophy one would expect from a man of Will Rogers' caliber, a man who had so many friends and no known enemies because he never met a person he ever disliked.

Every man's religion is good! It is good to the extent that he lives in accordance with the spirit of its goodness, faith and love.

This, perhaps, is the pertinent place to make a point to any reader who has up to this point felt repugnance for the various religious and Biblical references I have made. Such a person is sensing, by these reactions, within his own nature, the most common and perhaps deadliest negative form of "emotional thinking"—intolerance, prejudice, bigotry.

The "emotional thinking" of a negative nature must be combatted. Something must be done about it, and something can. For each one of you, and you alone—individually, can change an instinctive mental attitude that you possess. You will find such a change perhaps the most self-satisfying experience you have ever had.

Dr. Carrel, writing in *The Reader's Digest,* once said:

"If there is to be any regeneration of our people, it must take place in the small laboratories of our private lives. We must realize with all the intensity we can command, that refashioning our own character is not only the most satisfying and rewarding preoccupation of man, but is also the most important contribution we can make to society."

Happiness, then, is the direct result of knowing yourself. It is a self-made commodity—a do-it-yourself acquisition.

How many times have you seen a happy face and noticeably brightened yourself? Think what your being happy can do for others.

Man was made to be happy. Man was meant to be happy.

Don't let negative "emotional thinking" color your life with a dull gray coating. Utilize your waking hours to create happiness so that your Supraconscious will become accustomed to the happiness habit and take over your entire personality.

Happiness means health, it means longevity, it means success. Develop the happiness habit.

HAPPINESS IS NOT HAPPENSTANCE

All habits—good or bad—can be acquired.

With the constructive thinking you have been doing up to this point, your habits newly acquired are all good. There is no room for the bad.

Now you must learn to make a habit of one of life's greatest gifts—happiness.

The bad habit of monotony is the enemy of the good habit of happiness. You must banish monotony and its resulting unhappiness from your life.

At the back of this book there has been prepared for you enough unhappiness charts to last for several weeks. Start to use the first today.

Within a few weeks you will be nearer the goal of the happiness habit. But don't stop using your happiness chart. When you have used all that have been supplied here, make your own.

Keep on recording your monotony and unhappiness until you have achieved a true level of living.

Make your life a life of maximum happiness constantly.

XI

How To Conquer Disease

Perhaps the principal road to happiness is by healthiness. A happy mind lives in a well body. A sick body only houses an unhappy mind.

How are you to assure yourself health? How can you, without the study of medicine, set about to cure the bodily ills that make for mental ills, and the mental ills that create bodily ills?

You may feel that these questions are unanswerable—but they are not. You can, and you will, do just these things. You can, and you will, assure health for yourself. You can, and you will, find the kind of happiness that health brings.

Through countless ages man has battled disease.

From mumbo jumbo, to witch doctors, to the first glimmerings of science, and through to modern medicine, there has been a great battle to overcome the painmakers and killers of mankind—the diseases that struck from within.

Medical men have searched, delved and dug. They have carved up cadavers, experimented with injections, searched for drugs and "miracle cures" and come a long way in combatting the diseases that cripple, pain and kill.

But recently medicine has discovered a concept that, while it is new, is as old as time. This is the idea of the will to live.

More and more, through the years, physicians have noticed that some persons have wanted to recover from illness and others have not desired to live. The former group almost always did live. Among these people were effected what might be termed "miracle cures."

But, among those without the desire to live, even comparatively minor illnesses have proved fatal.

Why?

Medical science for a long time was at a loss to explain why what should have been almost certainly fatal illnesses were overcome and patients recovered when none but they themselves felt they would become well again. Nor could scientists explain why seemingly minor ailments proved fatal

172

to others, when everyone but the patient was positive that a cure was possible, easily and quickly.

It was psychiatry that finally began to investigate the so-called "will to live." Did a patient's mental attitude have anything to do with his recovery? Could a patient aid himself toward recovery, or could he prevent himself from becoming well again?

The results are well known to you: in earlier chapters you have read what has been discovered about psychosomatic illness. You have learned how the mind has been able to control the body.

The fifth and first propositions of the working hypothesis have served to show that it is possible to control your illness and to cure it—if you have the will to do so.

The fifth proposition, as you will remember, is that the Supraconscious has absolute control of the functions and conditions of the body. Therefore, there is no condition over which your Supraconscious has not the ability of control—if you want it to control.

The first proposition, that the Supraconscious is constantly amenable to control by the power of suggestion, means that desiring to get well strongly enough is all that the Supraconscious requires to help the organic system rid itself of that which is ailing you.

You must think of disease as something that creates discomfort for you. Think of it not as the word you know: that is, disease meaning illness. Think of it as the opposite of comfort, the opposite of ease: that is, as dis-ease.

What is your immediate physical reaction to something that makes you comfortable? You remove that thing, or move yourself away from it.

So it should be with dis-ease. You have to move toward ease—with the power of the Supraconscious.

A physician friend of mine set me straight one day when I seemed to be borrowing trouble about some prospective calamity. He said he always drew consolation from an old farmer's observation: "Mebbe 'taint so!"

The idea behind that little phrase is the entire key to the idea of utilizing the Supraconscious to bring to you that God-given power and wisdom to have health, happiness and success.

The idea that it isn't so is an important one in combatting dis-ease. It hinges on the very plan of substituting every negative thought with a positive one.

173

Suppose you try this experiment in a little notebook:

Every time you find something disturbing, or annoying, or irritating, or aggravating you, write down what it is. Then, above it, after a moment's clear thought, substitute a positive idea for the negative one.

Let us say that you are a motorist who is irritated by the fact that other motorists tend to make too much use of their horns, instead of their brains, in driving. In your notebook your entry will at first appear thus: Excessive horn-blowing drives me wild.

After you think about how to combat this annoyance, your entry will now take on the added word, while having the negative thought crossed out, thus:

Nothing
~~*Excessive horn-blowing*~~ *drives me wild.*

Perhaps you're a little irritable at your healthy, happily noisy children. Your tolerance of their happy overloud voices may make you enter in your notebook:

I can stand anything but noisy children.

On consideration, the positive thought would make this substitution:

I can stand anything *at all.*
~~*but noisy children.*~~

Simple? Yes, and quite effective in preparing your Supraconscious for the type of mental process that is going to make you a healthier person.

My main purpose in writing this book is to show you that within you—in your Supraconscious—there lies the power and wisdom of which I spoke. This power and wisdom, this understanding of the purpose of the Supraconscious, will help you cast the evil from you that brings with it illness and unhappiness—dis-ease.

That faith is a factor in healing has been proved by medical men over many years. There is much important evidence in favor of such a belief. Scientific research has given us definite proof that faith properly understood and applied is a powerful factor in overcoming disease and establishing health.

It seems to be that obviously this is what Jesus Christ meant when He said that "the Kingdom of God is within you." Christ said that truth would make us free. What is this truth and from what shall it free us?

The truth is that God is love. The healing power of God's love alone can free us from the ills and woes of the world. Man's dual nature is characterized by the negativeness of his savage ancestry and the spiritual attributes personified by Christ's love for all mankind.

You have seen how the human organism responds to mental suggestion and emotional stimuli. The relation of emotional reactions to the power of suggestion usually determines the condition of the organism commonly called health or sickness, or which I prefer to term ease and dis-ease.

If the human organism is functioning properly, it will resist the germs of disease as well as the negativeness of dis-ease. But if your resistance is lowered by negative emotional reactions, you are highly susceptible to ill health—organic and mental.

It is quite generally recognized now that most illness—disease and dis-ease—comes from within you. As I have discussed earlier, these ills are termed psychosomatic. They are caused by emotional disturbances which disrupt the harmonious functioning of the human organism.

The one man who has had perhaps the greatest influence in modern times on women's concepts of childbirth, Dr. Grantly Dick Read, makes an astounding assertion in his famous book *Childbirth Without Fear*.

"For my own part," he writes, "after thirty years of close association with physical and mental derangements of health I am persuaded without a shadow of doubt that with the exception of unforeseen accidents, the origin of every form of disease, both surgical and medical, whether hereditary or not, can be traced by careful investigation to the influence of fear upon the human mechanism."

Earlier in this book you read how the body reacts under the emotional stimulus of fear or anger, of which worry and resentment are the most common modern counterparts. You also read how negative responses can be caused by traumas of which you may have no conscious awareness.

The "feeling mind" which controls and directs bodily functions has no reasoning power. Its reactions are largely instinctive and it responds to negative feeling-attitudes just as it would to any physical danger or threat to the security of the organism. The repsonse is either a flight or a fight reaction.

Just as the cause of the most disease is within, so is the cure. Once you know this plain fact, the remedy is simple. You have learned how the organism changes its vibrational rhythm from harmony to discord in response to emotional disturbances. You must therefore learn to control your emotions. This control is the best way to keep the organism functioning harmoniously.

This control is also the best way to guard against the encroachment of dis-ease and disease. While cure is important once a healthy state has been lost, prevention of that loss is of greater importance by far.

Sometimes it is necessary to cure both functional and organic ills. When this becomes necessary simultaneously, the most effective way is to attempt harmonizing the human body. You must bring into play nature's own way of healing the diseased and dis-eased body. That is by spiritual therapy.

What is spiritual therapy? Its mechanics are quite simple. The most commonly used means of achieving this double healing is by prayer. An example of the so-called "miraculous power" of prayer is given by Dr. Rebecca Beard in her book *Everyman's Search:*

"Then we came to the great hurdle—the headless horseman, that frightening thing which still holds the majority of the people of the world in the grip of fear—cancer. Our thought was—perhaps we can do everything through prayer but this, and yet, in our intuitive knowing we realized we dared not step out into the world of spiritual healing until we were absolutely sure that there was no barrier, and no hurdle that could not be overcome through God's healing power.

"Because we had seen so many cancer sufferers we found this a tremendous hurdle to pass. We needed conviction, and we prayed, 'Father, show us a condition that is unquestioned, about which no one can rationalize. We want to see something that is so evident in its outward manifestations that everyone can see it. We want to see something that is called incurable. We want to see an instantaneous healing, and we want to see it complete and made possible without any agency but prayer.'

"The answer to our prayers was the healing of our friend, Alice Newton of Leavenworth, Kansas. It was not many weeks after we had prayed that she came to us in St. Louis. She had known me in Kansas City when I practiced there. This is what she said: 'I come because I have faith in you, and because I know you have something beyond medicine. I am in great need. Tell me the truth.' Her appearance when we first saw her shocked me. Her huge abdomen was larger than a woman

176

at full term pregnancy. She had the dreaded cachexia. Her emaciated body was scarcely able to carry the great burden. Her question was, 'Do you think that I can be healed with prayer and nothing else?' For just a moment I felt a sinking feeling. 'This is it,' I thought. 'You have asked for it. You wanted it.'

"You see, I did believe with my conscious mind, but my subconscious said, 'Help Thou mine unbelief.' Then I heard myself saying, 'Yes, Alice, I believe. But I want to see it. I need to see it.' 'All right,' she replied, 'I'll do it for you and for my husband. I will go home and map out a program and a schedule. I will follow it every day, and I have absolute faith now that our prayer will be answered, and the Lord will heal me.' She went home, canceled all social obligations, did simple things about the house, rested, walked in the open air, read her Bible, sang hymns, and prayed.

"Every day she repeated the same pattern. She wrote to us often and in none of her letters did she ever suggest failure. She confidently awaited the moment of her healing. You have no idea how this strengthened our faith. The unswerving faith of one person is a tremendous factor in building the certainty of God's power in their lives. 'Nor knowest thou what arguments thine own life to thy neighbor's creed hath lent.'

"Among Alice's friends was a wonderful doctor who visited her often, not as a doctor but as a friend. His medical knowledge made him insist that she permit him to tap her. It was curious, but the relationship of doctor and patient seemed to be reversed between them. It was she who would say to him, 'Don't you worry about me, Doctor.' She often consoled and encouraged him, but he would go on his way, sorry and unbelieving. A spiritual conviction and certainty such as hers is not easily gained. It is necessary to pay the price. Her constancy of purpose lasted over a period of two years. Finally, one night, with no special preparation, the miracle happened.

"At the time, her husband, a guard at the Leavenworth prison, was working from midnight until morning. Alice retired shortly after he left for work, and went to sleep as usual. As she slept she had a vision of the disciples asleep as Jesus came down the mountain side from his lone vigil of prayer. His face was full of sorrow as he looked at the sleeping men, then he glanced over and smiled at her. Immediately the scene changed. It was the day of the Crucifixion. The cross was being lowered into the hole that had been dug for it, the Master's body already nailed upon it. Torn with the thought of how the jar would hurt Him, she cried out, 'Oh my Jesus,' putting up her hand to steady his body and ease the suffering. At that moment her hand dropped to her abdomen and she awoke. Only then she realized that her abdomen was perfectly flat. The huge accumulation was gone! Immediately she felt all around her for moisture, thinking surely something had passed, but the bed was dry. There was no pain. Her spirit rejoiced, and she knew something wonderful had happened. So she turned out the light and waited.

"Her husband came home rather early that morning. He felt somehow that something had happened. His excitement was so great when he heard the news that, to relieve him, she asked him to go for her friend, the doctor, cautioning him not to tell. Alice was a woman with a marvelous sense of humor, so before the doctor came she slipped a pillow under the bed covers. She wanted to hear him scold. As he came in and stood at the foot of her bed, he shook a warning finger, saying, 'Alice, I told you to let me tap you.' She only smiled at first, then she said, 'Yes, Doctor, and I told you that God was going to take care of me. See what He has done,' and she pulled the pillow out and dropped it to the floor.

"The doctor was speechless for a moment, then he rushed around the bed and knelt at her side. His questions came short and fast in his excitement. 'What passed? What came away? Was there water? Was there blood? Did you perspire heavily?' Finally, his questions ceased, for her answers continued to be, 'No, nothing passed—nothing came away.' At last he said quietly, 'No one but God could perform a miracle like that.'

"She stayed in bed for a week because they thought it was wise. People passed through the house constantly to see her in the days that followed. At the end of the week she was weighed, and it was found that she had lost thirty-eight and a half pounds! That had disappeared overnight. And that was the answer to our prayer. That was a condition which no one could say had not existed. It could not be rationalized away. It was an instantaneous healing. No one could explain it. Where did thirty-eight and a half pounds of actual weight go in three hours? That was the miracle. I had wanted to see something which I could not explain. God has answered my prayer

"Later, Alice came to St. Louis and asked if I wished to examine her. This I did, and found every organ fresh and virginal as though she had never been ill. She lives today. This happening has had a strange sequel. During the past twelve years the Leavenworth paper and the *Kansas City Star* have mentioned this remarkable recovery each January on the anniversary of Alice's healing!"

Dr. Beard, who practiced medicine for twenty years before entering the healing ministry of spiritual therapy, has said that a "better understanding of our own emotional selves and a return to religious faith seemed to form the combination that holds the greatest promise of permanent help to any of us."

Is there any other explanation of such a miracle as the healing of Alice Newton? Medicine has discovered that in the normal course of events it takes the body almost a year to organically renew its cells. Yet you have read earlier how so-called miracles of faith healing appear to result from an accelerated process of organic repair. The extremely high vibrational rate of the thalamus, which quickens the processes of organic repair, usually is marked by some vivid mental picture—commonly known as a vision.

Visions stem from the practice of visualization—usually the practiced habit of praying with such deep feeling or subjective faith that mental pictures are formed in the "mind's eye," the occult sight of the Supraconscious mind. Visualization is a sign of increased acceleration of the vibrational frequency of the thalamus.

Spiritual therapy is not alone confined to the ministry of healing. Its greatest service to man is in furthering God's plan of evolution. Civilization is again at the crossroads of destiny. The only hope for the survival of man is the attainment of the goal for which he was created—the attainment of psychological and spiritual, as well as physical, evolution.

Such a development was predicted by the late French scientist Pierre du Noüy, in his *Human Destiny:*

"The moral perfection latent in a small minority will blossom in the majority, as will the universal comprehension and love radiated by Christ . . . They whose souls have been perfected in the course of their passage through their bodies, who have fully understood the conflict between the flesh and the spirit of which they have been the stage, have triumphed over matter, and they alone represent the evolutive group who are the forerunners of the superior race which is to come."

Too long have the mysteries of life been hidden behind the veil of mysticism! The human organism derives no power or benefits from the soul. The soul can do nothing for mind and

179

body. Its purpose is to carry "over" after the death of the physical organism.

Mind determines the condition of the body. The soul is conditioned by the quality of mind—in its passage through the body—as a great French scientist said.

"Miraculous cures seldom occur," wrote Dr. Alexis Carrel in *Man, the Unknown*. The reason is obvious. It takes a "heap of loving" (Alice Newton prayed daily for two years) to increase the vibratory rate of the thalamus enough to induce the phenomenal cataclysm that does the healing.

In other words, you must give before you can receive. This is the only basis on which the Law of Love works. Remember Christ's answer to the question "Which is the greatest commandment in the Law?"

Mankind has obviously retrogressed morally, mentally and physically. The evidence of this is the ever-widening spread of degeneracy—moral, mental and physical. Crime has increased, immorality has increased, disease has increased. All this is evidence of the fact that we have failed to comply with the Law of Love.

We have ceased to progress psychologically and spiritually. If we continue to move in this direction, we are heading further and further away from the good that is God.

God works His wonders—be they good or bad—through laws governing all His handiwork. Laws governing human nature are just as immutable as the laws that control cosmic forces. You would do well to heed the admonition of the Scriptures: "God is not mocked: for whatsoever a man soweth, that shall he also reap."

In spiritual therapy you find the "universal comprehension and love radiated by Christ." Universal comprehension can be acquired by cultivating the hidden power and wisdom of the "collective unconscious."

The key to this deeper intelligence is the love radiated by Christ. You must learn to use the power with which God has endowed you through the progressive process of evolution, just as Jesus used it. Did He not say: "He that believeth on me, the works that I do shall he do also, and greater works than these shall he do"?

Spiritual therapy affords one of the best means of preventing the ills of mind, body and soul, of making sure that we have ease rather than dis-ease. You must emulate the love radiated by Christ through the media of prayer, meditation and visualization.

Dr. Beard, talking of the discovery of the psychosomatic causes of high blood pressure and diabetes, said: "The medical world can give relief in disorders like these . . . but they do not offer complete cure.

". . . The answer," she continued, "is in the healing teachings of Jesus."

That moral aberrations, which are called sin, and physical ailments, or psychosomatic ills, stem from the same psychological source is disclosed by the following verses of Matthew IX:3-8:

"And, behold, they brought to him a man sick of the palsy, lying on a bed: and Jesus seeing their faith said unto the sick of the palsy: Son, be of good cheer, son, thy sins be forgiven thee.

"And, behold, certain of the scribes said within themselves, this man blasphemeth.

"And Jesus knowing their thoughts said, Wherefore think thee evil in your hearts?

"For whether is easier, to say, Thy sins be forgiven thee; or to say, Arise, and walk?

"But that ye may know that the Son of man hath power on earth to forgive sins, (then saith he to the sick of the palsy,) Arise, take up thy bed, and go into thine house.

"And he arose, and departed to his house.

"But when the multitudes saw it, they marvelled, and glorified God, which had given such power unto men."

Norman Vincent Peale, in his *The Power of Positive Thinking,* tells of investigations he has made into successful cases of spiritual therapy. He said he found five factors present in all such cases:

"First, a complete willingness to surrender oneself into the hands of God. Second, a complete letting go of all error such as sin in any form and a desire to be cleansed in the soul. Third, belief and faith in the combined therapy of medical science in harmony with the healing power of God. Fourth, a sincere willingness to accept God's answer, whatever it may be, and no irritation or bitterness against His will. Fifth, a substantial, unquestioning faith that God can heal."

So that you may prevent dis-ease, so that you may help to heal mind and body, you must draw upon one of the greatest resources available to man: the faith that heals, the ability to heal through spiritual therapy.

There are certain rules that I have discovered are easy to follow in the battle for ease and against dis-ease:

1. Have positive, affirmative faith so that you may release the deep spiritual power of God's loving care.

2. Remember that spiritual forces as well as the scientific techniques of medicine are important in healing.

3. Avoid disharmony—in your family, in your work, in your relationships with all people. Disharmony, disease and dis-ease are akin.

4. Visualize a picture of perfect health, happiness and vitality. Let this picture sink into the Supraconscious so that the Supraconscious level of the mind can control a positive thought pattern of healing.

5. Never become upset, worried or panicky in illness. This will only set up a pattern of negative thoughts which will be destructive and only create greater dis-ease.

They are five simple rules.

They are easy to learn and easy to remember.

They are simple, but between merely "understanding" them and "following" them there is as great a difference as there is between black and white.

Spiritual therapy can bring you new freedom from dis-ease.

It can show you for the first time what true ease means; not ease in the sense of leisure, but ease in the sense of love, the goodness of God, the happiness and wholesomeness of life and living.

This is the power of the Supraconscious.

This is the wisdom of the Supraconscious.

This is the power you have.

This is the wisdom you have.

It is yours to develop.

It is already within you.

It needs only to be discovered and encouraged.

FIGHTING THE BOGEYMAN OF DISEASE

Disease is often the result of dis-ease.

Emotion results in chemical and physical changes in the body. These changes are the feeling of everything you think.

Pleasant emotions produce changes that make you feel good.

Unpleasant emotions produce symptoms of illness.

To battle on the side of ease against the warring emotion of dis-ease, remember these five rules:

1. Have positive, affirmative faith so that you may release the deep spiritual power of God's loving care.

2. Remember that spiritual forces as well as the scientific techniques of medicine are important in healing.

3. Avoid disharmony—in your family, your work, your relationships with all people. Disharmony, disease and dis-ease are all related.

4. Visualize a picture of perfect health, happiness and vitality for yourself. Let this picture sink into the Supraconscious so that this wonder worker of your mind can control a positive thought pattern of healing.

5. Never become upset, worried or panicky in illness. This will only set up a pattern of negative thoughts which will be destructive and only create greater dis-ease.

XII

Discovering the
New Psychology

Has the anxiety of tomorrow spoiled today—and tomorrow? Do you panic at the idea of facing another day?

Certainly by this time you have realized the power of control you have over yourself. You now know that with this control no situation can become your master. *You* are the master of any situation.

With this realization, then, tomorrow—every tomorrow— is fully within your control. Your destiny is completely in your grasp. Its successes are all yours to achieve.

And you can laugh at its anxieties, its fears. For you know what these fears are, you understand the meaningless qualities of anxiety.

You are able to conquer today. And you are able to conquer tomorrow.

As I sat and wrote this book it was announced that reality was about to be given to a dream. President Eisenhower told the world that this country's scientists were about ready to place a man-made satellite in the skies. A little moon was to be rocketed up several hundred miles to travel about our earth at shattering speed and record scientific data we have never had before.

From this start, the reality of a platform in space to act as a way-station for space travel is a possibility within our lifetimes.

Incredible. Unbelievable. Yet true, completely true and possible. And all the result of a willingness to think ahead and believe.

As I read the President's words, I recalled the words of one of the great wise men this country has produced, William James: "Human beings can alter lives by altering their attitudes of thought."

That, James believed, was the greatest discovery of his generation. It is the greatest discovery of any generation— providing it is discovered and put to full use.

The discovery amounts simply to "think positive thoughts."

What are positive thoughts? They are good thoughts, they are loving thoughts, they are creative thoughts, they are decent thoughts. They are all the things that should be and, best of all, they don't allow any room in your mind for all the things that should not be—the negative thoughts.

Positive thoughts are dynamic thoughts. This is in complete harmony with God's Divine Plan of evolution. This plan is a threefold one—physical, intellectual and spiritual. It is a dynamic one; it is not a static one.

The Divine Plan will not tolerate standing still. It demands moving ahead, progression, reaching for new and greater things. It demands that life be lived on a positive level; it will not abide life based on negativism.

It is true that mankind can regress rather than progress. At the present time there is evidence of a regression in mankind. There is an alarming increase in degenerative disease, there is a widespread rise in crime, and even political thought has suffered in the emergence of totalitarian ideas that seek to undermine our democratic way of life.

Something must be done about this encroachment of negative thinking—something drastic.

The task of doing it lies with you. This is not a matter of "letting George do it." This has become a personal matter for every clear-thinking, intelligent and fair-minded individual.

It is up to you, as an individual, to set into motion positive thoughts that will help mankind progress, rather than regress.

More and more people are dying without ever knowing they had heart trouble. Millions have diabetes but do not know it. Arthritis is crippling countless other millions each year. Overweight, with its roots in unhealthy thinking, is ruining the lives of yet other millions. And cancer is becoming a dread to all.

Our criminal population is growing, and it is spreading through the teen-age ranks of the population so that it now encompasses more than a million juveniles.

And the same unstable emotional state is responsible for the psychological thinking behind the political ills of the world —Fascism and Communism. Worst of all, this political emotional unbalance has spread even to the educated classes.

Yet man has a great invention for self-help against all these scourges. That invention is religion. When properly used, it is virtually a panacea—a cure-all. But what has happened to religion? We no longer use it. We have relegated it to Sundays. Unhappily, it has become more and more a "Sunday affair."

A new philosophy of everyday life, based on a new psychology, is needed, because intellectual and spiritual growth depend upon psychological development based on knowledge of self.

Having read, absorbed and understood what has been outlined up to now in this book, and being intelligent and unbiased, you now know three things:

1. Man possesses a deeper intellectual faculty than his conscious mind.

2. This Supraconscious level of the mind can be developed through objective effort.

3. Our system of education and manner of living must be drastically changed if we are to make this effort and get the most out of life.

To achieve this goal, it is necessary to expand the consciousness with a profound awareness of the Supraconscious power and wisdom which have been endowed by the Divine Plan for your use.

To be consciously aware of these inner forces is to free your mind of the destructive effects of fears and other negativisms. The best way to get rid of the negativeness that is so harmful to your health, your happiness and the successful achievements of life, is to substitute positive thoughts for the negative emotions which are the biological heritage of the Supraconscious level of the mind.

You must never forget that it is natural for the Supraconscious to act automatically like a veritable tyrant until you learn to become its master.

The experience of a major-league baseball pitcher is a perfect example of what can be done by substituting positive thinking for negative emotion.

The pitcher was at a low ebb; his team had lost a series of games because he was pitching poorly. He was angry with his manager, annoyed at the fans and peeved at himself. This negative thought-pattern of emotions destroyed his self-confidence more and more. Each time he pitched, he sank deeper into the morass of negativism. He soon developed a complete defeat complex—he felt he could not possibly win a game for his team under any circumstances.

His wife persuaded him to join her church. There he learned how feelings of hatred and resentment combine to deteriorate the mind and the body.

186

His wife got him to join her in reading from the Bible every morning after breakfast. And at night they prayed together.

This routine of positive thinking bolstered his waning morale, despite the discouragement he felt at eventually having been sent down to a minor-league team.

Then one day the idea occurred to him that he might use his new-found religious feeling in the business of baseball. He found that allowing passages from the Bible to run through his mind actually helped him to relax when he got into a tight situation on the playing field.

Whenever he felt himself tiring, or felt that he lacked confidence to go on, he would step from the pitching mound and repeat to himself:

" 'But they that wait upon the Lord shall renew their strength; they shall mount up with wings as eagles; they shall run, and not be weary; and they shall walk, and not faint.' "

By applying this spiritual therapy to baseball, it wasn't long before this hurler was back in the major leagues. In addition, he opened an insurance agency in New York City and found that the same spiritual principles that worked for him on the diamond did the trick in selling insurance as well.

"They shall run, and not be weary." This quotation from Isaiah (40:31) is a fitting summary to a story told to me by Dr. Gerald M. P. Fitzgibbon, whose experiments in hypnosis were described earlier.

When I met Dr. Fitzgibbon, during the course of our conversation I asked him how he had happened to become a professional hypnotist. He related this experience:

"Many years ago I was participating in a marathon race and I had my heart set on winning it. I planned my pacing on the twenty-six-mile run carefully, but when I got a little beyond the halfway point I realized that I had not followed my plan carefully enough.

"I knew that I had set too fast a pace. So fast, in fact, that there seemed little hope that I would even last the entire distance. I slowed down a little, but soon—just as I figured—I started to tire.

"Then I started to pray. I prayed that I might have the strength to go all the way. Within a short time my prayers seemed to have been answered.

"I got my 'second wind'—and then as I tired again, I seemed to get 'third' wind and 'fourth' wind.

"I won the race!"

He told me that later he often thought about the "miracle" that had happened during that long run of twenty-six miles, three hundred and eighty-five yards. This experience interested him in the study of psychology. Eventually he found an answer to the phenomenon which brought him to start giving public demonstrations of the power of suggestion as an educational program.

Another extraordinary demonstration of the extranormal powers of the Supraconscious level of the mind is this story of a true happening which was published not too long ago in a widely read magazine:

". . . At that moment, a husky Negro appeared out of the darkness. "Can I help?" he asked. Deputy Sheriff Don Henry shook his head. Nobody could help if three trucks and a wrecker couldn't budge that cab, and by the time cutting torches and fire apparatus arrived it was going to be just too bad. The Negro calmly walked over to the cab, put his hands on the door and wrenched it off!

"Speechless, the crowd watched the Negro reach in the cab and tear out the burning floor mat. Then he put out the flames around Gaby's legs—with his bare hands.

" 'It was just about then that I caught a glimpse of the big fellow's face,' said one of the witnesses. 'At first I thought he was in a trance. Then I saw that set expression for what it was —cold, calculated fury. I'd seen it before—at Pearl Harbor, on Okinawa. I remembered thinking: Why, that guy's not calm, he's enraged. It was just as if he despised fire.'

"Swiftly, almost as if rehearsed, the Negro worked on, poking large arms into the truck cab. 'He straightened that steering wheel like it was tin,' the driver of the wrecker said. 'With his left hand on the brake pedal and his right on the clutch, he all but uprooted the whole works to free Gaby's feet.'

"But the crucial job wasn't done. The victim still lay encased in what witnesses called 'a squashed sardine can over a bonfire.'

"Patiently, then stubbornly, the big man struggled to squeeze in beside Gaby. The space was too tiny. Stepping back from the cab, he hesitated fleetingly. The flames were growing. He glared at them, slumped to a squatting position and began pushing into the cab, fighting crazily. At long last he was in far enough to rest his feet firmly on the floor board. He started rising slowly. His muscles bulged in the half-light and the sleeves of his shirt tore.

" 'My God, he's trying to push up the top!' a woman's voice called.

"Neck and shoulders against the caved-in cab roof, he pushed hard.

" 'We actually heard the metal give,' reported a farmer who had come to the scene. Discussing the rescue afterward, Deputy Henry shook his head, still baffled. 'And he held that top up until we could pull Gaby out.'

"In the excitement of attending to Gaby, no one thought to thank the Negro or even ask his name. Later at the hospital with Gaby, Deputy Henry told newsmen:

" 'The mysterious Samson disappeared as quietly as he'd come. If I hadn't witnessed it, I'd never believe a lone man could do a job we couldn't do with three trucks and a wrecker.' "

When this "mysterious Samson" was finally located, he told interviewing newspapermen an interesting—and significant— story. He said that he had seen his young daughter burn to death when a flash fire destroyed their home. With the mental picture burned into his brain, he said, he could not stand idly by and watch another human burn to death. The thought that a human was burning in that truck made him so furious that he had to do something about it!

Where did he get the superhuman power to accomplish such an extraordinary feat of strength? He told his interviewers he did not know—"unless God gave it to me," he added.

He was right! God had given him that strength. But it was in no way a "supernatural miracle." God has endowed everyone with the same power. This is the result of the processes of evolution. You have that power, if you have but the will to use it.

All you need is the desire to bring this power—and all your other great powers—into use. Often it is easiest to have some external occurrence "trigger" the machinery that will set loose your "hidden powers."

In the case of the man who saved the truck driver, the trigger obviously was his hatred of fire—fire which robbed him of one of his children. The sight of flames made him furious, for again he envisioned a human life being consumed —wasted.

The savage rage in this man's case was the emotional "trigger" that released a surge of extranormal strength that lies dormant in the Supraconscious level of the mind of every human. It was no different in its effect from the desire to win that "triggered" the emergency energy that enabled Dr. Fitzgibbon to win the marathon race.

There are hundreds of examples that could be cited as further evidence that you, as do all humans, possess much greater power and wisdom than you ordinarily use. It is unnecessary to cite more examples to you—you undoubtedly have read many in various publications and have heard of others, possibly involving people you know.

The first step toward making the greatest use of these deeper faculties of mind is to be fully convinced that these forces of the Supraconscious are extranormal, but not "supernatural."

It is the responsibility of education to effect this major change in popular thinking. Like human evolution, education must be progressive if we are to be taught how to live successfully in a changing world.

It was in comparatively recent times that people were thought "bad" because of the innate evil in their natures. It was believed that people "did wrong" because they were influenced—or even "possessed"—by the devil. That idea was the very basis of the goodness-badness theory of human behavior.

As education opened up more minds and people generally began to think for themselves, the age-old theory was supplanted by the idea that people could be taught to do right. This was the knowledge-ignorance theory. The advocates of this second traditional behavior theory were convinced that people could be taught the difference between "right" and "wrong." Once people were armed with this knowledge, they believed, "right" would be done.

As the science of the mind began to unfold, however, it became evident that factual knowledge is no assurance of "good" behavior. The two old theories were obviously based on erroneous foundations. A third theory was promulgated.

Where goodness-badness and knowledge-ignorance failed, the designers of this new theory said, their idea would prove more than adequate.

They called it the maturity-immaturity theory. The academic sponsors of this psychological theory concluded that all forms of misbehavior were the result of immature ways of solving problems.

So-called "bad" people, they agreed, were immature people. That is to say, they had failed to grow up emotionally. Consequently they behaved as do children—even to displaying childish (or immature) judgment and lack of self-control.

As sound as this theory seemed to be, it failed really to reach the root of the over-all problem. It did not answer the question completely, for it is quite apparent to even the most casual observer that many people, who apparently exercise excellent judgment in their private and business affairs, will at times do foolish things.

These people, particularly during times of stress, are prone to exhibit judgment that is completely immature. They are said to be emotionally immature people. They fall into the same category as the "bad" people we mentioned before—they failed to grow up emotionally.

I feel strongly that there is no such thing as an emotionally immature person. The people we have labeled that way are in reality "emotionally unstable."

What is the difference?

The emotionally unstable person allows negative thoughts to usurp his sense of reason. This is exactly like the uncontrolled emotional state that the celebrated neurologist Dr. C. Judson Herrick calls "thalamic dominance."

The instinctive and emotional brain—the "feeling" mind, the thalamus—is fully matured at birth, both structurally and psychologically.

The immense memory bank of the Supraconscious level of the mind contains the cumulative experience—both "good" and "bad"—of man's long trek of development from savagery to civilization.

This means that the human personality is basically not dual but multiple. Recent psychiatric experiments have uncovered the same fact. The most startling of these was a recent paper presented at a meeting of the American Psychiatric Association concerning a woman who had three distinct personalities. If you go back and reread Chapter V, "Your Incredible Memory and What It Can Do," now, you will note again the case history of the woman who was discovered to have four personalities, one of which was completely conversant in French while the others were unaware of the woman's ability to speak that language.

What deeper probing into the Supraconscious will show remains to be seen. It will, however, continue to discover the multiplicity of the human personality, possibly to extents that now seem fantastically unbelievable.

Just as the early belief in man's dual personality lead to

the formulation of the goodness-badness, the knowledge-ignorance and the maturity-immaturity theories, so the more enlightened concept of man's multiple nature leads to a new theory of behavior.

It is my belief that man, in his multiple nature, is motivated on a positive-negative basis. In my theory of positivism vs. negativism, I use the terms to mean constructive (positive) and destructive (negative).

I have shown you that the Supraconscious level of the mind is a veritable jungle of conflicting memories. The Supraconscious remembers all. Selectivity remains yours—once you develop the use of this level of your brain.

Under these circumstances it is obvious that the only way that there can be harmonious development of the human organism is by following the advice given by the recent popular song "Accentuate the Positive."

By putting accent on the positive and constructive memories of the Supraconscious, you acquire the power of attaining health, happiness, longevity and achievement.

The need to develop possitive thinking has never been greater. The emotional fear being pounded into every one of us with the threat of atomic warfare is enough to keep our adrenal glands in a constant state of emergency. This, added to the many other stresses and strains of "modern" living, makes for almost complete emotional unbalance and resulting physical unbalance and ill health—mental and organic.

Just how the primary emotions of fear and rage cause glandular disturbances that lead to various degenerative diseases when chronic feeling-attitudes, such as anxiety or resentment, upset the harmonious functioning of the endocrine gland system, has been fully outlined in an earlier chapter.

Two University of California scientists, Drs. C. H. Li and W. O. Reinhardt, recently discovered new evidence that the growth of the pituitary gland may be the cause of arthritis. They found that pure growth hormone would occasionally produce arthritic conditions in normal rats as well as all rats with adrenal glands and ovaries removed. The joint swellings, tenderness and other arthritic symptoms were relieved when hydrocortisone was given.

These experiments give confirmation to a theory suggested by many scientists, including Dr. Hans Seyle, that the pituitary keeps on producing growth hormones at a significant rate even after the body has grown to maturity and no longer needs the hormone for growth.

In most cases this is not damaging to early adulthood, the scientists say, because the cortisone produced by the adrenal glands combats the action of the growth hormones. But as people grow older the adrenals produce less cortisone. The growth hormone has no place to go, normal body growth having been completed. With not enough cortisone to combat this growth hormone, the hormone starts making the joints grow—hence arthritis.

It is unquestionable that a lack of cortisone is the cause of arthritis. But this deficiency is not due to old age or to adulthood. It is rather the other way around: people grow old because their adrenals produce less cortisone.

If your cortisone-producing machinery in the adrenal glands has not been impaired by needless flight-or-fight reactions—as described earlier—a proper balance will be maintained.

The major result will be, then, that the growth hormones of the pituitary gland will be utilized in a normal process of organic repair.

Instead of arthritis, you will have good health and long life!

The same biological reactions cause diabetes. Chronic anxiety and resentment keep the human organism in an almost constant state of "emergency" which was originally designed only for self-preservation during the long trek of mankind through the stages of savagery.

The "emergency" state was to help man fight, or flee, when danger appeared. But, like any piece of machinery, the human organism is subject to wear and tear. Chronic flight-or-fight reactions impair the insulin-producing capacity of the pancreas. Without the hormones that convert blood sugar into emergency energy, the sugar content of the blood becomes excessive. The result is diabetes.

The explanation of most heart attacks is similar—and just as simple. The biological processes of preparing the human organism for these unreal emergencies place needless strain on the heart and cause that organ to wear out prematurely. The result is a "heart attack."

One of the most widely mistaken notions is that heart attacks are caused by hard work, overexercise and the fast tempo of present-day living, says Dr. Paul D. White of Boston, the cardiologist who took care of President Dwight D. Eisenhower.

Heart specialists have found that half of all heart attacks occur while the victim is asleep—when the body is at rest!

When worry, or resentment, becomes chronic, these negative feeling-attitudes literally have a field day—at night, every night

—while the conscious mind sleeps. And while the conscious level of the mind is asleep, the Supraconscious level continues the mind's orgy of self-destruction.

As my friend Jacques Romano puts it: "It is slow suicide."

This "slow suicide" goes on in the Supraconscious, rather than its regular function of directing the processes of organic repair which normally revitalize and rebuild nerve and body cells during sleep.

Whether a heart attack occurs while one is awake or asleep is more often than not purely a matter of happenstance. It depends only on when the weakened organ happens to falter in its functional operation of pumping blood through the circulatory system.

Physicians are quite correct in warning their patients that too much eating and insufficient exercise contribute to heart attacks. The heart literally carries the weight of the body; the strain placed upon it when walking up a flight of stairs is equivalent to the weight of the body. The heavier one is, the greater the strain on this muscular, but small, organ.

While excessive weight in itself does not cause heart trouble, it is a factor that contributes to heart attacks. And the connection between chronic worry and overweight has been ably proved by such experts as Dr. Leonid Kotkin of New York City.

"Overeating provides a cloak for much anxiety," Dr. Kotkin writes in his recent book *Eat, Think and Be Slender*.

However, just because one has had a heart attack, this does not mean that he will die of heart disease. It has been said that it is never too late to mend. Even a heart weakened by years of flight-or-fight reactions can be strengthened by the formula of the Divine Plan—the formula of love.

This should be good news for thousands—especially harassed businessmen who worry needlessly about the tempo of their lives bringing on heart attacks.

"They are afraid to live for fear of dying," was the way the athletically inclined president of a New York pharmaceutical house, Dr. Theodore G. Klumpp, put it.

The connection between chronic worry and cancer has recently been proved just as obvious. The underlying cause is the same for cancer as it is for the other man-killers. Recent experiments have shown that the human organism, if given the opportunity to protect itself against cancer, will do so effectively.

A Los Angeles surgeon, Dr. Ian MacDonald, recently published findings which show that thousands of biopsies disclosed "scarring or minute destruction" where former clumps of cancer cells had fought a losing battle against the survival forces of the body.

Here, then, were human organisms prepared to fight disease from within; organisms not riddled with anxieties. Dr. MacDonald has come to the conclusion that four of five persons have "a built-in body defense" against cancer. I believe everyone has such a defense, if only it is allowed to function.

It has been my observation that people who are afflicted with cancer have gone through a lengthy stage during which they were afflicted by worry or grief, envy or resentment. Although they may have been unaware of this basic anxiety and the devastating effects of the negative feeling-attitudes they have harbored, such has been the case.

Medical science is convinced that others of the dreaded mankilling diseases have their roots in similar trouble—the flight-or-fight, the "emergency," processes of the body being too constantly used and the consequent wearing-out of the body's healing ability.

Generally speaking, it seems quite obvious that you can become afflicted with a degenerative disease when imbalance or deficiency of the endocrine gland hormones allows the process of organic repair, called metabolism, to slow down.

Your mental "flower garden" is no different from the garden in front of your home. If you neglect to cultivate it, weeds take root.

Utilization of positive, that is constructive, thoughts on the conscious level of intellect will uproot the mental weeds of negative, destructive "emotional thinking" at the level of the Supraconscious.

Therein you have the formula of harmonizing the functional operations of the entire human organism.

All truly great men have consciously or unconsciously developed these deeper mental and spiritual values. The case of Abraham Lincoln is typical. Unexpectedly, he had the power to pay back with interest those who had discredited, discounted and ridiculed him.

Lincoln showed no sign of wounded vanity or pride, however. In the fires of suffering, his nature had been purged of all vindictiveness. When asked why he did not repay his enemies in kind, he answered those who urged him to disregard his innate feeling of clemency:

"You have more of the feeling of personal resentment than

I have. Perhaps I have too little of it, but I have never thought it paid."

You, be you sixteen or sixty, can learn now to use the positive-negative theory of living.

First, remember that your greatest enemy is anxiety. In any of its forms—envy, resentment, worry, grief—it is the killer.

Second, realize that anxiety is the result of negative thinking.

Third, and most important, understand that positive, constructive, thinking is the natural enemy of anxiety. It is the perfect antidote for the poison of panic that seeps into the human organism and kills by "slow suicide."

It is never too late to repair, to mend, to regrow, to rebuild. That is to say, it is never too late to start living.

The best technique is to set a conscious check on yourself four times daily—a "radar trap" to spot any poison of panic that may be slipping through into your system, so that it can work its killing effects on you through your Supraconscious when you are asleep.

Make the first check-point your hour of awakening every day. Do you feel bright and cheery? Willing to face the day and whatever it may hold? Well rested from your slumber? Happy at the prospect of living longer, being more successful?

Your radar-check should show a "yes"—and a truly meant one—for each question. A "no" anywhere along the line means that negativism crept into your Supraconscious during the night. Watch out for it tonight.

At noon, make radar-check number two. Before you start your lunch ask yourself: Was the morning successful? Have you been able to prevent any reverses, no matter how large, from upsetting you? Have you been able to allow no one to irritate you? Do you really feel like eating? Will you enjoy your meal and not suffer indigestion because of an upsetting morning?

Again, obviously, the answers must be "yes" or else trouble is beginning to brew for you.

Before heading for home in the evening, check out a third time: Has the day been satisfactory? Did you achieve harmony with everyone with whom you came in contact? Did you overcome all the problems that cropped up? Are you looking forward to returning to your home and family?

Snare any little "no," no matter how small it is. If you don't, it will grow quickly out of bounds. A "no" is like a weed: its roots are deep, it strengthens quickly and grows speedily.

Before falling asleep comes the most important check-point of the day: Are you looking forward to tomorrow?

Only one question, but such an important one.

The poison of panic grows in "yesterdays." The flower of felicity grows in "tomorrows."

Make all your "tomorrows" happy todays, so that your life will be long and healthy, successful and vital.

THE LAWS OF THE NEW PSYCHOLOGY

The new psychology is formulated on the fact that man's dual nature is based on positivism vs. negativism.

Its three rules are three steps to intellectual and spiritual growth in both health and long life.

1. Anxiety is the killer. In any of its forms—as envy, resentment, worry or grief—it is your greatest enemy.

2. Anxiety is the result of negative thinking.

3. The natural enemy of anxiety, therefore, is positive thinking.

Positivism is the perfect antidote for the poison of panic that seeps into the human organism and kills by "slow suicide."

The four-times-a-day radar check is your best guarantee against the encroachment of negative thought and anxiety.

1. Every day when you awaken ask yourself:

"Am I bright and cheery?

"Am I willing to face the day and all it will hold?

"Am I well rested from my sleep?

"Am I happy to be able to live longer and be more successful?"

EVERY ANSWER MUST BE YES—TRULY MEANT.

Even the slightest inkling of a no means that negativism has made some headway during the night.

WATCH OUT FOR IT TONIGHT!

2. At noon every day ask yourself:

"Was my morning successful?

"Did I prevent any reverses—no matter how large— from upsetting me?

"Did I allow no one to irritate me?

"Do I really feel like having lunch now?

"Will I really enjoy my meal and not have indigestion because of some upset this morning?"

EVERY ANSWER MUST BE YES—TRULY MEANT.

If there is even a little no, there's trouble brewing for you this afternoon.

STOP IT!

3. Before you head for home every evening ask yourself:

   "Has the day been satisfactory?

   "Did I achieve harmony with everyone with whom I came in contact?

   "Did I overcome each and every problem that presented itself?

   "Am I looking forward eagerly to going to my home and family now?"

EVERY ANSWER MUST BE YES—TRULY MEANT.

No matter how small a no is, it will soon grow out of bounds. It is like a weed.

ROOT IT OUT!

4. The most important radar-check of the day is before falling asleep. Ask yourself:

   "Am I looking forward to tomorrow?"

THE ANSWER MUST BE YES—TRULY MEANT.

A no here is a danger flag.

PULL IT DOWN!

XIII

How To Use Your
Hidden Powers

There is within you complete power over the functions and conditions of your body.

This has been proved time and again. It has been done in this book in the process of expounding, and proving, the propositions of the working hypothesis that was set forth at its beginning.

Perhaps it is best, before you go further, to re-examine the seven propositions of the working hypothesis at this point. This will enable you to see how each has been proved by experiment, natural and scientific, and how these powers—now recognized for what they are and accepted—can be put to the greatest use.

The seven propositions of the Golden Gift, to reiterate, are:

1. The Supraconscious is constantly amenable to control by the power of suggestion.

2. The Supraconscious is incapable of independent reasoning by the processes of induction.

3. The power of the Supraconscious to reason deductively from given premises to correct conclusions is practically perfect.

4. The Supraconscious is endowed with a perfect memory.

5. The Supraconscious has absolute control of the functions and conditions of the body.

6. The Supraconscious has the power to communicate by means other than the recognized channels of the five senses.

7. The Supraconscious is capable of intuition and perception of the laws of nature.

The question that naturally should now arise in your mind —and it undoubtedly has—is: "What am I to do with the power that is within me?"

What *you* are going to do with this great Golden Gift is, of course, up to you alone.

You can use it for the greatest benefit to self and mankind. Or you can allow it to lie unused and wasted.

If you prefer to make use of this "hidden power," you must now learn how it can be aroused at will, under certain requisite conditions, for many purposes, including the alleviation of human suffering.

Skeptics have long taken a negative attitude toward the belief in mental therapy. I recall quite vividly one man with whom I discussed this theory saying: "Even if good can be derived by credulous people from any system of so-called mental therapy, it can never be of any benefit to me, because I don't believe in such things!"

"But you are making a great mistake!" I explained to this man, adding, "And don't feel that the mistake you make is in any way a personal one. It isn't. It is almost a universal one!

"It is a mistaken belief such as that you just expressed that permits many petitions of sincere pilgrims to holy places to go unanswered.

It is my own belief that the faith of the conscious mind has nothing more to do with the requisite mental attitude beyond consciously submitting thoughts to the Supraconscious level in accordance with the great law of suggestion that underlies all human relationships.

"The faith required for therapeutic purposes is purely a subjective faith," I explained further. "It is only attainable upon the cessation of active opposition on the part of the conscious mind.

"This is the faith that is required by man to tap the great resources of the accumulated intelligence of mankind that is stored in the Supraconscious."

I tried to explain to the man that in this modern age, subjective faith is the key to the "hidden power" of human nature.

"Subjective faith, then, as you term it," my friend said, "is much the same as superstition was when it was the emotional force that induced the magic of ancient days."

"Exactly," I replied.

The man was forced to agree that he had been the victim of mistaken thinking.

It was not many months later that I had a letter from this man telling me that by using subjective faith he had succeeded in helping his wife overcome a lengthy and painful illness which had made life in his family miserable for many years.

Under all systems of mental therapy the perfect passivity of the patient is required as the first essential condition. Of course it is desirable to gain concurrent faith both on the conscious and Supraconscious levels of the mind. That is the mental attitude attained by those who induce therapeutic cures through the medium of prayer.

But it is not absolutely necessary if the patient, in good faith, makes the necessary autosuggestions. This can either be done consciously in words or by submitting to the suggestions of a therapist.

The many examples of suggestion through hypnosis are ample proof of this fact.

No matter what the system of mental healing used, the conditions are essentially the same. The whole science of mental healing can be summarized in two words: passivity and suggestion.

The first requisite is perfect passivity and receptivity on the part of the patient. This means simply the suspension of the functions of the conscious level of the mind for the time being. This will allow the Supraconscious level of the mind to receive the impressions directed by suggestion and act on them.

Of course, ideally, a state of profound hypnosis is generally considered the most favorable condition for the reception of suggestions—whether they be made orally or mentally.

Whenever, by passivity, the patient becomes subjectively receptive to the corrective suggestions of the therapist, he is at least partially induced into a hypnotic state. Frequently the patient is wholly hypnotized.

If the therapist can place himself in a similar hypnotic state, the result of the suggestions upon the patient will be all the more effective.

The reason for this is a very simple one. The suggestions to the Supraconscious level of the patient's mind are conveyed telepathically from the Supraconscious level of the therapist's mind.

If both the patient and the therapist are in a partially hypnotic state, they are en rapport on the Supraconscious level. The Supraconscious of the therapist, having been given direction in advance, can then convey the correct suggestions to the patient's Supraconscious.

The Supraconscious level of the patient's mind, being controlled by such suggestion, exercises its complete control of the functions and conditions of the body to restore a normal state of health.

Nonetheless, it is not necessary that either the patient or the therapist become even partially hypnotized.

If the requisite element of faith or confidence has been established in the Supraconscious level of the patient's mind, the hypnotic state is not a necessity. But a concurrence of both objective and subjective faith is required in such cases to produce effective results.

It has been claimed by some mental therapists that faith on the part of the patient is not an essential prerequisite to successful healing. Some people may choose to believe that. But a close observer will see that the statement is made primarily for the purpose of inspiring faith subjectively in a doubting patient.

For example, a prospective patient approaches the therapist with an expressed lack of faith. The patient says: "I understand that it is necessary that your patients have faith before they can be healed. If that is the case, I cannot be helped by mental treatment because I am hopelessly skeptical."

To this, the therapist may reply: "Faith is not necessary in my method. I do not care what you believe. I can help you nonetheless."

This usually is satisfactory to a prospective patient. If he submits himself for treatment then, he has all the faith essential for a successful cure—that is, subjective faith. And, oddly enough, the patient is undoubtedly quite unaware of this expression of faith.

This is but a "trick of the trade." It is a commendable one, for it gives the patient the required faith and accomplishes the therapy without any great struggle to re-educate the patient.

Some therapists will not use such "trickery." Jesus Christ, for example, refused to use any falsehood, even if the end seemed to justify the means. He always told His followers very frankly that faith was essential.

The words of Jesus are as true today as they were when He proclaimed to mankind the secret power in a single word that epitomizes the entire science of psychotherapy—FAITH.

Here we see the efficacy of His admonition: "What things soever ye desire, when ye pray, believe that ye receive them, and ye shall have them" (Mark XI:24).

The success of psychotherapy, depending as it does upon the mental attitude of the patient, may not be lasting. If the corrective suggestions do not remain dominant in the patient's Supraconscious, the cure may not be permanent.

A patient may, for example, be so elated with the success of the treatment that he talks about it to an acquaintance who may be skeptical. The result is that his confidence is weakened by his friend's expression of incredulity or doubt.

The patient's enthusiasm may easily be dampened by a

storm of ridicule. The Supraconscious level of the patient's mind, ever amenable to control by the power of suggestion, is adversely influenced by his associates' unfavorable attitude. Without being consciously aware of it, the patient loses faith.

In such a case, if the ailment has had a mental origin, the patient may even suffer a far more severe and serious attack than he did originally.

Christ seemed fully aware of this danger. It is written that when He healed a person in private He usually enjoined him: "See thou tell no man."

The very example of the skepticism of friends or relatives undoing the work of the Golden Gift is proof that the Supraconscious is constantly amenable to control by the power of suggestion. This is especially so when the individual is not aware that his mind is being influenced by the attitudes of others.

How careful you have to be in guarding against negative ideas, whether they are expressed by others or originate in your own mind!

This is why your daily fourth check-up against negative thinking is the most important. The final fifteen minutes of every day are the moments that are going to plant the seeds of thought for your Supraconscious to consider through your sleeping hours.

If you think constructively, if you think positive thoughts, just before falling asleep at night there is less possibility that the Supraconscious level of the mind will be disturbed by dwelling on some of the disagreeable happenings of the day.

DO NOT FAIL TO MAKE YOUR FOURTH CHECK-POINT OF THE DAY! Before you read any further, go back to the last chapter and read again the process of checking against negative thoughts so that it is well absorbed by your conscious and will become a routine controlled by your Supraconscious.

You have seen the results of suggestion in hypnotic sleep. Remember: natural sleep is no different from hypnotic sleep. The thoughts you plant in the mind before falling asleep are the thoughts upon which the mind will dwell. The suggestions you plant are the suggestions the mind will carry out.

The results of hypnotic suggestion are, in a word, amazing. This is because the more perfectly objective intelligence can be held in abeyance, the more effectively the Supraconscious can perform its functions of directing the bodily organs in physical normality.

The Supraconscious level of the mind is as amenable to control by suggestion during natural sleep as it is during induced—or hypnotic—sleep.

Therefore the most favorable condition for the transference of therapeutic suggestions from the therapist to the patient is when both are in a state of natural sleep.

Little need be said here regarding the mode of operation. The method is as effective as it is simple. All that is required on the part of the therapist is that he shall be possessed of an earnest desire to cure the patient, and that he shall concentrate his mind, just before going to sleep, upon the task in hand and direct his Supraconscious to occupy itself during the night in conveying therapeutic suggestions to the patient.

The communication between the Supraconscious levels of the therapist's and the patient's minds is achieved by mental "telegraphy"—telepathy. You will recall what Dr. Carrel said about the phenomenon of "miraculous healing":

"There is no need for the patient himself to pray, or even to have any religious faith. It is sufficient that someone around him be in a state of prayer."

To this end the therapist must accustom himself to the assumption that his Supraconscious is like a distinct entity. It must be treated as though it were separate and apart from the conscious level of the mind and therefore it has to be guided and directed in the work to be done.

You know that no part of the human organism functions as a separate unit. But for the purposes of autosuggestion it is desirable to look upon your Supraconscious as a "willing servant" which will carry out the wishes and directions of its master, your conscious mind.

The work is possibly more effective if the therapist knows the particular ailment with which the patient is afflicted. He will then be able to give directions more specifically. But this may be left to the natural instinct and latent wisdom of the Supraconscious.

Everyone possesses the power to alleviate human suffering, to a greater or lesser degree, by this unique method. It is not a means by which money can be earned—but it has compensation far more valuable than money.

Aside from the pure satisfaction of doing good, there is a practical reward in every effort to heal the sick by this method. Every sincere effort to convey therapeutic impressions to the patient during sleep is inevitably followed by a dreamless sleep on the part of the therapist. Try it yourself and see.

This means simply that the Supraconscious is free from the usual conflicts of mind that usually cast their reflections across the threshold of consciousness in the form of dreams.

It would seem that the Supraconscious, following the suggestions of the therapist, occupies itself so completely with the work it is directed to do that it has little time to indulge in the emotional conflicts that ordinarily "worry" the human nervous system while one sleeps.

The physical environment of the sleeper, therefore, fails to produce impressions strong enough to cause the dreams that ordinarily result from the mental impressions of the happenings of the day.

Thus the therapeutic suggestions imparted during sleep react favorably upon the therapist, and his own health is promoted by the very act that aids the health of the patient. Dr. Carrel said: "Generally the patient who is cured is not praying for himself, but for another." This constructive attitude is conducive to greater acceleration of the processes of organic repair and therefore beneficial to the therapist.

You have been shown how the Supraconscious level of the mind is constantly influenced by the suggestions of the individual's conscious level of the mind. This is the normal relation between the two segments of the mind.

Ordinarily, objective control is exercised unconsciously. That is to say, you are not aware of the interactive processes of the two levels of the mind—the "feeling" level and the "reasoning" level—explained in the chapter on brain power.

Once you do recognize this fact, you have not only arrived at the principle that lies at the root of all true psychological science, but you are then prepared to accept the primary proposition which underlies the science of mental therapy:

Man controls by suggestion the operation of his own Supraconscious, even though the suggestion be in direct contradiction to his own objective belief.

This is unqualifiedly true, even though suggestion may be contrary to reason, experience, or the evidence of the senses.

If, therefore, such drastic results can be produced when opposed by the strongest instincts of man's own nature—the instincts for survival—how much easier must it be to produce equally amazing results when operating constructively in harmony with these instincts. That is, along the lines of least resistance.

It must be quite evident to you, now, that autosuggestion can be employed to great advantage for therapeutic purposes.

Indeed, the power of self-help is the most important part of mental therapy.

Without this power, psychotherapy is of comparatively little value or benefit to anyone. And with it goes the power to resist disease—to prevent sickness as well as to cure it.

The old axiom that an ounce of prevention is worth a pound of cure holds just as good in psychotherapy as it did in organic remedies.

If you can attain the power to hold yourself in the mental attitude that will enable you to resist the encroachments of disease, you have mastered the great secret of psychosomatic medicine. This is the hidden power that is yours to use.

That you can do it as well as anyone else is a fact that has been demonstrated beyond question. The best workers in the field of Christian Science give more attention to teaching their pupils and patients how to help themselves than they do in instructing them how to help others.

The fundamental principles which make mental therapy possible were outlined in Chapter VII, "Live Longer and Love It." They bear repeating now:

1. The Supraconscious exercises complete control over the functions and conditions of the body.

2. The Supraconscious is constantly amenable to control by suggestions of the conscious mind.

3. These two propositions being true, the conclusion is obvious that the functions and conditions of the body can be controlled by suggestion from the conscious level of the mind.

Perhaps it would be wise to turn back to that chapter and reread the words of my friend Jacques Romano. In those words you will find the proof of this proposition.

The whole science of mental therapy is embraced in these three basic principles. They contain all that you need to know when you attempt to heal yourself or ward off the encroachment of disease.

The process of making a particular application of these principles is equally simple.

The main purpose of mental therapy is to arouse the catalytic power of the Supraconscious level of the mind and focus its curative force directly on the ailment or disease.

The five senses of perception are the channels through which exterior stimulation is communicated to the brain. Medicine has determined that the stimuli of what one sees, hears, touches, tastes and smells pass through the thalamus—

wherein is housed the Supraconscious—before the impulses reach the conscious mind to become conscious thoughts.

Psychologists tell us that more than eighty per cent of the mind's activity ordinarily is the result of what one *sees*. It is obvious, then, that the Supraconscious, being in the path of such stimuli before they are even consciously recorded, can be aroused to its greatest effort by the process of seeing than by any other means of sensory stimulation. The act of seeing with the physical eyes has a counterpart in seeing with the "mind's eye."

This is the great secret of visualization. It has been found that you will worry because you have made a mental picture of your troubles, real or fancied.

"If you can relax the muscles of your eyes, you can't worry," wrote Albert Edward Wiggam, widely known psychologist. "If you can quit looking at your troubles, they will disappear.

"These statements are made on the basis of twenty years of experiment by Dr. Edward Jacobson of the Physiological Laboratory of the University of Chicago. They are supported by sixty years of related experiments by scientists all over the world.

"No more important discovery for health and happiness has ever been made in the studies of the body and mind.

"To convince yourself, you should first notice that if you have lost money, or a loved one, or feel inferior, or fear you may lose your job, or are jealous, or have had a lover's quarrel, or your rent is overdue, you have pictures—visual images—in your mind of the things or persons involved.

"You will be astonished to discover you are always looking at your mental worries and troubles."

Creating these mental pictures, this visualization, must be directed by your will. You cannot permit your imagination to run riot. It has been said that imagination is a good servant but a poor master.

I personally employ a combination of visualization and affirmation to increase the vibrational rate of the Supraconscious preparatory to employing autosuggestion.

Here is how it is done:

1. Take a piece of paper and pencil and write on it any affirmation. You might use something like "Be still and know that I am God!"

(Because of inherent superstition—or you can call it faith if you like—the "hidden power" of the thalamus is activated by the mere mention of the word "God." The thalamus, as you remember, is the seat of the Supraconscious. It is a mental dynamo which generates the electrical vibrational force that makes the human organism tick. The Supraconscious is more susceptible to suggestion when its vibrational force has been increased to higher frequency than is normally required to maintain functional harmony.)

2. When you are able to visualize the written affirmation in your mind's eye with your physical eyes closed, you have succeeded in turning on the catalytic power of your Golden Gift—the Supraconscious—literally to perform miracles of healing.

(The extraordinary rapid acceleration of the processes of bodily repair, which Dr. Carrel classified as "miraculous healing," has been explained to you earlier in this book.)

3. Practice this until you are able to project the "visual image" anywhere from head to toe. This is the way to channel the curative power of your Supraconscious directly to the afflicted spot or organ.

4. Once you have acquired complete control, the next step is to mentally command the Supraconscious specifically to rid you of a particular pain, ache, discomfort, tension, congestion or ailment.

You must remember that the Supraconscious has to be treated as a separate and distinct entity. That, of course, it is not; it is inseparably united with the human organism as a whole. But it is essential that you treat it separately.

Constant reiteration of the command to the Supraconscious will give you therapeutic aid and produce the desired results eventually. When this effect is distinctly felt, the matter should be dismissed from your mind and your attention directed to other things.

If any remnants of pain or discomfort remain, ignore them, for the Supraconscious has been put on the job. Once your Supraconscious tackles a job, it will be completed. But you must give it continued conscious support by feeling completely confident of its ability to cure you.

At the very start, the only real difficulty and obstacle in the way of success you will find as a "beginner" lies in the fact that you lack confidence. The education of your whole life has been such as to cause you to look with distrust upon any but material remedies. There is no inclination to persist in your efforts.

If *this* book is not sufficient to bolster your confidence in

208

your own ability to cure most of your ailments and render yourself immune to most of the diseases that humanity has fallen heir to, you should, upon finishing this book, read: *The Doctor Alone Can't Cure You* by Rolf Alexander, M.D.; *Doctors of the Mind* and *How Never to be Tired* by Marie Beynon Ray; *Take it Easy* by Arthur Guy Mathews, Ph.D.; *Healing Mind, Body and Purse* by Frederick G. Lieb; *Managing Your Mind* by S. H. Kraines and E. S. Thetford; *It's All in Your Mind* by John Davis; *Within You is the Power* by Henry Thomas Hamblin; and *Freedom from Fear* by Lester L. Coleman, M.D.

These works cover many aspects of what has been demonstrated in this volume. The practical application of that knowledge is summed up for you in this book.

The first vital essential to effect mental therapy is faith—deep subjective faith.

Secondly, you must never fail to realize that the suggestions conveyed by your conventional education are what you must combat, neutralize and overcome by stronger and more emphatic countersuggestion if you are to succeed.

Writing in *It's All In Your Mind*, John Davis contributes these enlightening facts:

"Experiments in hypnotism have shown that suggestion (which is only the act of implanting an idea in another's mind) can cause an increase or decrease of the sugar content of the blood stream; and for this reason suggestion is now being used to treat diabetes. Suggestion, which directly affects only the mental realm, can even bring about organic changes in the bodily tissue.

"A classic example is the old-time "conjurer" who conjured warts off the subject's hand by making suggestive motions, as if grasping the wart in his hand, and repeating some such phrase as, "I've got it now. It will disappear within ten days." There is no doubt that this has been done, but the only magic involved was the magic of suggestion; implanting the idea within the subject's subconsciousness that the wart was going away.

"Doctor Cleckley, a world famous neurologist at the University Hospital, Augusta, Georgia, has told me that he has removed a great many warts and benign growths by hypnotic suggestion. I have personally seen a large bed-sore, inflamed and speckled with pus pockets, completely disappear within three days following a suggestive treatment, although a specialist had been treating it with salves, drugs, and ray treatments for six months with no results.

"I have seen cured, with one suggestive treatment, a case of arthritis of ten years' standing. The patient could hardly walk and stated that he had not had a good night's sleep for years. Before he could get out of bed in the morning, it was necessary for his wife to massage his legs with liniments.

"After the one suggestive treatment, more than two years ago, he has had no more trouble, and can run, jump and climb stairs with no discomfort. Of course, some of the old-school materialist-minded doctors would say that this case of arthritis had not been cured by suggestion, but that only the symptoms had been removed. Evidence in this and other cases, however, seems to indicate the contrary.

"Coué, who cured everything from diabetes to glaucoma with suggestion (there are those who will recall his famous "Every day in every way I am getting better and better") was adamant that organic diseases yield to suggestion more readily than do functional or nervous disorders. Doctor Walsh, of Fordham University, has said, 'Analysis of statistics of diseases cured by mental influence shows that its results have been more strikingly manifest in organic than in the so-called nervous or functional diseases.' And Dr. James Pages, in lecturing on surgical pathology, says, 'There is scarcely an organ the nutrition of which may not be affected by the mind.'

"Dr. Harry Lipton, psychiatrist in the U.S. Public Health Service, has demonstrated to me very convincingly that ideas can bring about an organic change in tissue. Doctor Lipton uses suggestive treatments extensively and has cured amnesia, stammering, and all manner of other disorders by this means. The most striking examples of the power of thought upon body tissue are the cases where shrunken limbs have been rebuilt.

"Doctor Lipton showed me a picture of a prisoner who had been shot through the thigh. The nerve had been replenished, but the patient was unable to use his leg. The leg had drawn upward until the foot was almost up to his hip, and for several years this man had walked upon a peg-leg strapped to his knee.

"Then Doctor Lipton began a series of suggestive treatments. In six months, the leg had straightened out almost entirely; the atrophied muscles had regained some measure of their former strength; and it was possible for the patient to walk with the aid of a specially built shoe. The pictures of the 'before' and 'after' in this case would convince even the most skeptical person that thought can change tissue."

Do not feel that it is necessary to resort to hypnotic treatment to change your thinking and improve your bodily health.

As an intelligent person who has understood what you have read, there is no reason why you should not be able to accomplish the very same things others have accomplished.

The examples of hypnotism are given only to illustrate just what the human mind is capable of. The reason that hypnosis often produces such spectacular results is that it affords an excellent method of implanting an idea in the Supraconscious.

The Supraconscious is impersonal. It will not reason why or question any suggestion offered to it. As it is a creative organism, it will go to work immediately to transform the suggestion into fact.

It makes no difference who plants the suggestion in your Supraconscious. There is no reason why you, as an intelligent being, cannot quite effectively plant any suggestion in your own Supraconscious. You can do so as effectively as any hypnotist, and there is no need for you to utilize hypnosis.

Despite the years of background education you will have to overcome to get through to the Supraconscious, it is only the person of inferior intelligence who will require the help of a hypnotist to make contact with his Supraconscious.

You must have confidence in yourself.

You must not allow the slightest doubt to nullify the effectiveness of your suggestions.

You must be prepared to combat all the counter-efforts of your habitual everyday thinking, for this and the emotions you entertain also filter down to your Supraconscious and have their influence on it.

You must be prepared to combat the negative thoughts of your conscious. They, along with all your other thoughts, eventually filter through to the Supraconscious and work quite as effectively as hypnotic suggestions, but counter to your therapy thoughts.

"Praying without ceasing" is merely keeping a constant watch over your thoughts. If you constantly think of ill health and constantly talk about your aches and pains and troubles, you are impressing the idea of ill health and trouble on your Supraconscious. For the Supraconscious, having the power to influence bodily functions, proceeds to realize these thoughts in your body.

211

Fear, anger, hatred, pessimism and destructive thinking have their influence on you. They make you ill, just as if you had transmitted a clear message to your Supraconscious saying: "Make me sick."

You must not beg the subjective forces to make you sick. Yet some people do exactly that!

You can utilize this knowledge so that you learn the importance of acquiring right thinking habits. Only with these habits will you learn how to control the creative forces of the Supraconscious. Then your autonomic, or sympathetic, nervous system will be within your own control.

This power is yours. You have only to discipline the use of your reason. You have but to exercise properly your free will.

The effectiveness of mental therapeutics has been proved by the countless number of so-called "faith cures." You have read of many. The magazines and newspapers often wonder at these phenomena. Perhaps you, too, have wondered. Perhaps you have even been inclined to doubt. Yet such cures are possible, if only you have faith, patience and perseverance.

Take, for instance, the case of Frederick Elias Andrews of Indianapolis. This man's story is a perfect example of the power of suggestion through the medium of repeated affirmation.

"I was about thirteen years old," writes Mr. Andrews, "when Dr. T. W. Marsee, since passed over, said to my mother, 'There is no possible chance, Mrs. Andrews. I lost my own little boy the same way, after doing everything for him that it was possible to do. I have made a special study of these cases, and I know there is no possible chance for him to get well.'

"She turned to him and said, 'Doctor, what would you do if he were your boy?' and he answered, 'I would fight, fight, as long as there is a breath of life to fight for.'

"That was the beginning of a long drawn-out battle, with many ups and downs, the doctors all agreeing there was no chance for a cure, though they encouraged and cheered us the best they could.

"But at last the victory came, and I have grown from a little, crooked, twisted cripple, going about on my hands and knees, to a strong, straight, well-formed man.

"Now, I know you want the formula, and I will give it to you as briefly and quickly as I can.

"I built up an affirmation for myself, taking the qualities I most needed, and affirming for myself over and over again, 'I am whole, perfect, strong, powerful, loving, harmonious and happy,' till I could wake up in the night and find myself repeating, 'I am whole, perfect, strong, powerful, loving, harmonious and happy.' It was the last thing on my lips at night and the first thing in the morning.

"Not only did I affirm it for myself, but for others that I knew needed it. I want to emphasize this point. Whatever you desire for yourself, affirm it for others, and it will help you both. We reap what we sow. If we send out thoughts of love and health, they return to us like bread cast upon the waters; but if we send out thoughts of fear, worry, jealousy, anger, hate, etc., we will reap the results in our own lives.

"Man is the sum of his own thoughts; so the question is, how are we going to entertain only the good thoughts and reject the evil ones? At first we can't keep the evil thoughts from coming, but we can keep from entertaining them. The only way to do this is to forget them—which means substitute something for them. This is where the ready-made affirmation comes in.

"When a thought of anger, jealousy, fear or worry creeps in, just start your affirmation going. The way to fight darkness is with light—the way to fight cold is with heat—the way to overcome evil is with good. For myself I never could find any help in denials. Affirm the good, and the bad will vanish."

For the beginner, the battle will be hard. It is the first-time effort at controlling the Supraconscious that is the most difficult.

And as a beginner, you must persist until you are cured. After that first time, you will find each successive time that there will be less resistance to overcome from the patterns of habit.

Once you triumph over illness, mental or organic, the reasoning of the conscious level of your mind no longer interposes itself as an obstruction. Soon it concurs in the truth of your suggestion.

Once you possess both objective and subjective faith in your own power, you will find that you can operate with your Supraconscious on a line of no resistance whatever.

Once you attain this point, the rest is easy.

You now have acquired the ability to effect, say, an instantaneous cure of a headache. For you can quickly put a stop to any pain.

You are on the verge of being able to direct your own body to cure itself, to replenish itself, to regenerate and grow anew.

How few illnesses there are that are not the result of—and

encouraged by—psychosomatic disturbances! Certainly a broken bone will not be set by the Supraconscious, but its capacity to heal will be hastened. And so many of the illnesses that afflict man are amendable to control by the mental processes.

Perhaps you have stopped for a moment and said to yourself: "This doesn't seem credible; it's impossible!"

Let us recapitulate then, for an instant.

The process of applying the principles of autosuggestion of the cure of ailment and dis-ease is completely demonstrable by scientific truths.

You are not called on to deny the existence of matter.

You are not asked to deny the reality of the disease that affects you.

You are not advised to avoid a doctor. Quite the contrary, you are told directly to seek the aid and comfort of your family physician. It is the only logical thing to do, especially if an illness fails to respond rapidly enough to your own mental therapy.

Thorough examination of thousands of cases of mental therapy has pointed to one thing: no cure ever was effected by this method until the Supraconscious level of the patient's mind was impressed with a belief in the efficacy of the means employed. No cure ever will be effected without this belief. This is the basic requirement of every form of mental therapy.

Christ enjoined upon His followers the simple scientific fact that faith on their part was a condition precedent to their reception of the benefits of His healing power. He compelled His followers to believe by publicly demonstrating that power.

The few simple rules stemming from His teaching and laid down here are all that is required to become proficient, with a little practice, in the science of self-healing.

They are simple rules, but they are rules you must believe.

They are rules you must understand intelligently.

They are rules you can understand because you are intelligent.

They are not mere theory, without practice. The science of healing is as old as mankind.

Max Long, in his *The Secret Science Behind Miracles,* tells how the ancient Kahunas of Hawaii used the magic powers of suggestion to heal the sick and also to evoke fatal illness by means of a "death prayer."

Thomson Jay Hudson, almost a century ago, successfully used a means of healing not unlike that described here.

The science of healing has been demonstrated again and again. It is obviously eminently practical: not only as a means of healing disease and dis-ease but also as a means of warding off their encroachment.

Once you have mastered this "hidden power" of the Golden Gift you will find its chief value in the almost unlimited power which it gives you to prevent disease. It is this very power that Dr. MacDonald describes in telling how the human body wards off cancer in four out of every five persons.

You have only to retain the mental attitude of denying the power of disease to obtain mastery over you.

When you recognize the first symptoms of approaching illness, start immediately a vigorous course of therapeutic suggestion. Direct the Supraconscious to focus its healing powers on the organ or section of the body involved.

Prevention is far more simple than cure.

By persistently following the course of attack outlined here you will soon discover that you possess perfect mastery over your own health. This is one of the greatest of your hidden powers.

YOUR HIDDEN POWERS HARNESSED FOR HEALTH

The power of suggestion is so strong, so powerful, so mighty that it can bring to you bodily healing of a sort than can only be termed "miraculous." Yet there is no miracle about this. By combining the powers of visualization and affirmation preparatory to employing autosuggestion you can cure your own self-induced ailments and render yourself immune to many of the diseases to which mankind has fallen heir.

Here are the rules of visualization and affirmation put to use:

1. On a piece of paper write any affirmation.

2. Visualize that affirmation in your mind's eye, with your physical eyes closed.

3. Practice this until you are able to project a "visual image" anywhere in your own body.

4. Thus being able to channel your visual image, the curative powers of the Supraconscious can be used to rid you of pain, discomfort, ache, tension, congestion or ailment.

To effectively bring these powers into use by yourself, you must:

1. Have confidence in yourself.

2. Allow no doubts to nullify the effectiveness of your suggestions.

3. Be prepared to counteract all efforts of your habitual everyday thinking that may be contrary to your curative desires.

4. Never "beg" the subjective forces to make you ill by using such phrases as "such-and-such (or so-and-so) makes me sick."

XIV

How To Live Twenty-Four
Hours A Day

Are you always pressed for time?

Have you ever felt that the days are too short? Or been annoyed that the weeks have too few days? Or found to your consternation that the months seem to disappear before you know where they've gone?

Have you often wondered how much better off you would be if the days have more than twenty-four hours; if perhaps they were twenty-eight hours long?

Your days seem short because you are limited to using the waking hours for productivity. You, as do millions of your fellow men, believe that the powers of thinking—be they conscious or Supraconscious—are limited to those waking hours. Thus, even if you are an Edison with the ability to get by on only four hours sleep a day, you are able to utilize productively not more than twenty hours of your day.

You are not alone in realizing how little time there is—even if you could use all twenty-four hours in every day.

But, utilizing the powers of the Supraconscious, you can use all twenty-four hours in each and every day.

Your gain can be phenomenal! Your life can be made thirty-three per cent longer. This is the first step toward accomplishing the Life Limitless.

The average person sleeps eight hours a day. If you could make use of that eight hours constantly, you would make an immediate gain of one whole day in every three.

You can earn more than two whole days in every week!

You can have for your exclusive use months that are forty instead of thirty days long!

You can increase each year of your life to sixteen months!

The advantages of this new *time-power* are endless. Your gains can be limitless.

Is there some great secret to extending time—and life? Is there some great formula you have to buy or acquire?

NO! The great secret of time-power is already within you.

You possess it now! And you are quite ready to use it if you have learned the lessons of the previous chapters.

Your waking hours have now added to your productivity, health and happiness by the simple use of your Supraconscious powers.

But those powers are not with you only during your waking hours. They are with you all the time!

The thirty-three per cent bonus on life you can take for yourself is those hours of bodily sleep.

The wonderful machine in your skull needs little rest. All it asks is fuel. It wants to be fed—well and regularly. When you sleep, its period of dormancy is infinitesimal. Unlike your physical body, it is capable of going for days without any rest whatsoever.

Yet most of us let all that fallow field lie dormant for one-third of our lives. Even if part of that time it does not lie dormant, we have not yet learned to recognize the fact that our brains are working longer hours than we are, and that we should tap that source of wonderful time-power.

The great secret of time-power is what I term sleep-thinking.

A famous psychologist once wrote of his even more famous brother: "He goes to sleep at night thinking about a problem and wakes up with the right answer."

The psychologist is Dr. Herman Baruch; his brother is Bernard Baruch. Is it any wonder then that the man who owns this well-trained mind and utilizes this time-power is a multimillionaire and advisor to presidents?

One of the most outstanding demonstrations of sleep-thinking is found in the explanation given by Napoleon Hill of how he developed his Supersense, which he terms the "sixth sense."

Writing in his book *Think and Grow Rich,* Hill states:

"Somewhere in the cell structure of the brain is located an organ which receives vibrations of thought ordinarily called "hunches.""

"So far science has not discovered where this organ of the sixth sense is located, but this is not important. The fact remains that human beings do receive accurate knowledge through sources other than the physical senses. Such knowledge, generally, is received when the mind is under the influence of extraordinary stimulation."

We have already learned that the organ to which Hill refers is that segment of the brain called the thalamus. It receives thought vibrations which Hill calls "hunches" and which we know are manifestations of the Supersense.

We, too, also know that the rate of vibration of the thalamus can be greatly accelerated by the technique of visualization, a process of stimulating the mental activity called creative imagination.

Hill's method of cultivating creative imagination is unique and effective.

Just before falling into a state of sleep every night, he would shut his eyes and create a mental picture. This picture, which he would see in his imagination, was that of a group of prominent men of past history.

The men would gather to act as a mystic council of "Invisible Counsellors." The group included Ralph Waldo Emerson, Thomas Paine, Thomas Edison, Charles Darwin, Abraham Lincoln, Luther Burbank, Napoleon Bonaparte, Henry Ford and Andrew Carnegie.

Every night, over a period of years, Hill held an imaginary council meeting with this illustrious group.

This is how he describes one of the meetings:

"I had a very DEFINITE PURPOSE in indulging my imagination through these nightly meetings. My purpose was to rebuild my own character so it would represent a composite of the characters of my imaginary counsellors. Realizing, as I did, early in life, that I had to overcome the handicap of birth in an environment of ignorance and superstition, I deliberately assigned myself the task of voluntary rebirth through the method here described.

"Being an earnest student of psychology, I knew, of course, that all men have become what they are, because of their DOMINATING THOUGHTS AND DESIRES. I knew that every deeply seated desire has the effect of causing one to seek outward expression through which that desire may be transmuted into reality. I knew that self-suggestion is a powerful factor in building character, that it is, in fact, the sole principle through which character is builded.

"With this knowledge of the principles of mind operation, I was fairly well armed with the equipment needed in rebuilding my character. In these imaginary council meetings I called on my Cabinet members for the knowledge I wished each to contribute, addressing myself to each member in audible words, as follows:

" 'Mr. Emerson, I desire to acquire from you the marvelous understanding of Nature which distinguished your life. I ask that you make an impress upon my subconscious mind, of whatever qualities you possessed, which enabled you to understand and adapt yourself to the laws of Nature. I ask that you assist me in reaching and drawing upon whatever sources of knowledge are available to this end.

" 'Mr. Burbank, I request that you pass on to me the knowledge which enabled you to so harmonize the laws of Nature that you caused the cactus to shed its thorns, and become an edible food. Give me access to the knowledge which enabled you to make two blades of grass grow where but one grew before, and helped you to blend the coloring of the flowers with more splendor and harmony, for you, alone, have successfully gilded the lily.

" 'Napoleon, I desire to acquire from you, by emulation, the marvelous ability you possessed to inspire men, and to arouse them to greater and more determined spirit of action. Also to acquire the spirit of enduring FAITH, which enabled you to turn defeat into victory, and to surmount staggering obstacles. Emperor of Fate, King of Chance, Man of Destiny, I salute you!

" 'Mr. Darwin, I wish to acquire from you the freedom of thought and the courage and clarity with which to express convictions, which so distinguished you!

" 'Mr. Lincoln, I desire to build into my own character the keen sense of justice, the untiring spirit of patience, the sense of humor, the human understanding, and the tolerance, which were your distinguishing characteristics.

" 'Mr. Carnegie, I am already indebted to you for my choice of a life-work, which has brought me great happiness and peace of mind. I wish to acquire a thorough understanding of the principles of organized effort, which you used so effectively in the building of a great industrial enterprise.

" 'Mr. Ford, you have been among the most helpful of the men who have supplied much of the material essential to my work. I wish to acquire your spirit of persistence, the determination, poise, and self-confidence which have enabled you to master poverty, organize, unify, and simplify human effort, so I may help others to follow in your footsteps.

" 'Mr. Edison, I have seated you nearest to me at my right, because of the personal co-operation you have given me, during my research into the causes of success and failure. I wish to acquire from you the marvelous spirit of FAITH, with which you have uncovered so many of Nature's secrets, the spirit of unremitting toil with which you have so often wrested victory from defeat.'

"My method of addressing the members of the imaginary Cabinet would vary, according to the traits of character in which I was, for the moment, most interested in acquiring. I studied the records of their lives with painstaking care. After some months of this nightly procedure, I was astounded by the discovery that these imaginary figures became apparently real."

Whether or not Mr. Hill has the right answer to the phenomenon of sleep-thinking, there has been placed before you sufficient evidence in the preceding chapters that "somewhere in the cell-structure of the brain is located an organ which receives vibrations of thought ordinarily called 'hunches.' " This faculty is the Supersense.

Mr. Hill says he is not a believer in, nor an advocate of, "miracles," for the reason he has enough knowledge of Nature to understand that Nature never deviates from her established laws.

Some of Nature's laws are so incomprehensible, says Mr. Hill, that they produce what appear to be "miracles." Mr. Hill says that the Supersense "comes as near to being a miracle as anything I have ever experienced, and it appears so, only because I do not understand the method by which this principle is operated."

Mr. Hill says there is one thing he does know: "that there is a power, or a First Cause, or an Intelligence, which permeates every atom of matter, and embraces every unit of energy perceptible to man.

"This Infinite Intelligence converts acorns into oak trees, causes water to flow down hill in response to the law of gravity, follows night with day, and winter with summer, each maintaining its proper place and relationship to the other.

"This Intelligence may, through the principles of this philosophy, be induced to aid in transmuting DESIRES into concrete, or material form."

Mr. Hill says he has this knowledge because he has "experimented with it—and has EXPERIENCED IT."

A famous psychologist once said, "There is a deep tendency in human nature to become precisely like that which you habitually imagine yourself to be."

Apropos of this, Mr. Hill has said that he had the "very definite purpose of rebuilding his own character as it might represent a composite of the characters of his imaginary counsellors."

The reason autosuggestion, as employed by Mr. Hill in

preparation for sleep-thinking, literally works wonders is explained fully in earlier chapters. Having grasped the full significance of these chapters, you now can see the true meaning of such phenomena as so-called "spiritism."

Had the late Arthur Edward Stilwell only comprehended the marvelous mechanism of his Supraconscious, instead of interpreting the experiences of his Golden Gift in terms of "spirits," what a boon his life might have been to education, and through public instruction, to faltering humanity!

When people do not understand a phenomenon in the general category of extrasensory perception, they are prone to call the incident a "miracle" and attribute it to some supernatural cause.

This is exactly what Arthur Stilwell did. He used his Supersense to attain fame and fortune. This he managed to do through the medium of sleep-thinking. But he insisted to the day he died that "spirit guides" were responsible for most of his extraordinary achievements.

Arthur Stilwell was a sensitive and dreamy youngster. While still in his childhood, he acquired the habit of drifting into trances. In these self-induced hypnotic states he received extranormal knowledge which he believed came from a "spirit world."

When he was fifteen he learned during a sleep-thinking session that in four years' time he would meet and marry a girl named Genevieve Wood. It was not long after his nineteenth birthday that he met Jenny Wood at a church festival. After a brief courtship they were married—just as his Supersense had foretold.

Following his marriage, he took a job as clerk with a trucking company. The inspiring voices continued to counsel him during his sleep. His sleep-thinking advisors told him to go west and build a railroad.

Arthur Stilwell was a farm boy. He had hardly finished high school. He knew little about business and nothing at all about financing, and especially about railroading. Yet he felt impelled to venture westward under the continuous urging of his sleep-thinking advice.

He quit his job and moved to Kansas City. There he worked at various jobs. With the help that came to him from sleep-thinking, his success was uncanny. At the age of twenty-six, he began building his first railroad after having acquired the necessary financial backers.

Believing that he was being guided by superior intelligence

from a "spirit world," Stilwell insisted upon sleeping alone, to the bewilderment of his charming young wife.

It is related that, when vexed by some engineering problem he would place drawing material on a table at his bedside. In the morning he would recall exactly what his sleep-thinking had told him—and details of the plans would be written on the paper.

On one occasion, Arthur Stilwell was "advised" in a sleep-thinking session to build a railroad from Kansas City to the Gulf of Mexico. The logical terminus for the new line was Galveston, Texas. But the railroad tracks were laid to a point only fifty miles from Galveston when Stilwell had a strange vision.

He saw a great tidal wave engulf the city of Galveston, crushing buildings and drowning inhabitants. Having learned the value of heeding the promptings of his sleep-thinking, he construed the vision as a warning not to use Galveston as a port terminal for his new railroad.

Stilwell ordered the location of the rail line changed. He directed that the terminus be at a new location, upon which site was later built a city named Port Arthur in his honor. A few days after the completion of the railroad, a tidal wave swept up the Gulf Coast. The city of Galveston was devastated, just as Arthur Stilwell had seen in the "preview" of the terrible disaster during his sleep.

Arthur Stilwell made millions of dollars. He lived a long happy married life. He credited everything to "spirit guides" which he thought advised him while he slept.

From what we now know of the astounding reach, power and wisdom of the Supraconscious level of the mind, there is no doubt that Arthur Stilwell actually had succeeded in tapping the extranormal resources of his Supraconscious while he slept. He benefited by using time-power.

The hours of sleep can be utilized for greater use of your productivity if only you desire it. Time-power is yours to utilize.

The secret is in visualization.

Just before falling into the final state of sleep at night, you must imagine in your mind's eye whatever problem is facing you. In this way you can transmit it to the Supraconscious to answer or solve for you.

The work your Supraconscious can accomplish is unlimited. The knowledge it can draw upon is universal. The answers it will give to your problems are perfect—if your Supraconscious is working correctly.

One of the most successful ways of accomplishing the mental therapy that we discussed in the previous chapter is during sleep. Indeed, perfect rest and recuperative slumber can be assured under almost any circumstances at the word of command from your conscious.

Even dreams can be controlled in this way. If you are troubled by distressing dreams—the result of negativism—you can change their "current" or prevent them altogether, by energetically commanding the Supraconscious to control this.

It is especially effective in directing the Supraconscious to aid in the healing of some other person to use the powers of the Golden Gift during sleep.

If you habitually do this at the time of going to sleep, you will not only be certain of obtaining recuperative sleep for yourself, you will also procure the contentment and peace of mind that always results from a consciousness of having done "good" for your fellow man.

The exercise of the power of the Supraconscious in this manner is never a tax upon your vital force. It always, in fact, rebounds to your own benefit.

The reason is obvious. The normal condition of the Supraconscious level of the mind, while the conscious mind is asleep and the body is resting physically, is that of increased activity. This is its technique of recuperation and rebuilding the body.

If the activities of your Supraconscious are directed into pleasant channels, your bodily rest is perfect and your recuperative powers extended to their maximum.

It is for this reason that mental therapy by means of sleep-thinking is better for all concerned than any of the other methods of mental therapy known to mankind.

By sleep-thinking, you are following the pattern of nature. Nature employs the subjective powers at a time when they are normally active and at their best. This occurs when they are revitalizing the fatigued organs of the body and rebuilding their cellular structures.

In acting on the commands of the conscious mind, given just before falling asleep, the discordant impressions that too often disturb the sleeper and disrupt recuperation are overcome by the more potent suggestion.

Your sleeping hours are the basis of the foundation of a Life Limitless.

Your sleeping hours are the source of the time-power, which

in turn is the source of a vast increase in your living benefits.

By developing your Supraconscious to the point where you can utilize sleep-thinking, you are adding through time-power one-third again as much productive living as you now use at maximum.

There is only one rule you need to follow to make time-power work for you:

Just before falling into the final state of sleep every night, imagine in your mind's eye whatever problem is facing you.

That is the rule for transmitting to the Supraconscious that which you wish it to answer or solve for you.

That is the rule for bringing into play the wonderful gift of sleep-thinking.

GIVING YOUR DAY ITS DUE

With the lessons on self-suggestion and the abilities you have now acquired in utilizing your Supraconscious, you have reached the great step of increasing your life by time-power.

If you can utilize every one of your sleeping hours for Supraconscious thought and planning, you are giving yourself a bonus of extending your life by making every day truly a twenty-four-hour day.

The gains of this new time-power are limitless, once you use the powers of sleep-thinking.

There is only one simple rule to follow to utilize time-power.

Just before you fall into your final state of sleep at night imagine in your mind's eye the problem to which you require a solution.

Thus you will transmit to your Supraconscious the necessary information for it to work on through the night.

XV

Making Your Life Vital

The world is undergoing vast changes.

A crisis is at hand.

Whether civilization will suddenly disintegrate on the rocks of physical, mental and moral degeneracy will be determined by the decisions our leaders make now and during the years ahead.

Involved in this new, and greatest, crisis with which we are faced are the wondrous discoveries science has made. We are on the threshold of unleashing physical forces of which man has hardly dreamed.

The atom has been split—will we use this new unlimited energy source for violence and destruction? Or will it be the means of material progress beyond anything man has dared to imagine possible?

But science has another discovery—and this is one that you can use to help fashion a means of saving mankind from self-destruction.

Everywhere, everyone must be made conscious of the powers within the mind of man. It is these powers, the "hidden powers" of the Golden Gift, which have to be unleashed to accomplish this necessary humanitarian task.

You, and you alone, are capable of taking off the wraps that hide the power of the Golden Gift. You must develop the powers of the Supraconscious, both for yourself and for your fellow man.

You must demonstrate in your own life that there is an amazing power of vastly superior intelligence *within* every human being and that this power is of mammoth proportions compared with their conscious minds.

Show the world you have discovered that a deeper intelligence permeates all things. Prove that we all are akin to the elements of the entire universe through the medium of natural laws.

It has been difficult for the average person to conceive of a body of matter, such as the human organism, as being "alive" with some kind of "spirit force" or "soul" to "give it life."

But life is a part of God's Divine Plan.

Life manifests itself in an endless stream of magnetism from countless suns, which we know as stars, upon your planet.

Life sets things in motion. No power known to man can stop it.

To continue to grow, you must obtain that which is essential for your growth. You must encourage the processes of organic repair, which are known as metabolism. Positive "emotional thinking" must supplant the negativism that disrupts the creative functions of the body.

Thought is the only means by which mankind can achieve individual and collective growth. It is, therefore, the key to human progress.

On the mental level, like attracts like. That means simply that mental vibrations respond only to the extent of their vibratory harmony. It should be clear, therefore, that thoughts of creative abundance will respond to similar thoughts of the subjective intelligence.

In other words, you have to make mental images of the things you desire. Affluence from without will be attracted only if we can imagine affluence within.

If you put your "heart"—that is, your Supraconscious mind—in your work, you are bound, by the Law of Attraction, to succeed.

This God-given power depends upon a consciousness of power. Unless you are conscious of this power, you cannot use it.

Unless you use it, you will lose it.

The question people have been asking themselves and their counsellors for generations is: "Is there really an unknown power, a force, an influence, that some people understand and are able to use to achieve success?"

Many of the questioners have thought that this power is "luck." And obviously there is such a thing as luck. It is the combined power and influence of three elements of the laws of nature working creatively in conformity with God's Divine Plan of evolution. These are (1) the Law of Suggestion, (2) the Law of Attraction and (3) the Law of Compensation.

To invoke the creative power of these elements of the laws of nature, you must assume a favorable mental attitude:

1. You must tell your Supraconscious mind exactly what you want.

2. You must desire it with all your "heart."

3. You must have complete confidence that you will attain it.

The reasons for this are apparent from what we have learned in the foregoing chapters:

1. The Supraconscious is constantly amenable to control by the Law of Suggestion and functions best through the technique of visualization.

2. Desire is the emotional force that arouses the creative power of the Supraconscious and causes the Law of Attraction to put into action the vibrational currents necessary as a means to the desired end. Or as one writer put it, "The Flame of Desire supplies the heat for the Steam of Creative Action."

3. Confidence, or faith, is the mental factor that governs the Law of Compensation.

You can help make this very day the beginning of a new era. You can accomplish this by changing your method of thinking from an unconscious haphazard process that forgets or ignores individual responsibility to a systematic technique that puts you in conscious control of your inner creative forces.

Until all of us become consciously creative, distribution of material things can contribute little or nothing toward the solution of individual world problems. Grandiose schemes for "sharing the wealth" can only lead to chaos. Inequality of wealth is not due to unequal distribution of possessions. It is due, rather, to unequal degrees of success in complying with the creative laws.

The creative source is within you.

It is not bound by circumstances beyond your control.

You must remember this always—the creative source is within you.

Think creatively. Train your mind to it. Form new habits of thinking. Shake off the negative influences of your past life or previous heritage.

Train your mind. Remember that thoughts are not actually "things." They do not actually create "things."

But thoughts do attract "things" and influence events.

Remember the Law of Suggestion and the Law of Attraction.

Remember the "hidden power" you possess. It is this "hidden power," this Golden Gift, which can be made to work for you the wonders of God.

Remember that Jesus Christ said, "He that believeth on me, the works that I do shall he do also, and greater works than these shall he do."

Man has, unfortunately in the past been inclined to explain the powers of the Golden Gift in terms of soul-power. If, however, this great power was an attribute of the soul, it should only work for the "good" of mankind. Yet you have seen that this power can and does work for "evil" equally as well as for "good."

Constructive emotion is the stuff of which spirituality is made. For human emotion is the means by which the "hidden power" of the Supraconscious is released. And destructive emotion is a force which weakens the human spirit.

The "feeling mind"—the thalamus—generates the electrical vibrations that constitute the "life force" of the human organism. This energy is set in motion by the impulse we call emotion.

Spiritual force, then, is a higher rate of thalamic vibration than is necessary for normal functioning of the human organism.

The power that highly accelerated vibrational force has is untold and tremendous.

It is this power which you possess. It is this power which you can unleash for your own gain, your own happiness, your own health, your own longevity.

You possess power to communicate mentally. You possess power to see mentally. You possess power to heal mentally. All these powers can be activated by your own efforts, by your emotions. It is your emotions which dictate the quality of the feeling mind.

You produce your own results in life according to the quality of your thoughts.

You possess a "magic" in your mind. But only through your individual co-operation with God's Divine Plan for the evolution of immortal man can you use this "magic" to attain health, wealth, happiness and longevity.

Only when you are ready to believe absolutely that there is "magic" in your mind, only when you are ready and anxious to make it work, can you achieve all that this "magic" is capable of bringing to you.

Start to reread this book now. Study the nature of man once again. Study how this brain works. Learn of the "magic" that lies in the qualities of hypnotism, extrasensory perception and the "collective unconscious."

Remember that all the things man has in the past called "supernatural" are natural—it is the nature of man's mind. These things are truly extranormal. They are part of the powers that belong to anyone who attains conscious control of his Supraconscious forces.

Reread the chapters that outline how the mind influences the body, how powerful prayer is, how the mind can heal. Absorb these facts. Act on them.

You, and you alone, must assume responsibility for your own spiritual development. This must be accomplished by elevating your own consciousness through positive thinking.

You must also teach your children and family that they have within their minds these creative forces that will make them truly children of God and heirs of heaven.

To the skeptical I can only point out the number of distinguished persons of this present hectic day who are reaching some of these same conclusions.

For example, we have shown that mental health cannot be considered apart from physical health. Such distinguished doctors as Dr. Morris Fishbein, formerly of the American Medical Association, and ministers such as Dr. Norman Vincent Peale, of the Marble Collegiate Church in New York, are speaking their minds on these matters.

The American Academy of General Practice—an association of family doctors—is carrying on an educational plan for its members so that the doctors may better be able to consider emotional and mental problems when they treat their patients for stomachaches or heart palpitations.

Medical authorities all over are telling the world that emotional problems are universal and there is nothing shameful about them. Fear, anger and guilt have been named by these doctors the greatest enemies of our general well-being.

In another area, practical and highly successful business executives are practicing creative thinking. And a recent press dispatch quoted a corporation head as stating that religion is a practical thing and that there is a guidance above man's own intelligence and experience which can unfailingly be found by prayer and faith.

There are daily illustrations of achievement against so-called "insurmountable obstacles." Prominent people have recognized the seriousness of the problems we face today. The current trend to mental, physical and moral degeneracy is being seen as a miscarriage of the natural laws that govern human nature.

The thinking world is beginning to realize that all the dangers that besiege you can be met with the greatest weapon you possess: your thoughts and your emotions.

But you have to learn to use them.

Concerning the power of emotions, Dr. Grantly Dick Read, exponent of "natural childbirth," wrote to me: "The mother who is afraid is chemically different in many ways from the mother who knows no fear . . ."

Dr. Read said that the mother who has fears therefore gives a direct "legacy of psychological inhibitions" to her child. He added, stressing the vital importance of his work and of its relationship to the ideas inherent in the whole study of your "magic" mind, "the nature of the birth of a child will lay the foundations for the nature of the generations to come."

The primary purpose of the Supraconscious level of your mind is to keep the human organism functioning harmoniously.

To maintain this harmony within yourself, you must bear in mind all the things which have been emphasized earlier in this volume.

Two things are of prime importance in the practice of that "magic," that creative force, that Golden Gift, with which you are endowed.

The first is the working hypothesis of principles concerning the wonderful powers of the Supraconscious:

1. The Supraconscious is constantly amenable to control by the power of suggestion.

2. The Supraconscious is incapable of independent reasoning by the processes of induction.

3. The power of the Supraconscious to reason deductively from given premises to correct conclusions is practically perfect.

4. The Supraconscious is endowed with a perfect memory.

5. The Supraconscious has absolute control of the functions and conditions of the body.

6. The Supraconscious has the power to communicate by means other than the recognized channels of the five senses.

7. The Supraconscious is capable of intuition and perception of the laws of Nature.

The second is the suggestive affirmation to be repeated often and believed in:

"I am whole, perfect, strong, powerful, loving, harmonious and happy."

This sums up best what you are trying to achieve. But any other affirmation that better suits an occasion may be used.

The purpose of this suggestive affirmation is to keep negative emotions from usurping reason and destroying peace of mind. It will induce a high level of creative thinking through functional harmony of the whole organism.

It works—like magic!

"Magic," said Karl du Prel, "is nothing but unknown natural science."

The eminent theosophist A. P. Sinnett said: "The powers with which occultism invests its adepts include, to begin with, a control over forces of nature which ordinary science knows nothing about."

"Magic," wrote Jollivett-Castelot, "is by no means, as most outsiders imagine, the negation of science. Quite to the contrary, magic is science but science with synthesis, almost integral science—its horizons being the absolute, the infinite in unity.

"It is not, in truth, science which will ever explain magic to the people but it is magic which will progressively cause to be understood the doctrines of science which today are still in their infancy; it is magic which will develop in their true sense the apparent mysteries of nature."

The academic knowledge you have acquired concerning your own evolutionary nature should convince you of the need—the necessity—of self-help. Once we are given the implements of self-improvement, God expects each one of us to develop the inherent qualities that constitute our spiritual beings. That means simply the exercise of your creative faculties and of the Supraconscious level of your mind to perfect yourself physically and intellectually. This can be accomplished by substituting positive feeling-attitudes for negative ones and acting on the ideas generated in our transformed minds.

As an individual, you must feel and take a common interest in and with all people, regardless of race, creed or color.

You will profit best by helping others to succeed.

World peace and a solution of world problems could be quickly realized if all the peoples of the world would simultaneously visualize a state of international social harmony with health, happiness and prosperity for all.

The way can be found not only to enjoy health, wealth and happiness for yourself, but also to lead all mankind in the direction of intellectual and spiritual growth.

You are constantly creating and recreating yourself by passing on every conscious idea to your Supraconscious. Psychologists say that ninety per cent or more of your mental activity is unconscious.

Therefore you must act upon your knowledge. In so doing, you can help re-create the world.

This is what God has charged you with.

You cannot, you dare not, escape thought.

Proper creative thinking will make you free. It will make the world free. And it will make your life useful, purposeful and rewarding.

THE RULES FOR A NEW LIVING

You must have faith in the fact that you have the power within yourself to do with your life what you will.

And you must use this power.

The longer you allow it to stand idle, the less you will be able to use it.

It becomes a matter of use it or lose it.

The best way to use this power is to assume the most favorable mental attitude:

1. Tell your Supraconscious exactly what you want.
2. Desire it with all your "heart."
3. Have complete confidence that you will attain it.

XVI

It's Your Life—Take It From There!

You have crossed the threshold into a new world!

It is, as Alfred, Lord Tennyson, once wrote, a "new world which is the old."

You are still you; the world is still progressing day by day, and you are still a part of it. But you are new, and your world is new!

From this day on you can hold your head high—not out of snobbery, but out of happiness.

From this day on you can smile—not out of simplicity, but out of happiness.

You have made the discovery of a new life. Here is the life you once asked "to live over again." Here is the living over again. And it is not the same old life, the one filled with fears and panic, the one replete with envy and hate.

You are a person who has discovered the magic of living. You know the magic power that is in your mind. You understand how to make every day happy and complete.

And you have discovered that, by so doing, those you love dearly, those who are around you day by day, all have gained by your gain.

This is a discovery you must not take lightly. This is a lesson you delved deeply into yourself to learn. This is a magic that you want to use for "good."

Therefore remember the dozen rules of your "magicianship."

FIRST, let no week start without reacquainting yourself with the seven propositions of the working hypothesis:

1. The Supraconscious is constantly amenable to control by the power of suggestion.

2. The Supraconscious is incapable of independent reasoning by the process of induction.

3. The power of the Supraconscious to reason deductively from given premises to correct conclusions is practically perfect.

4. The Supraconscious is endowed with perfect memory.

5. The Supraconscious has absolute control of the functions and conditions of the body.

6. The Supraconscious has the power to communicate by means other than the recognized channels of the five senses.

7. The Supraconscious is capable of intuition and perception of the laws of nature.

Before each week starts, you must reread these propositions and understand the powerful effect of the Supraconscious and the control you have over it.

SECOND, allow no bedtime to pass without using the power of suggestion upon the Supraconscious. By constant practice you will be able to achieve the trigger-quick control of your Golden Gift which will make your life a new one.

THIRD, set aside some part of each day—preferably a time when you can meditate in peace—to do some "refilling" in the memory storehouse.

Empty out the "file" of ills. Create and fill to overflowing the "file" of "good" and happiness.

Destroy the negative thoughts—the hates and evils, the poisons and passions that maim.

Cultivate the positive thoughts—the happinesses, the goodnesses and the joys of life in which flourish health and long life.

FOURTH, every minute of every day, love. Once you have learned to love, you will have learned to live.

This is an emotion that must pervade your body constantly. Don't let hate encroach upon the territory of love within you. Don't relax your vigil for a moment, for hate is a deadly evil, a crawling, creeping destroyer of your welfare.

Today and always, love, love, love!

FIFTH, depend on prayer. Prayer is the master power. Pray when you are alone. Pray in a quiet place. Free yourself from destructive emotions. Relax both physically and emotionally. And concentrate on the simple truth.

SIXTH, use your Faith Factor. Believe with all your "heart" and mind. Accept faith within your Supraconscious so that you can change your life by thinking and doing.

Faith will accomplish miracles for you—but you must believe.

SEVENTH, think happiness, live happiness, be happiness. Remember that happiness is a do-it-yourself commodity. It is self-acquired. And it is the fuel on which the mental engine runs.

You were made to be happy; you were meant to be happy. Don't fail to take advantage of this gift. Don't allow a gray coating of dullness to discolor your life.

Happiness means health, longevity and success.

EIGHTH, remember the power and the wisdom.

Destroy dis-ease by having affirmative faith in God's loving care; by avoiding disharmony in your everyday living; by visualizing good health.

The power and the wisdom are the keys to true ease—the ease of love, of happiness and wholesomeness in life and living.

NINTH, utilize the positive-negative psychology of living —the new psychology.

Anxiety in any of its forms—envy, resentment, worry, grief —is a deadly enemy. It is the negative approach to living. Its natural enemy is positive, constructive thinking.

Keep watching your negative-positive level by the four radar checks daily: upon awakening (to assure yourself that happiness lies ahead); at noon (to assure perfect assimilation of your meal); on the way home (to assure harmony within the family); and at bedtime (to assure restful sleep and interest in the new day).

TENTH, crusade against illness by overcoming the patterns of habit. Achieve both objective and subjective faith in your power so that there will be no resistance from any ailment, mental or organic.

This is the "hidden power" you have which will deny disease any mastery over you. Therapeutic suggestion is the direct line to longevity. It is the key to healing powers.

Remember, practice will make perfection. Perfection will achieve prevention. Prevention is more simple than cure.

ELEVENTH, give yourself the extra life that you want so that you can "live it over again." Every night at bedtime, concentrate on the problems that face your day ahead. Allow your Supraconscious to add one-third to your life.

Increase your life span not only chronologically, but by extending the capacity of each and every day.

Imagine in your mind's eye your problems. Transmit them thus to your Supraconscious. Build the foundations for a Life Limitless.

TWELFTH, make yourself vital. Exercise your creative faculties. Perfect yourself physically and intellectually.

Enjoy health, wealth and happiness.

Re-create yourself, make your life useful, purposeful and rewarding.

There is magic in your mind!

Allow this magic to help you enjoy living. Allow it to show you the zest that is possible in your life.

Keep this book close at hand. Reread it as often as possible. Practice the rules of living a long and happy life. Practice the rules of using your Supraconscious to its utmost limits.

Don't be afraid to tax the powers of the Supraconscious. It is a remarkable machine. The greater it is taxed, the harder and more perfectly does it work.

Use the lessons you have learned faithfully and you will get results you never believed possible.

You will astound yourself with what is in store for you.

You have the secret of adding years to your life—and the secret of adding life to your years.

Discover yourself—and the magic power of your mind— and you have discovered a new world!

There are indeed many unknown dangers lurking in the vast
unknown. This danger is real, but you must see, since the same
unknown danger is there in the rest of the ordinary waking rea-

THIS IS AN UNHAPPINESS CHART!

	8 AM	9 AM	10 AM	11 AM	NOON	1 PM	2 PM	3 PM	4 PM	5 PM	6 PM	7 PM	8 PM	9 PM	10 PM	11 PM
Sunday																
Monday																
Tuesday																
Wednesday																
Thursday																
Friday																
Saturday																

Here is how it works. As shown in Chapter 10 of this book, you must evaluate every hour as it ends—at least for the first week or two. Later, and until you can reach the true level of living in which you achieve the maximum of happiness and the minimum of monotony, you can evaluate your hourly rating at the end of each day.

This is how to mark the chart:

If what you did during each hour brought you monotony for MORE than twenty minutes, blacken that square with a pencil or pen. If, however, LESS than twenty minutes of that hour was filled with dull and monotonous happenings, leave it blank.

At the end of the week total the number of filled-in squares and the number of blank squares. Enter the result here:

There are _____ filled-in squares; there are _____ blank squares.

There are _____ more _____ squares than there are _____ squares.

If there are more filled-in squares than blank ones, you are well past the danger point and have exceeded your monotony limits.

If there are more blank squares than filled-in squares, you are below the danger point. But you must have twice as many blank squares as filled-in ones to be heading away from danger and into happiness.

Continue filling in these charts until fewer than one fourth of the squares are filled in.

The heights of happiness are yours when you can show a chart that has 90 per cent or more of the squares left blank at the end of a week.

THIS IS AN UNHAPPINESS CHART!

	8 AM	9 AM	10 AM	11 AM	NOON	1 PM	2 PM	3 PM	4 PM	5 PM	6 PM	7 PM	8 PM	9 PM	10 PM	11 PM
Sunday																
Monday																
Tuesday																
Wednesday																
Thursday																
Friday																
Saturday																

Here is how it works. As shown in Chapter 10 of this book, you must evaluate every hour as it ends—at least for the first week or two. Later, and until you can reach the true level of living in which you achieve the maximum of happiness and the minimum of monotony, you can evaluate your hourly rating at the end of each day.

This is how to mark the chart:

If what you did during each hour brought you monotony for MORE than twenty minutes, blacken that square with a pencil or pen. If, however, LESS than twenty minutes of that hour was filled with dull and monotonous happenings, leave it blank.

At the end of the week total the number of filled-in squares and the number of blank squares. Enter the result here:

There are _____ filled-in squares; there are _____ blank squares.

There are _____ more _____ squares than there are _____ squares.

If there are more filled-in squares than blank ones, you are well past the danger point and have exceeded your monotony limits.

If there are more blank squares than filled-in squares, you are below the danger point. But you must have twice as many blank squares as filled-in ones to be heading away from danger and into happiness.

Continue filling in these charts until fewer than one fourth of the squares are filled in.

The heights of happiness are yours when you can show a chart that has 90 per cent or more of the squares left blank at the end of a week.

THIS IS AN UNHAPPINESS CHART!

	8 AM	9 AM	10 AM	11 AM	NOON	1 PM	2 PM	3 PM	4 PM	5 PM	6 PM	7 PM	8 PM	9 PM	10 PM	11 PM
Sunday																
Monday																
Tuesday																
Wednesday																
Thursday																
Friday																
Saturday																

Here is how it works. As shown in Chapter 10 of this book, you must evaluate every hour as it ends—at least for the first week or two. Later, and until you can reach the true level of living in which you achieve the maximum of happiness and the minimum of monotony, you can evaluate your hourly rating at the end of each day.

This is how to mark the chart:

If what you did during each hour brought you monotony for MORE than twenty minutes, blacken that square with a pencil or pen. If, however, LESS than twenty minutes of that hour was filled with dull and monotonous happenings, leave it blank.

At the end of the week total the number of filled-in squares and the number of blank squares. Enter the result here:

There are _____ filled-in squares; there are _____ blank squares.

There are _____ more _____ squares than there are _____ squares.

If there are more filled-in squares than blank ones, you are well past the danger point and have exceeded your monotony limits.

If there are more blank squares than filled-in squares, you are below the danger point. But you must have twice as many blank squares as filled-in ones to be heading away from danger and into happiness.

Continue filling in these charts until fewer than one fourth of the squares are filled in.

The heights of happiness are yours when you can show a chart that has 90 per cent or more of the squares left blank at the end of a week.

INSPIRATION PAD

In Chapter 5 of this book there is outlined the method of recording the results of your "inspirational" thoughts. The following pages are provided so that you can record these thoughts right in the book that is teaching you how to reach this level of your Supraconscious and how to use these thoughts.

Follow these rules so that you can make the most of your memory and your Supraconscious:

1. Upon awakening think deeply to reveal to yourself any ideas that have pushed to the conscious surface during your sleep hours.

2. Write them down here. A catch phrase is sufficient, especially if there has been more than one thought.

3. Later in the day reread what you have written here.

4. Apply the creativeness of your memory to your problems.

5. Use this note pad all through the day—or in the night should you awaken with a "flash" of inspiration.

6. Never disregard any single thought of the "hunch" or "sixth sense" variety. Note it down here immediately it makes itself known to you.

7. Such inspirational thoughts that come to you during the daytime hours, reread before you fall asleep at night. Meditate on them and allow them to reach your Supraconscious so that they can be "processed" there.

8. In the morning, reread again the thoughts of the day previous so that you can give your Supraconscious the opportunity to supply you with the proper evaluation of these inspirational ideas.

INSPIRATION PAD

_____

_____

_____

_____

_____

_____

_____

_____

_____

_____

_____

_____

_____

_____

MEBBE 'TAIN'T SO . . . !

In Chapter 11 of this book is explained how negative thoughts can cause dis-ease, which in its way will cause disease.

Negative thoughts are ill thoughts. They must be quickly changed to positive ones.

In the space provided on these pages, keep a record of your negative thoughts and how you have successfully combatted them by changing them to positive thoughts.

Two examples of how to effect this change are listed below:

I can stand anything ~~but noisy children~~ at all.

~~Excessive horn blowing~~ Nothing drives me wild.

_____

_____

_____

_____

_____

_____

_____

_____

_____

_____

_____

_____

_____

_____

_____

_____

_____

_____

_____

_____

_____

THE RULES OF PRAYER

(Clip this card. On this side are the five rules of successful prayer power. On the reverse side are the rules for using the formula of love. Keep it in your wallet, or pocketbook, at all times. Refer to it often. These two sets of rules are the key to happiness and health and will bring you the golden harvest of life.)

1. Pray when you are by yourself.

2. Pray in a quiet place.

3. Free yourself from destructive emotions.

4. Relax physically and emotionally.

5. Concentrate on a simple truth and do not wander from it.

THE BATTLE OF EASE AGAINST DIS-EASE

1. Have positive, affirmative faith so that you may release the deep spiritual power of God's loving care.

2. Remember that spiritual forces as well as the scientific techniques of medicine are important in healing.

3. Avoid disharmony—in your family, in your work, in your relationships with all people. Disharmony, disease and dis-ease are akin.

4. Visualize a picture of perfect health, happiness and vitality. Let this picture sink into the Supraconscious so that the Supraconscious level of the mind can control a positive thought pattern of healing.

5. Never become upset, worried or panicky in illness. This will only set up a pattern of negative thoughts which will be destructive and only create greater dis-ease.

THE FORMULA OF LOVE

At least once each night before you fall asleep, and again once each day—preferably when you awaken in the morning and have not yet encountered the strain of your day's work—repeat either or both of these thoughts:

The proper name for God in man is LOVE!

and

Thou shalt love the Lord thy God with all thy heart, and with all thy soul, and with all thy mind. Thou shalt love thy neighbor as thyself.

At any time during the day when you encounter stress or strain, determine the exact cause of your moment of grief and (inserting the word or phrase that best signifies it in the blank space) repeat this thought so that the formula of love can work for you:

I love _____ as I do myself!

THE RULES FOR A NEW LIFE

You must never lose faith in the fact that you have within you the power to do with your life exactly what you will.

Use this power, for if it is allowed to lie fallow it will diminish and disappear.

USE IT OR LOSE IT.

Tell your Supraconscious exactly what you want.

Desire it with all your "heart."

Have complete confidence that you will attain it.

THE PANIC-POISON RADAR TRAP

This four-times-a-day radar check is your best guarantee against allowing any of the poison of panic to slip into your system. Panic brings about anxiety. Anxiety is a killer—in any of its forms: envy, resentment, worry or grief.

1. EVERY DAY WHEN YOU AWAKEN, ASK YOUR-SELF:

    Am I bright and cheery?

    Am I willing to face the day and all it will hold?

    Am I well rested from my sleep?

    Am I happy to be able to live longer and be more successful?

    EVERY ANSWER MUST BE—"YES"

2. EVERY DAY AT NOON ASK YOURSELF:

    Was my morning successful?

    Did I prevent any reverses, no matter how large, I may have had from upsetting me?

    Did I allow no one to irritate me?

    Do I really feel like having lunch now?

    Will I really enjoy my meal and not have indigestion because of some upset this morning?

    EVERY ANSWER MUST BE—"YES"

3. EVERY DAY BEFORE GOING HOME ASK YOUR-SELF:

    Has the day been satisfactory?

    Did I achieve harmony with everyone with whom I came in contact?

    Did I overcome every problem that presented itself?

    Am I looking forward to going home to my family now?

    EVERY ANSWER MUST BE—"YES"

4. EVERY NIGHT BEFORE FALLING ASLEEP ASK YOURSELF:

    Am I looking forward to tomorrow?

    THE ANSWER MUST BE—"YES"

USING YOUR HIDDEN POWERS

By combining the powers of visualization and affirmation you have within you the power of curing self-induced ailments and rendering yourself immune to many of the diseases to which we of mankind have fallen heir.

Here are the rules of visualization and affirmation as they should be put to use. At the end of this page there is a blank space; use it to record your affirmations so that you can be able to concentrate on them while reading this book.

1. In the space below, write any affirmation.

2. Visualize that affirmation in your mind's eye, with your physical eyes closed.

3. Practice this until you are able to project a "visual image" anywhere in your own body.

4. When you are thus able to channel your visual image, the curative powers of the Supraconscious can be used to rid you of pain, discomfort, ache, tension, congestion or ailment.

To bring these powers effectively into use by yourself, you must:

1. Have confidence in yourself.

2. Allow no doubts to nullify the effectiveness of your suggestions.

3. Be prepared to counteract all efforts of your habitual everyday thinking that may be contrary to your curative desires.

4. Never "beg" the subjective forces to make you ill by using such phrases as "such-and-such (or so-and-so) makes me sick!"

My Affirmations:

THE RULES OF THE SUPRACONSCIOUS

Clip this page and keep it at your bedside.

Each night when you have achieved muscular relaxation and have freed your conscious of the petty thoughts of the day, read this seven-point lesson.

At first read it aloud. Later, when you have acquired the gift of absorption and concentration, read it silently.

1. The Supraconscious is constantly amenable to control by the power of suggestion.

2. The Supraconscious is incapable of independent reasoning by the processes of induction.

3. The power of the Supraconscious to reason deductively from given premises to correct conclusions is practically perfect.

4. The Supraconscious is endowed with a perfect memory.

5. The Supraconscious has absolute control of the functions and conditions of the body.

6. The Supraconscious has the power to communicate by means other than the recognized channels of the five senses.

7. The Supraconscious is capable of intuition and perception of the laws of nature.

BELIEVING IS DOING!

(Clip this card. Place it in your shaving mirror, on your dressing table, in the sun visor of your car, near the kitchen sink—anywhere that you will see it early each and every day.)

I CAN ONLY BE SUCCESSFUL AND HAPPY IF I HAVE HUMBLE BUT REASONABLE CONFIDENCE IN MY OWN POWERS.

Index

255